שַׁעֲרֵי בִינָה

GATES OF UNDERSTANDING

ויפתח יי אלהינו לנו ולכל ישראל אחינו בכל מקום
שהם . . . שערי בינה

May the Lord our God open the gates of understanding, for us and for all our people, wherever they may be.

Piyyut
SEFARDIC LITURGY

שַׁעֲרֵי בִּינָה

GATES OF
UNDERSTANDING

A companion volume
to
SHAAREI TEFILLAH: GATES OF PRAYER

Edited by
LAWRENCE A. HOFFMAN

Notes to *Shaarei Tefillah*
by Chaim Stern and A. Stanley Dreyfus

PUBLISHED FOR THE
CENTRAL CONFERENCE OF AMERICAN RABBIS
BY THE
UNION OF AMERICAN HEBREW CONGREGATIONS

5737   New York   1977

LIBRARY OF CONGRESS CATALOGING IN PUBLICATION DATA

Main entry under title:

Shaarei binah   Gates of understanding.

In English.
1. Prayer (Judaism)—Addresses, essays, lectures.
2. Reform Judaism—Addresses, essays, lectures.
3. Jews. Liturgy and ritual. Daily prayers
(Reform, Central Conference of American Rabbis)—
Commentaries. I. Hoffman, Lawrence A., 1942–
II. Jews. Liturgy and ritual. Daily prayers
(Reform, Central Conference of American Rabbis)
III. Title: Gates of understanding.

BM660.S43   296.7'2   77-23488
ISBN 0-8074-0009-2

Contents

CONTENTS

Acknowledgments

MANY THANKS are due my two co-editors Rabbi Chaim Stern and Rabbi A. Stanley Dreyfus. Rabbi Stern's poetic sensitivity, so evident in *Gates of Prayer,* is here matched by the scholarly precision of his Notes and his synopsis of the Sabbath service themes. Rabbi Dreyfus co-edited the Notes, providing particularly meticulous research into past editions of the *Union Prayer Book* as well as a comprehensive table of scriptural readings. Moreover, it is Rabbi Dreyfus who has been charged with the responsibility for overseeing the many aspects of liturgical renewal which this book describes and of which it is a part. It is he who first conceived of *Shaarei Binah,* and who has guided me at every step along the way to its completion.

Shaarei Binah is a compendium of significant observations made by people of considerable wisdom and insight. Some are alive in person; others only in the thoughts they bequeathed to us. We are all indebted to these teachers of noble vision: those mentioned expressly in the Contents, certainly, but countless others as well, who were teachers of teachers, and whose anonymity in no way denies their real presence.

Rabbi Joseph Glaser, Rabbi Leonard Schoolman and Rabbi Elliot Stevens deserve more than passing credit too. Books are not just written, they are produced; and these, my colleagues, have worked assiduously to realize the dream of publishing this one. So many people were enlisted in their aid: Ralph Davis who oversaw the complexities of layout, design, and overall publication; Vivian Mendeles who combines typing expertise with unique devotion, commitment and initiative; and Miriam Jefferson, Ellen Weinberg, and Laurie Rutenberg, who helped proofread these pages.

It was my wife, Sally, whose support emboldened me to take on this project and whose love sustained me throughout it. To her it is dedicated.

LAWRENCE A. HOFFMAN

שַׁעֲרֵי בִינָה

GATES OF UNDERSTANDING

Introduction: The Liturgical Question

Lawrence A. Hoffman

> Only three times before this Shabbat, in the one-hundred-two year history of our Union, could a new prayerbook have been consecrated at a General Assembly.[1]

With these words Rabbi A. Stanley Dreyfus presented *Gates of Prayer* to the Reform movement: an historic event certainly, celebrating the fruition of a century of organized Reform Jewish life in America, and heralding the birth of a new liturgy for the Reform community of the future.

In fact, *Gates of Prayer* is not the first but the second landmark in this liturgical rebirth. A Passover Haggadah, sensitively edited by Rabbi Herbert Bronstein and handsomely illustrated by Leonard Baskin, was the harbinger of this epoch of liturgical creativity,[2] and *Gates of Prayer* is still to be followed by *Gates of Song,* a compendium of liturgical music; *Gates of the House,* a manual for home devotion and ritual; and *Gates of Repentance,* a High Holiday prayerbook.

So it is against a background of comprehensive liturgical renewal that this book should be viewed. Though accompanying *Gates of Prayer* specifically, its actual subject is prayer in our time. This is, therefore, not a prayerbook, but a book about prayer; and its focus is worship generally, Reform Jewish worship specifically, and most particularly, Reform worship of today.

Since public worship for Jews is the recitation of a fixed liturgy, this book can also be considered a book about liturgy, a word which the dictionary defines as "a form of public worship" or "a collection of formularies for the conduct" thereof. But however broad this dictionary definition of liturgy may be, modern scholarly investigation has tended to approach the subject in one particular way. Since this usual interpretation is not prevalent in the collection of essays reproduced here, it is important to know what that interpretation is, how it came into being, and why it was omitted from our sampling. To appreciate fully what this book is, it is necessary first to see what it is not.

Rabbis throughout history were passionately involved in prayer, and therefore wrote both commentaries on it and treatises about it. Yet they never described themselves as liturgists. For them, prayer was but one undifferentiated aspect of a Jewish way of life which they took for granted. They might just as easily have written books on the dietary laws or any other aspect of Judaism to which they took a liking and for which there was a thirst for more knowledge.[3] Their method, in any case, was entirely the same: to search Jewish literature and practice for precedents which could guide the pious Jew in his quest for a more thorough understanding of the divine will.

It was the modern world of the nineteenth century which wrested liturgical study from the realm of medieval piety and conceptualized the possibility of studying it objectively.[4] Those who pioneered this scientific study were, by and large, men steeped in the Jewish tradition from childhood, who discovered the scholarly approach of secular academia later in life. Their mission became the application of that approach to the lore they had learned earlier. Yet they, like the rabbis who preceded them, did not perceive liturgy as an independent subject. Though their scientific methodology was different, they, too, were as apt to write monographs on any aspect of the immense totality of Rabbinic tradition as they were to study liturgy.[5] Their field was Rabbinic literature and, if they studied prayer, they did so from a perspective of viewing prayers as liturgical literature.

Their methodology can be described as historical. Its aim was to trace the development of a prayer through time. Understanding the evolution of the subject was equated with understanding the subject itself. The result was almost two centuries of learned debate on how a given prayer arose, what political or social events influenced its growth, and so on. Needless to say, this literature about prayer makes for fascinating reading. To know, for example, that part of the *Yizkor* service may be related to the Crusades; or that the familiar Shabbat poem, *Lecha Dodi,* is a sixteenth-century poetic acrostic with mystical metaphoric allusions, is to add great dimension to the act of worship. So this book could have remained faithful to the classical model of liturgical study by constituting a collection of outstanding essays on the history of Jewish prayers.

But reason dictates a different course. The history of prayers has been dealt with elsewhere.[6] This book is devoted to the realization that Reform Jewry today is embarking on a new era in liturgical practice.

4

The essays assembled here, therefore, are related not to that general literature which constitutes Jewish prayer through the ages, but to the specific liturgical renaissance in which we happily find ourselves. *Gates of Understanding* is descriptive of *Gates of Prayer* insofar as that prayerbook epitomizes such liturgical rebirth. But in a fuller sense our subject is the Reform Jewish community for whom *Gates of Prayer* is intended.

So we have taken the liberty of defining liturgy more broadly than scholars of the past have allowed. Our subject is not the history of any particular prayers, and certainly not literature. Our concern is prayer as a Jewish activity, here and now; it is a particular prayerbook, *Gates of Prayer,* and the entire worship experience which that book represents. The essays here articulate several thoughtful perspectives which *Gates of Prayer* reflects. Moreover, since our underlying assumption is that a prayerbook illuminates the lives of those who use it, the reader will find the following pages to be no simple book review, but an analysis of the living relationship between a book of prayer and a community that prays. We begin, necessarily, with some historical considerations, but our focus is preeminently on the community of today, and our real subject is nothing less than the contemporary act of worship and the contemporary worshipper behind it.

In the first and smallest section of the book, we consider whence we came. How does Reform worship, generally, relate to its past? What are some basic symbols and ideas that mark the synagogue service? What visions guided the American founders of our movement? Jakob Petu-chowski's essay, "Some Basic Characteristics of Jewish Liturgy," summa-rizes with exceptional clarity the essential nature, structure, and ideas of the classical Siddur. His lucid description allows us to let the early masters of Reform Judaism speak for themselves, so it is followed by three illustrative portraits of American Reform's formative years.

David Einhorn was one of the many exciting personalities whose influence was to prove enduring. His prayerbook, *Olat Tamid,* became the basis for the *Union Prayer Book.* Kaufmann Kohler, an outstanding theological spokesman, and the second President of the Hebrew Union College, was Einhorn's son-in-law, and he described his late father-in-law's principles in an address before the Central Conference of Ameri-can Rabbis in 1909. His eloquent description of Einhorn's conception of liturgy and worship is reproduced here. It is remarkable how some of Einhorn's observations made as early as 1837—particularly his views on the equality of women—still have a contemporary ring. The Con-ference also discussed the importance of synagogue music, and selec-tions from its first significant debate on the subject make up our next selection. One of the speakers was Isaac Mayer Wise, the institutional architect of the Reform movement. Finally, to present a picture of nascent Reform worship as it was actually practiced, we reproduce a news item drawn from an 1854 edition of Isaac Mayer Wise's English weekly, *The American Israelite*.

Having portrayed the past and the motivating principles still very much at work in the Reform community, we turn to the present. Some of the articles were written decades ago, but they merit inclusion because their timeless quality is as evident now as then. Since their authors spoke from a Reform perspective, they cited the only Reform prayerbook in general use at the time, the *Union Prayer Book*. They are included here, however, not for what they have to tell us about that volume, but for the significance of their insight for us, today. Since so many of them dealt with theological concerns, we have entitled the next section, "What We Believe," and subsumed under that title those treatises which deal specifically with prayer, represent a spectrum of current theological options, and may be encountered in at least some of the services of *Gates of Prayer*.

The articles in this section represent different conceptions of God and of prayer, and are in large measure mutually exclusive. Yet, despite their different perspectives, all authors claim to stand within the bounds of Jewish tradition, and all see worship as a significant part of life. To introduce the debate we present a discussion of "The Language of Debate and the Language of Prayer," by Abraham Cronbach. A traditional yet Reform perspective follows: Samuel Cohon's "Three Paths to the Holy," which explores the mystical, the *halachic* (or legal), and the philosophic approaches within Judaism. The reader may consider the next four articles as optional contemporary theologies, and apply Cohon's and Cronbach's insights to them. What linguistic model do the authors use? Do they represent the mystical, the *halachic*, or the philosophic approaches to God? What are the practical consequences of their theoretical approach for the actual act of prayer?

Eugene Borowitz's "The Individual and the Community in Jewish Prayer," represents what is perhaps the dominant theoretical stand in our movement today, Covenant Theology. Henry Slonimsky's "Prayer and a Growing God" is a personal and poetic statement which suggests an as yet imperfect God evolving together with humanity to realize an ideal world. For both authors, God is personal; meeting us, confronting us, making demands on us. "No Retreat from Reason," by Roland Gittelsohn, presents quite a different image. There is still God, as there is prayer, and there is certainly no absence of divine imperatives. But these terms are understood in a different way. Alvin Reines ("Polydoxy and The Equivocal Service") concludes the theological section with his own critique of what he calls "Conversation Theism," and argues for an alternative grounded in a highly unique view of the essence of Reform Judaism. All of these theological options are present in varying sections of *Gates of Prayer,* and readers may judge for themselves which they wish to draw on for the theoretical basis of their own worship.

We then turn to the third section which explores the variables which, together, constitute the worship experience itself. Much has been written on the relative ability—or inability—of modern people to attain such an experience at all. Illustrative of these articles on "the problem of prayer" is Ely Pilchik's "Stumbling Blocks to Prayer." With admirable precision, Pilchik illustrates three problems of prayer for our generation. Are they still as problematic as they seemed to be when this article was written (1967)? Since they are existential barriers arising from the inherent nature of contemporary life, you may simply examine your own being to determine their validity.

By contrast, the topic of the function of the prayerbook in the worship experience has received relatively little treatment. "Affirmation and Study" by Israel Bettan does explore one aspect of that topic and is, therefore, included to represent the prayerbook's role in providing a worship experience. To what extent, he asks, should a prayerbook reflect moral guidance and impart ethical preachments? This leads naturally to Joseph Gutmann's informative discussion of the role of art in providing "The Environment of Prayer," and a parallel piece by William Sharlin on the place of music. Gutmann's brief synopsis of the Jew's historical fondness for artistic symbolism is as informative as his critique of present synagogue art is challenging. Sharlin examines such crucial matters as the process of musical influence, the threat—as well as the promise—of secularity, and the crucial factor of the worshipper's "religious intent."

My own concluding chapter, "The Liturgical Message," provides a comprehensive model by which a prayerbook can be studied. It unifies many of the disparate themes contained in the other articles, and relates them to Reform liturgy and Reform Jewish identity of our time.

Finally, we include the notes for *Gates of Prayer* itself. They are prefaced by a synopsis of the themes of the major services, and followed by a table of scriptural readings for the annual synagogue cycle. Chaim Stern, the general editor of *Gates of Prayer,* has written the former; A. Stanley Dreyfus, Chairman of the CCAR Liturgy Committee, and Visiting Lecturer in Commentaries at the New York branch of the Hebrew Union College-Jewish Institute of Religion, has compiled the latter. The notes themselves are the product of both Rabbi Stern and Rabbi Dreyfus, who are to be commended for assembling

INTRODUCTION

them so masterfully. It is our hope that they will provide a ready reference source to enrich the act of prayer.

NOTES

1 The complete text of Rabbi Dreyfus' remarks follows:

Only three times before this Shabbat, in the one-hundred-two year history of our Union, could a new prayerbook have been consecrated at a General Assembly: only in 1895, in 1918, in 1940. For over a third of a century the present *Union Prayer Book* has ordered our worship in synagogue and in home and has served as the gate through which two generations have entered into Jewish living.

Yet, as early as a decade ago, many voices, lay and rabbinic, and foremost among them Maurice N. Eisendrath, of blessed memory, importuned for a new prayerbook, which should recall the tragedy of the Holocaust, reflect upon the miracle of Israel's rebirth, and offer guidance and hope to our people in these fearfully perplexing times.

In response to that reiterated demand, the Central Conference of American Rabbis has published *Gates of Prayer: The New Union Prayerbook*. The book, first outlined under the wise direction of Rabbi Robert I. Kahn, was edited, and in largest measure written by Rabbi Chaim Stern, deeply sensitive poet, brilliantly gifted liturgist. *Gates of Prayer* retains many a treasured passage from the *Union Prayer Book*. Like the *Union Prayer Book* it draws chiefly upon the old *Siddur,* preserving classic prayers which have been the vehicle for Jewish devotion over centuries and millennia. To these much has been added that speaks in the accents of today, that invites us to probe our Jewish identity, to define our values and to refine our conduct. All of this, old and new, is gathered up into orders of worship that, please Heaven, will satisfy the spiritual needs of a Reform community which is united in its quest after holiness, but which chooses diverse ways to attain its goal. And because it respects these diverse ways, because it does not seek to force all our people into a single liturgical pattern, *Gates of Prayer* is truly a liberal prayerbook.

The services in *Gates of Prayer* were repeatedly evaluated in eighteen congregations, large and small, representative of the constituency of the Union. The manuscript was revised again and again upon the basis of comments received from rabbis and laity, and the final draft was overwhelmingly approved by vote of the membership of the Conference. Thus the volume embodies the contributions of very many beyond the Liturgy Committee itself. It may fairly be described as the handiwork of American Reform Jewry.

This new prayerbook we have named *Shaarei Tefillah, Gates of Prayer,* because our Rabbis affirm that the way to God which is prayer can never be permanently obstructed. But for most of us that way is impeded: the gates of prayer have been so long disused that we can hardly lift the latch, push aside the portals. May this book swing open those gates to us; through it may we come to know the solace and the joy of dialogue with the Highest.

So, in the name of the Central Conference of American Rabbis, its President, Rabbi Arthur J. Lelyveld; its Executive Vice-President, Rabbi Joseph B. Glaser; its Officers and Executive Board; and in the name of all who toiled that this book might be; I proudly present to you, Mr. Matthew Ross, Chairman of the Board of Trustees of the Union of American Hebrew Congregations, and to you, Mrs. Irving Benjamin, President of the National Federation of Temple Sisterhoods, and to each of you assembled here *Shaarei Tefillah, Gates of Prayer. Navo-ah she-arecha.* Come now, let us enter the gates!

2 *A Passover Haggadah,* Herbert Bronstein, ed. (New York: Central Conference of American Rabbis, 1974). Other books mentioned in this paragraph are scheduled for publication at various times between 1977 and 1979.

3 The earliest prayerbooks, in fact, do contain halachic material not immediately relevant to worship. The first one, *Seder Rav Amram Gaon,* (ninth century) presents detailed regulations governing preparation for Sabbath and holidays; *Machzor Vitry,* the major prayer manual of the medieval Ashkenazic world (Northern France and Germany) includes many pages on such matters as the dietary laws, the making of *tsitsit,* and laws pertaining to the holidays.

4 See, for example, Michael A. Meyer, *The Origins of the Modern Jew* (Detroit: Wayne State University Press, 1967), pp. 144–162.

5 Leopold Zunz, for example, the epitome and one of the founders of this movement known as the Scientific Study of Judaism included the first major study of the Liturgy as simply one chapter in his book, *The Historical Development of the Synagogue Sermons of the Jews.*

6 Some basic historical data have been summarized in the notes to individual prayers at the back of this book, pp. 177ff.; for further information on the history of Jewish prayers, see Israel Abrahams, *A Companion to the Authorised Daily Prayer Book* (1922, Reprint. ed. New York: Hermon Press, 1966); Abraham E. Millgram, *Jewish Worship* (Philadelphia: Jewish Publication Society, 1971); Joseph Heinemann with Jakob J. Petuchowski, *Literature of the Synagogue* (New York: Behrman House, 1975); Jakob J. Petuchowski, ed., *Understanding Jewish Prayer* (New York: Ktav, 1972); Jakob J. Petuchowski, ed., *Contributions to the Scientific Study of Jewish Liturgy* (New York: Ktav, 1972). On Reform Liturgy, see Jakob J. Petuchowski, *Prayerbook Reform in Europe* (New York: World Union for Progressive Judaism, 1968); relevant sections in David Philipson, *The Reform Movement in Judaism* (1907, Reprint. ed. New York: Ktav, 1967); W. Gunther Plaut, *The Rise of Reform Judaism* (New York: World Union for Progressive Judaism, 1968); W. Gunther Plaut, *The Growth of Reform Judaism* (New York: World Union for Progressive Judaism, 1965); and Lou H. Silberman "The Union Prayerbook: A Study in Liturgical Development," in Bertram Wallace Korn, ed., *Retrospect and Prospect* (New York: Central Conference of American Rabbis, 1965), pp. 46–80.

Part One

Whence We Came

Some Basic Features of Jewish Liturgy*

Jakob J. Petuchowski

Jakob J. Petuchowski, Research Professor of Jewish Theology and Liturgy at the Hebrew Union College-Jewish Institute of Religion, is an influential thinker, esteemed teacher, and prolific writer. The following selection, taken from his definitive work, *Prayerbook Reform in Europe*, provides a concise account of Jewish Liturgy's traditional structure, and the considerations which led to liturgical reform in the Jewish communities of Western Europe.

What is the essential order or flow of ideas which constitutes the traditional service? To what extent are the editors of a Reform prayerbook free to alter the classic structure of the liturgy? Is there a contemporary equivalent to the medieval *piyyut* which a liberal prayerbook might utilize? I have inserted parenthetical page references to *Gates of Prayer* to enable the reader to compare that volume with Petuchowski's description of the *Siddur*, and, thus, to suggest answers to the above questions.

Judaism is a liturgical religion. Herein Judaism differs from some other religions which rely on hymns and *ex tempore* prayer exclusively. Judaism has its prayerbook. It, too, knows of the free outpourings of the pious heart, of the prayer uttered by the individual in his joy and in his anguish. But, in addition to those private expressions of devotion, Judaism has, for use in both synagogue and home, the fixed liturgy which is known as the *Siddur*. The name itself (meaning "order") indicates that Jewish prayer follows a definite and established order or arrangement. So much indeed has the *Siddur* become a part of Judaism that even sects which have broken away from Judaism have taken with

---

*Originally published as Chapter Two of *Prayerbook Reform in Europe* (New York: World Union for Progressive Judaism, 1968), and entitled "Some Characteristics of Jewish Liturgy."

them the idea that there should be a fixed liturgy. The Samaritans have a fixed liturgy. So do the Karaites. Even the liturgical tradition of the early Christian Church was, at least in part, indebted to the worship services of the synagogue.

A second fact to be borne in mind is that scholars are able to speak of a *history* of Jewish liturgy. History implies development. It means growth and change. The *Siddur* did not come into existence all at one time. Many generations contributed to its evolution, and perpetuated within its pages their love of God, Torah, and Israel, their joys and their sorrows, their contrition and their exaltation, their memories and their hopes.

Biblical psalmists, Pharisaic interpreters, Rabbinic sages, medieval bards, commentators and philosophers, and more recent mystics and poets—all had their share in the formation of the *Siddur.* Moreover, the existence of various rites—such as the Sephardi, the Ashkenazi, the Italiani, the Yemenite, etc.—within the Tradition itself testifies to the important role played by local needs as well as by local talent. Yet all of the rites, with all their divergences and unique *minhagim* (local customs), have enough basic material in common to be recognizable as mere varieties of the same fundamental structure of Jewish prayer which was laid down in Mishnah and Gemara, and formalized in the Geonic period.

The fact of evolution and change, moreover, must not be misunderstood. With a few rare exceptions in the realm of synagogal poetry, the evolution of the *Siddur,* until the rise of modern Reform Judaism, has been in one direction only. It has always been a case of adding more, never one of omitting. Every age would leave traces of its own devotional experience, but never at the expense of that of its predecessors. There are pages in the Talmud which take us straight into the liturgical workshop of Rabbinic Judaism, and demonstrate to us how the liturgy came to be fixed. Different rabbis suggest different prayers for the same occasion. In doing so, each one tries to do justice to one, rather than to another, tradition. But the final decision is not couched in terms of "either/or," but of "let us say all of them!"[1]

Then, again, there are prayers which were, at first, nothing but the private prayers of individual teachers. But, on account of the reputation of the teachers, or of the intrinsic merit of the prayers, or on account of both, such prayers found their way into the statutory service and became part of the fixed liturgy. We can illustrate this with the following example. "Prayer" *par excellence* for the ancient Rabbis was the prayer of the so-called Eighteen Benedictions. After the structure of the Eighteen Benedictions had become formalized, provision was made in the daily service for the private prayer of individuals. This rubric was called "Supplications," or "The Falling on one's Face," in view of the posture of prostration assumed by the worshipper for this section of the service—the Eighteen Benedictions having been recited in a standing position. While, at first, this rubric of the service was meant to enable the individual to couch his private prayer in his own words, the Talmud records the prayers which some of the teachers used to offer on that occasion.[2] After a while, the private prayer of Mar the son of Rabbina—"O my God, guard my tongue from evil, and my lips from speaking guile . . ."—was incorporated into the liturgy at this point [*GOP*, pp. 70/71]. As a consequence, the period for private "Supplications" was shifted to a position *after* the recitation of Mar's prayer. For a time, the period set aside for "Supplications" was still regarded as the domain of private prayer. In due course, however, official liturgical texts were provided for the "Supplications" as well. [*GOP* omits them.]

This illustration may serve to highlight two problems in connection with the traditional liturgy. On the one hand, it shows how the service grew by constant additions. On the other hand, it raises the question of the place of individual prayer within the framework of a liturgical service. Both of these problems are related to the apparently contradictory claims, known already to the Talmud, of *keva* (fixed times and fixed liturgy) and of *kavanah* (inwardness and spontaneity). Yet traditional Judaism affirms both principles, and Abraham J. Heschel has shown how they are reconciled.[3] The fixed times of prayer, he says, are part of "the order of the divine will." They are an immeasurable aid to us when we are in no mood to pray, and by thus forcing oneself to pray he may be saved from the danger of losing the ability to pray altogether. Again, the fixed liturgy may admittedly be nothing more than a makeshift arrangement. Ideally, perhaps, man should pray in his own words, and the liturgical formulae were fixed only when, because of the Exile, men had lost the art of spontaneous prayer. But that is only part of the story. If reciting the words of the liturgy is a "prayer of empathy" (man deriving inspiration from the words on the page in front of him), and is thus contrasted with the prayer of "self-expression," we ought to remember that even in the latter man is making use of *words*, and words are by nature external. Why not, then, use the words which have been proved to be efficacious by millenial use?

But the synthesis of *keva* and *kavanah*, of the fixed and the spontaneous, of the printed word and the inward intent, is a synthesis which gives birth to its own dialectic. One generation's expression of *kavanah* becomes the next generation's heritage of *keva*. The example we have given above of the daily rubric called "Supplications" demonstrates this. So does the history of the *piyyut,* that artistic creation of the medieval synagogal poets, which, at first, aimed at an alleviation of the routine character of the service, and which, in due time, was itself to become so much a matter of liturgical routine that its removal was demanded in the very name of *kavanah.* And, when we come to the nineteenth century, to the rise of Reform Judaism, the old balance between *keva* and *kavanah* had to be struck all over again, and a new synthesis came into being.

The basic structure of the Jewish public worship service is simple enough. In its original form it consisted of "The *Shema* and its Blessings" [*GOP,* pp. 31–35, 55–59], and of—what the Rabbis called—"The Prayer," i.e., a composite of eighteen (later, nineteen) benedictions on weekdays [*GOP,* pp. 60–70], and of seven benedictions on Sabbaths and festivals [*GOP,* pp. 306–313]. The *Shema* comprised Deuteronomy 6:4–9 (which the Rabbis called, "The Acceptance of the Yoke of God's Rulership"); Deuteronomy 11:13–21 (which the Rabbis called, "The Acceptance of the Yoke of the Commandments"); and Numbers 15:37–41 (which, on account of its last verse, the Rabbis referred to as "The Exodus from Egypt"). The three Biblical passages were surrounded by a framework of "blessings," i.e., really eulogies in which God was praised for various aspects of His dealings with the world in general, and with Israel in particular.

The first "blessing" before the *Shema,* in the morning service, praised God as the Creator of light, who daily renews the work of creation [*GOP,* p. 55]. In the evening service, this "blessing" took the form of praising God, who, "by His word, brings on the evening twilight" [*GOP,* p. 32]. The second "blessing" before the *Shema,* identical in content for both morning and evening services, though differing in the wording employed, praised God for the love He has shown Israel—a love manifest in Israel's possession of the Torah [*GOP,* pp. 32–3, 56]. In the morning service, the *Shema* was followed by one "blessing," in which the contents of the *Shema* were affirmed as true and enduring, and in which the theme of the Exodus from Egypt, mentioned in the third paragraph of the *Shema,* was developed—both in terms of the memory of God's past redemptive acts, and in terms of the future messianic hope [*GOP,* pp. 58–9]. A similar "blessing" followed upon the *Shema* in the evening service [*GOP,* pp. 34–5], where, however, yet another "blessing" followed—one which invokes God as the Guardian "who spreads out the tabernacle of peace" [*GOP,* p. 35].

The rubric, "The *Shema* and its Blessings," thus constituted the creedal affirmation within the Jewish worship service. It proclaimed the monotheistic faith, and Israel's loyalty to the divine commandments; and it linked that proclamation with an affirmation of the doctrines of Creation, Revelation, and Redemption.

That the *public* worship originally began with the first "blessing" before the *Shema* is still evidenced by the fact that, to this day, the first "blessing" before the *Shema* is preceded by the Call to Worship ("Praise ye the Lord, to whom all praise is due!") [*GOP,* pp. 31, 55], even though, for many a century now, this Call to Worship has been preceded by a great deal of other liturgical material. Prayers which were originally meant to be recited by the individual in his own home, prayers connected with rising from one's bed, washing one's hands, putting on one's belt, etc., were transferred to the beginning of the synagogue service [*GOP,* p. 286]. So were passages from Scripture and Rabbinic literature which the pious Jew was meant to study every day before he began his statutory prayer [*GOP,* p. 285]. And so were psalmodic passages from Scripture which, at first, were likewise a matter of private, rather than of public, worship [*GOP,* pp. 290–297].

Nor did the actual "blessings" of the *Shema* remain in the short and simple form in which they were originally couched. For example, the first "blessing" before the *Shema,* dealing, as we have noted, with God as the Creator of light, was elaborated by later mystics who saw the heavenly luminaries as angelic beings, and who, therefore, gave free rein to their fancy in describing the praises uttered by the angelic choirs [*GOP,* pp. 315–317].

"The Prayer" which followed the "*Shema* and its Blessings" was the rubric which provided petitionary prayer, prayers for forgiveness, for instruction, for personal and national welfare, etc. That is to say, it provided that on weekdays [*GOP,* pp. 62–66]. On Sabbaths and festivals, the petitionary prayers were replaced by a single one of gratitude for the gift of the Sabbath or the festival [*GOP,* pp. 309, 518–20]. Yet the first three and the last three benedictions of "The Prayer" remained the same for Sabbaths, festivals, and weekdays. Those six benedictions dealt with (a) the God of the fathers, who would send a redeemer to their children [*GOP,* p. 60]; (b) the mighty acts of the Lord, manifest particularly in the resurrection of the dead [*GOP,* pp. 60–61]; (c) the holiness of God which is proclaimed by Israel on earth even as it is by the angels on high [*GOP,* pp. 61–62]; (d) the request that the worship service be acceptable to God [*GOP,* p. 66]; (e) gratitude for God's providence [*GOP,* p. 67]; and (f) a prayer for peace [*GOP,* p. 70].

The benedictions making up "The Prayer" also underwent elaborations, and they were changed to take into account the changed circumstances of Jewish life. For example, the benediction we have mentioned under (d), above, originally read as follows: "Have pleasure, O Lord our God, in the service of Thy people Israel, and accept in favor the fire-offerings of Israel and their prayer." It concluded either with "Praised art Thou, O Lord, who accepts the service of His people Israel," or with "Praised art Thou, O Lord, whom we serve in reverence."[4] This benediction goes back to the days when the sacrificial cult of the Jerusalem Temple was still practised. After the destruction of the Temple, a prayer for the acceptance of sacrifices was no longer in order. Instead, it was changed into a plea for the acceptance of *prayer* and for the *restoration* of the sacrifices. It now reads as follows: "Have pleasure, O Lord our God, in Thy people Israel, and in their prayer. Restore the sacrificial service to the inner sanctuary of Thy house; and receive in love and favor both the fire-offerings of Israel and their prayer. And may the service of Thy people Israel ever be acceptable to Thee. And let our eyes behold Thy return in mercy to Zion. Praised art Thou, O Lord, who restorest Thy divine presence to Zion."

If "The *Shema* and its Blessings" and "The Prayer" were the original components of the public Jewish worship service, they did not remain its sole contents. We have already seen that the rubric of "The *Shema* and its Blessings" is now preceded by a number of other rubrics. Likewise, "The Prayer" came to be followed by other liturgical materials. Reference has already been made to the history of the rubric called "Supplications." This was followed by other prayers as well. It almost seems that Jews were reluctant to bring their service to a conclusion. The actual end was postponed more and more—by the addition of more psalms, more prayers, and the repeated recitation of the *Kaddish*.

Yet, even before those latter additions were reached, there came other components of the worship service. There was a reading from the Torah on the mornings of Sabbaths, festivals, Mondays, Thursdays, New Moons, and all special feast and fast days. There was also a Torah reading on Sabbath afternoons; and a lesson from the Prophets followed the Torah reading on the mornings of Sabbaths and festivals and on some special days during the afternoon service as well. The custom in Palestine had been to read through the entire Pentateuch within a period of three years or three and a half years. The Babylonian custom was to read through the entire Pentateuch in one year; and the Babylonian custom ultimately prevailed everywhere. It was left to some congregations espousing the cause of modern Reform Judaism to revert to the old Palestinian custom. It should furthermore be remembered that, in the early Rabbinic period, the Hebrew readings from the Scriptures were followed by an Aramaic translation or paraphrase. There was also an exposition of the Scriptures—the antecedent of the modern sermon. The Aramaic paraphrase ultimately lapsed, and the homilies, too, fell into oblivion before the beginning of the modern period. There were, indeed, wandering preachers who entertained and edified congregations in Eastern Europe on Sabbath afternoons. But the regular rabbis confined themselves to legal expositions twice a year, on the Sabbath before Passover, and on the Sabbath before the Day of Atonement.

The place of homiletics was taken by inserts into the prayers, the *piyyutim.* In the Palestinian rite, there seem to have been *piyyutim* for every Sabbath of the year. Elsewhere, *piyyutim* were recited on the festivals and on special Sabbaths only. *Piyyutim* are poetic compositions which develop the themes of the particular occasion, weaving the law and the lore of the day into the warp and woof of the liturgy. Scholars are still debating the precise occasion in Jewish history which gave rise to the introduction of *piyyutim.* Was it the legislation of the Emperor Justinian, in the sixth century, prohibiting the exposition of Scripture in the synagogue? In that case, the Jews circumvented this prohibition by incorporating this exposition into the prayers which they were allowed to recite. Or was it some other manifestation of government interference with Jewish practice, perhaps in Babylonia rather than in the Byzantine Empire? Perhaps we shall never know for sure. But one thing we do know. Quite apart from any external pressure, there was an inherent dynamic in the Jewish liturgy which led to constant elaborations. We have already referred to the mystical embellishments of the first "blessing" before the *Shema* in the morning service. This had nothing to do with government interference. Other liturgical poetry was likewise independent of such considerations. It is the old conflict between *keva* and *kavanah,* between the fixed and the spontaneous elements of the worship service which is, at least in part, responsible also for the introduction of *piyyutim.* The Jewish worshipper was not satisfied merely to recite his father's prayers. He wanted to pour out his own heart before God, to "sing unto the Lord a new song."

The classical structure of the liturgy makes no distinction between one festival and another. The service is the same for Passover as it is for Pentecost and Tabernacles. Only the mention by name, of the particular festival in question—and sometimes, though not always, the Scripture lesson being read—distinguishes one festival service from another. By means of the *piyyutim,* the meaning of each and every festival was brought out more clearly in the liturgy; and a service on Passover was truly a Passover service, a service on Tabernacles was distinctly a Tabernacles service, and so forth. The *piyyutim*, therefore, served the purpose of revitalizing the synagogue service.

That is not to say that the *piyyutim* were, at first, universally welcomed. Any *addition* to what has become traditional is as much of a *reform* as any *omission* from what has become customary. The legal authorities of Judaism fought fiercely against the introduction of the *piyyutim*—quite as fiercely as they were to fight, centuries later, against any suggestion that the *piyyutim* be omitted. For one thing, there was objection to introducing one kind of subject matter into a prayer which deals with something else. This was a general objection, and, as such, it was not even specifically directed against the *piyyutim*, although, of course, it lent itself to that purpose. Take, for example, the case of the first "blessing" before the *Shema* in the morning service. We have described it as a praise of God who is the Creator of light. Not in its original version, but before the time of Saadia Gaon (10th century), this "blessing" was made to include the wish, "O cause a new light to shine upon Zion, and may we all be worthy soon to enjoy its brightness" [*GOP*, p. 317]. Saadia Gaon objected to the insertion of that wish—not, be it understood, because he objected to the messianic hope as such, but because he regarded the first "blessing" before the *Shema* as a prayer dealing with the *physical* light, which must not be interrupted by mentioning the quite different—and metaphorical—messianic light.[5] If a mere sentence, voicing the messianic hope, could be regarded as an illegitimate interruption of a prayer, it is easy to imagine how much greater must have been the objection to the insertion of long and involved poetic passages which, to give but one example, discuss in great detail the various aspects of the Sinaitic Revelation *within* the structure of the first three benedictions of the Prayer of the Seven Benedictions in the morning service of Pentecost.

But the legalistic objections had to give way to the strong popular desire for this innovation in the liturgy. A compromise was reached by insisting that, whatever the subject matter of the poem, towards its end it must lead into the theme of the prayer in which it is inserted. With this proviso more or less followed, the *piyyutim* became an integral part of the traditional Jewish liturgy. They represented the victory of *kavanah* over the exclusive domination of *keva*. Yet, as we have already had occasion to see, one generation's expression of *kavanah* becomes the next generation's heritage of *keva*. This was in a very special sense the case with the *piyyutim*. Most of the poets who wrote *piyyutim* must have had very learned congregations in mind. Their compositions presuppose an intimate knowledge on the part of the worshipper of the totality of Biblical and Rabbinic literature, an ability to catch the slightest hint, and a mind which is a veritable concordance and cross-index.

To illustrate this latter point, it suffices to take but one line of a very early composition for the festival of Tabernacles. The Hebrew text, literally translated, says: "As Thou hast saved the mighty ones in Lud with Thee, when Thou didst go forth to the salvation of Thy people, so do Thou save us."[6] What the poet *intends* to say is the following: "As Thou hast saved Israel together with Thyself in Egypt, when Thou didst go forth, etc." The word for "mighty ones" *(elim)* can also be read as "terebinths," and, in Isaiah 61:3, Israel is called "terebinths of righteousness." Consequently, the word *elim* (terebinths) can be used as a name for Israel. As for Lud, we read in Genesis 10:13 that "Mizraim begot Ludim, etc." But *Mizraim* is Hebrew for Egypt, and, if Ludim be the offspring of Egypt, then Ludim (or, in the singular, Lud) could likewise be used as a name for Egypt.

That this kind of style fascinates the scholar and challenges his ingenuity goes without saying. He either has the requisite knowledge at his finger tips, or he can study the various commentaries which have been written on the *piyyutim,* supplying the necessary cross-references. (Yet no less an expert in the classical sources than the twelfth-century Bible commentator Abraham Ibn Ezra was quite vehement in his objection to the very style of the *piyyutim.*)[7] But it is also clear that the worshipper without the requisite background in Hebraic scholarship can only experience the height of boredom during the recitation of the *piyyutim*—a boredom which will lead to conversation with his neighbor, and to an inevitable disturbance of the decorum. Or—and this is hardly any better—he may devoutly recite page after page of words which are utterly incomprehensible to him, regarding them as some kind of magical incantation. In either case, the inclusion of *piyyutim* in the liturgy of necessity leads to a considerable prolongation of the worship service.

If we have devoted what might appear to be an undue amount of space to a discussion of the *piyyutim,* then the explanation for that is to be found in the fact that, long before any more thoroughgoing reforms of the worship service were undertaken, nascent Reform Judaism directed its major offensive against the *piyyutim.* They were the *bête noire* of the early Reformers. There is something ironic, and even pathetic, in the spectacle of Reform Judaism—the champion of *kavanah*—declaring war on what was, after all, the major expression of *kavanah* in an earlier age, and in seeing the arch-traditionalists, the spiritual heirs of those who initially opposed the introduction of *piyyutim* with all their might, as the zealous defenders of the *kavanah* which, in the course of the centuries, had itself become *keva*. (A rather lone Reform voice was that of Gustav Gottheil who, at the 1869 Israelite Synod in Leipzig, pleaded: "I fully recognize the rights of the present to change the prayer, but I believe that the religious consciousness of other times also has the right to find expression in our prayers. I do not believe that our time, with its cold rational direction, is especially suitable to create warm, heart-stirring prayers. And for these I would rather go back to the warmer religious sentiment of antiquity, and let it supply us with such prayers. Therefore, I must speak out against the generally condemnatory judgment against *piyyutim*.")[8]

The very struggle about the *piyyutim* underlines one of the major features of the evolution of the traditional Jewish liturgy. There was, indeed, evolution. There was development, and there was growth. But, as we have already noted, it was all in one direction only: that of constant *addition*. Once something had been incorporated into the liturgy, one did not let go of it any more. To this day, the Orthodox Jew prays, on every Sabbath, for the welfare of the Babylonian exilarchs and the heads of the Babylonian academies[9]—institutions which have ceased to exist many centuries ago. But the prayer remains!

It was this kind of extreme conservatism in our liturgical development which, by the time the nineteenth century had come around, set the stage for the liturgical task of modern Reform Judaism.

NOTES

1 See, for example, b. *Berakhot* 11b.

2 B. *Berakhot* 16b, 17a.

3 Abraham J. Heschel, *Man's Quest for God*. New York, Scribner's, 1954. See especially pp. 64ff.

4 See Rashi to b. *Berakhot* 11b, s.v. *va'abhodah*.

5 Cf. *Seder Rav Amram*, ed. Frumkin. Vol. I, p. 192.

6 Philip Birnbaum, ed., *Daily Prayer Book*. New York, Hebrew Publishing Co., 1949, pp. 683f. Note that, though this prayerbook is supposed to be "translated and annotated," this passage and similar ones remain untranslated. No simple translation could ever do justice to them.

7 See Ibn Ezra's commentary on Ecclesiastes 5:1. Cf. also the collection of traditional objections to the *piyyutim* in A. A. Wolff, *Die Stimmen der ältesten glaubwürdigsten Rabbinen über die Pijutim*. Leipzig, 1857.

8 W. Gunther Plaut, *The Rise of Reform Judaism*. New York, WUPJ, 1963, p. 184.

9 Birnbaum, *op. cit.*, p. 377.

David Einhorn's Guiding Principles*

Kaufmann Kohler

David Einhorn was born in Bavaria in 1809, and educated at the famed Yeshiva of Fürth, as well as the universities of Würzburg and Munich. After a stormy career in Europe, he migrated to America, becoming the rabbi of Har Sinai Congregation in Baltimore. In 1858, he published a prayerbook in German and Hebrew to which he gave the title *Olat Tamid*, "The Perpetual Offering."

In part, *Olat Tamid* was Einhorn's response to a Rabbinic conference held in Cleveland in 1855. Isaac M. Wise, the moderate leader of Reform Jewry, had attended and signed a conservatively oriented document designed to unite disparate elements of Jewish opinion in the United States. Under pressure from the right, he had even subscribed to the binding nature of Talmudic Judaism, an act which the more radically inclined Einhorn denounced as treason in a blistering editorial in the Jewish press. Wise's prayerbook, *Minhag America*, had mirrored its author's relative conservatism by including much Hebrew, which Wise still saw as the basic language of prayer, and generally showing relatively little deviation from the traditional liturgical structure. Einhorn's *Olat Tamid* quickly became a widely accepted alternative to Wise's liturgy.

Einhorn's son-in-law, Kaufmann Kohler, reached prominence as a rabbi in Detroit, Chicago, and, finally, New York. In 1903 he succeeded Wise as the second President of the Hebrew Union College. He wrote a well-known account of Jewish theology, and was paramount in assembling the Pittsburgh Conference of 1885, from which a Reform platform emerged. The *Union Prayer Book* is in large part a combination of Einhorn's *Olat Tamid* and the theological platform that was adopted in Pittsburgh.

The following selection represents Kohler's understanding of some of the principles which guided his father-in-law. It speaks for itself, and

*From the *CCAR Yearbook* 19 (1909): 215-270. It was written for the centennial of Einhorn's birth, and entitled, "David Einhorn, the Uncompromising Champion of Reform Judaism."

the reader may determine the extent to which Einhorn's concerns are still timely, and the degree to which his solutions to those problems are still acceptable.

In Frankfort-on-the-Main in 1845,* . . . Einhorn at once became conspicuous by his pointed, lucid and pronounced utterances. Against Frankel's insistence upon the maintenance of the Hebrew language in the Synagogue liturgy, he remarked that "while the Talmud leaves no doubt as to the permissibility of the vernacular in the liturgy, he would urge its use in the divine service as a necessity today. Hebrew is the language of the study of the Law. As long as prayer was mainly the cry of the oppressed Jew, the scarcely intelligible Hebrew sufficed. Now people need prayer as the simple expression of their innermost thoughts, convictions and sentiments. This can only be attained through the mother-tongue." For this reason he unequivocally opposed the committee's distinction between a subjective and an objective necessity of using the vernacular in the service. "Sentiment is praiseworthy," he said, "but not that morbid sentimentalism which paralyzes, nay, kills all spiritual life. By striking the rock of a dead language we can not bring forth living waters to quench the thirst of the people" (Proceedings, p. 27; 49).

As the first speaker on the Committee's report, which proposed the mention of the Messianic idea in the liturgy to the exclusion of all political aspirations, Einhorn at once points to the underlying principle. "For the Talmudic Jew," he says, "the Messianic hope is inseparable from the whole ceremonial law, on the full observance of which his salvation depends. Only the sacrificial cult in a restored Temple and State would work atonement for him; hence his wonderful abiding hope in the restitution of its former glory. Our views have entirely changed. We no longer believe in the atoning power of sacrifice and priesthood connected with the holy land. We stand upon the ground of prophetic Judaism which aims at a universal worship of God by righteousness. Israel's political overthrow, formerly bewailed as a misfor-

---

*[Ed. note: The reference is to the Frankfort Conference of 1845, when the subject of Hebrew and German as languages for prayer was debated. Zacharias Frankel (1801–1875) argued that, although Jewish law permitted large-scale use of the vernacular, wisdom dictated maintaining the priority of Hebrew if only for its symbolic value. The conference voted that Hebrew was advisable, but Frankel interpreted the resolution as being insufficiently strong. Hebrew, for him, was essential, not merely advisable. He subsequently declared his ideological independence from the Conference and founded what he called "the positive historical school." It is from this school that American Conservative Judaism claims its origins.]

tune, in reality is its forward move toward its larger destiny. Prayer took the place of sacrifice. From Israel's midst the word of God was to be carried to all parts of the earth, and new religious systems were to aid in this great work. The Talmud moves in a circle, whereas we today believe in progress." "The Messianic idea (which I formerly took to be a substitute for the immortality idea) expresses, in my opinion, the hope of both earthly and heavenly salvation. There is nothing objectionable therein. The belief in Israel's election also contains nothing that is repugnant. On the contrary, it should be retained in the service as expressing the claim of an undeniable privilege, as it engenders in the Jew a feeling of reassuring self-consciousness over against the ruling church." Accordingly, Einhorn wanted all the petitions for the restoration of bloody sacrifices and of political independence eliminated, and have put in their stead the Messianic prayers so framed as to express the hope for a spiritual rebirth and the uniting of all men in faith and in love by the agencies of Israel" (*Proceedings, p. 74f.*). Thus we see here all the points accentuated that formed the basis of Einhorn's theological system, and especially of his Prayerbook.

Of course, he voted for the reading of the Haftarah lesson in the vernacular, expressing regret that the reading of the Torah lesson in the vernacular could not at once also be voted for *(p. 134)*. The book of Esther, only, did he want read in Hebrew alone *(p. 137);* the reason, though not stated, is obvious. Quite characteristic is the reason given for the then discussed abolition of the custom of calling up seven men for the reading from the Torah: "It should not appear as if woman was excluded from the benefits of the Torah" *(p. 144)*. In regard to the playing of the organ on Sabbath, while agreeing with the arguments offered by others, that the same law that abrogated the prohibition of certain work in the Temple of old holds good also in our Synagogue, he adds the elucidating remark that "the distinction between the ancient Temple and the Synagogue made by the Talmudists is due to their adherence to the belief in the sacrificial cult which we no longer share. Hence, our Synagogue takes the place of the ancient Temple" *(p. 147)*.

As Referee of the Committee on the Position of Woman, . . . Einhorn undertakes to show that "the inequality of woman in the Mosaic Law forms part of the ancient priestly system of castes, which need not and should not be kept up in a higher state of religious education, whereas Rabbinism beholds in woman an inferior creature altogether, excluding her from the greatest privileges of religion in the Synagogue and public life and lowering her to such an extent as to institute a special benediction for man, thanking God that he was not made a woman. We have long outlived the notion of natural inequality of men in regard to holiness. The distinctions made by Holy Writ have, for us, only relative and temporary value. It is, therefore, our sacred duty to declare, with all emphasis, woman's perfect religious equality with man. It is true, life, which is stronger than all theory, has already accomplished much in this respect, but much is still wanting, and even the little that has been accomplished still lacks legal sanction. It therefore behooves us, as far as it is possible, to declare the religious equality of woman, both as to her duties and her rights and privileges, to be in accord with the Jewish law. We have the same right to do so as had the Synod of Rabbenu Gershom eight hundred years ago when passing new religious decrees in favor of the female sex. The Talmud, with reference to the Mezuzzah, says: 'Should the men only have the promise of the lengthening of their days and not also the women?' So say we in regard to woman's religious life. Let us reclaim her spiritual powers for the religious community; they have been kept back too long" *(III, 253–265).*

The Debate on Music*

The following is a significant portion of the first large-scale debate in the Central Conference of American Rabbis on the role of synagogue music. The fact that it occurred as early as 1892 indicates that the rabbis' concern for liturgical music was rivaled in importance only by their desire for an appropriate liturgical text. From the beginning, their goal was both to breathe life into the service and to unify disparate local customs by providing common hymns which all congregations could sing.

As in other matters related to the service, the background for this discussion is Reform in Europe. Of the composers and singers who contributed to the development of synagogue art music there, perhaps the two most notable are Salomon Sulzer (1804–1890) and Louis Lewandowski (1821–1894). It would be impossible to do justice to either man without expanding this limited introduction into an essay of considerable length.[1] Probably of greatest significance from our perspective, however, is one particular reform: the mood which Sulzer, especially, established, and which became standard in Reform temples throughout America.

> His first task was to abolish the prevailing chaotic mood of worship. The "Schreien" and "Nachsagen" of the Judenschule were immediately done away with. He defined the province of the cantor, designated that of the congregation, and created a new factor in the service, the choir, which was to compliment the function of both.[2]

Thus, when the Conference met to discuss the role of music in worship services, a ready model lay before them: the presentation of traditional Jewish music in an artistic form capable of stirring the hearts of the assembled worshippers, such as Sulzer himself had achieved in his pioneering work in Vienna.

The immediate issue to which there was no ready solution, however, was the determination of a common hymnal in which such artistic arrangements of appropriate music could be presented. A variety of

*From *CCAR Yearbook* 3 (1893): 24–30.

hymnals were available for adoption, but none was deemed acceptable in its present form. On the other hand, the need to publish some musical accompaniment for the *Union Prayer Book* resulted in the Conference's taking immediate steps to assemble whatever music there was. The account of that effort deserves to be summarized, not only because it demonstrates the supreme significance that liturgical music had in the minds of rabbis from the very beginning of the Reform movement, but also because the process of formulating a hymnal then, demonstrates quite well the difficulty inherent in first writing a prayerbook and then demanding instant music to accompany it; a problem facing us just as much today as it did in 1892.

The 1892 debate resulted in the rabbis' resolving to send their favorite texts to the fledgling Cantors' Association of America, so that the words might be set to music. Since, however, there was no guarantee that the rabbinic Conference as a whole would officially accept the lyrics selected by its individual members, the cantors were loathe to begin the arduous task of musical composition. But a year later (1893) the rabbis voted to wait on the cantors no longer, and instead, to issue a collection of whatever music they could find, for temporary use at least. This decision apparently prodded the reluctant Cantors' Association to compose some new tunes, and a volume was produced. (It was an interim edition; the first official hymnal did not appear until 1897.)

In 1895, the President of the Cantors' Association, Alois Kaiser of Baltimore, complained that his colleagues had been given too little time for their work, and that they had not even been supplied with a complete text of the proposed prayerbook from which to work. He concluded that the hastily produced product contained, of necessity, "little of permanent value."[3] To his surprise, however, its deficiencies had not prevented the book from being received enthusiastically across the country. The CCAR committee report of that year described it as containing "tunes . . . so simple as to enable the congregation to join in the singing," and "many [which] do not lend themselves to congregational singing . . . [but] may be used for private edification and devotion."[4]

Yet discontent with the state of synagogue music was voiced year after year. In 1909, the dismal failure to promote congregational singing, and the realization that many hymns were of Christian origin, made universal in character by expurgating Trinitarian references, led the CCAR to mandate someone to comb the libraries of Europe, to "examine all the literature of devotion and poetry in German, English and French that is at all accessible," in the hope of locating sufficient Jewish material that might be utilized. Nevertheless, two years later, the Conference noted that even though over 10,000 copies of the hymnal had been sold, most congregations probably did not make actual use of it.

So in 1912, the Conference invited Rabbi Israel Aaron of Buffalo to speak on "The Reintroduction of Congregational Singing." After reviewing the long history of Jewish congregational singing, he concluded:

It is rather strange that with this long and honorable testimony behind it, the endeavours to reinstate congregational singing have been so discouraging. In spite of the publication of the *Union Hymnal* and other hymn compilations—perhaps, some might say, because of them—in few, if any, of our larger congregations do even a minority of those assembled on Sabbath or Holidays really sing the hymns. A dozen or so scattered and courageous souls may hum along with the choir, but there is hardly a suggestion of the full-volumed joyful noise we have a right to expect. There is a well-defined feeling that the choir should do all the singing because they can do it better and because they are paid to do it.[6]

A survey undertaken in November of that year revealed, "the most surprising result . . . that the *Union Hymnal* is even less generally used than has been assumed."[7]

The next few decades witnessed constant revisions designed to make the hymnal authentically Jewish, musically sophisticated, and inviting of congregational participation. Yeoman service was performed by men like A. Z. Idelsohn (1882–1938) who worked tirelessly collecting authentic Jewish folk melodies, and who argued for a return to the traditional practice of chanting from the Torah;[8] and Abraham Binder (1895–1966) who almost singlehandedly edited the new *Union Hymnal* of 1932, which reflected the rising East European influence in the movement.

The musical style had by now changed dramatically from the early days when Christian hymns and anthems outnumbered Jewish melodies in the Reform synagogue. But the basic pattern by which songs were sung remained the same. The 1930 committee report to the CCAR convention, for example, still lists as one aim the stimulation of congregational singing. There were many notable exceptions to be sure, but even Binder's masterful arrangements of traditional folk melodies were not entirely successful in evoking the "full-volumed joyful noise" of congregational participation called for back in 1912. The *Union Songster* of 1960, edited by Eric Werner and Malcolm Stern, though intended for religious school use, was adopted as a general congregational hymnal in many temples, and its judicious selection of musical options did alleviate the difficulty to some extent. But, as Malcolm Stern summarizes, "Within a decade after its appearance, music from Israel and from the youth camps of American Jewry made much of the prior music of Reform Jewry obsolete."[9]

I have devoted such considerable space to the Reform movement's search for a viable musical idiom in order to dispel the popular misconception that the current unhappiness with congregational passivity is a recent phenomenon. The record indicates unequivocally that full congregational participation has been much sought after since the first debate in 1892; and that the existence of many magnificent hymns, edited and reedited by the finest scholars and musicians, did not suffice to move the majority of worshippers to sing together. Clearly the basic problem went much deeper than the quality of songs, or their arrangement in specific hymnals. And we shall have to examine the matter further later in this book.

At this moment in time, then, the Reform movement has spawned a considerable repertoire of magnificent music; it has fought the notion that non-Jewish hymnology need form the nucleus of synagogue songs; and it has both salvaged and nurtured authentic Jewish musical motifs of the past. Yet much has not changed through the years. The challenge of evoking congregational participation is still with us. The procedural anomaly of first selecting prayer texts and only then demanding that they be set to music still prevails. Contemporary Jewish composers must be encouraged, if our musical heritage of the past is to be supplemented by compositions of the present. The very definition of "*Jewish* music" as well as the role such music should play in the service are matters which have yet to be determined.

The following passage is taken from the original 1892 debate which expressed these issues so well. The reader may compare it with William Sharlin's contemporary perspective (pp. 122ff.) and the discussion on worship "choreography" provided in the concluding chapter, "The Liturgical Message."

Resolved, That the hymn-book by the Rev. Dr. I. M. Wise be adopted as the hymn-book of American Jewish Reform Congregations and a committee of five be appointed to revise and add such selections of other hymns to it as they may see fit.

Resolved, That the Cantors' Association of America be requested to furnish appropriate music for the same.

The following discussion then took place.

Rabbi Guttman:*

You will agree with me that the Jewish Synagogue is indeed sadly in need of Jewish music. We can indeed say we sing, but our music is not the outgrowth of Jewish production. We sing Methodist music and Presbyterian and Catholic. I may say that my congregation may not be a praying congregation, but my congregation is a singing congregation. And I see the time come when hymnology, when singing in the Jewish Synagogue, will bring life and new spirit into our congregations. There are about 330,000 members of the Christian Endeavor Society at present here in New York City, and I see by this morning's paper that they opened their services with a song service. And I have often attended these Methodist and other denominational services, and it is the song in the Christian church which is the power and is really the secret force that gives them this power, and I think we ought to do

---

*[Ed. note: Rabbi Adolph Guttman (1854–1927), rabbi in Syracuse, N.Y., from 1883–

likewise in the Jewish church. We ought to have congregational singing. In Jewish Reform Congregations they do not pray, and they ought to sing. And this Cantors' Association could do a great deal for us. . . . If we call upon the Cantors' Association the members of that Association are perfectly capable and willing to furnish us Jewish music. And, therefore, I would ask the members here present to vote favorably upon this resolution.

The Rev. Dr. Kohler was then called to the chair, while Dr. Wise made the following remarks:

That which the preceding speaker said is a truth which ought not be overlooked. We have built up an American Synagogue, an American Congregational Organization, which is unique in itself, in correspondence with the American spirit, with the American liberty and with the American present and future. I believe that as we now worship we ought be as American as possible, namely, as American Israelites. And that which has grown out of the American Jewish spirit, that ought to be preserved. While we can not preserve all the original prayers that have been written, if I had been on the Committee, I certainly would have voted that all those prayers in German or in Hebrew or in English, which were produced originally by American minds shall be preserved, and ought to be preserved in the Union Prayer Book. Then it would have been a Union Prayer Book and an American. But this appears hardly possible to-day because the prayers which have been produced are too numerous. But not so in hymnology. That hymnology is the soul of all live worship and always was, we have the best evidence in Scripture itself. The Scriptures have been preserved through various centuries; those preserved contain very little prayer, but contain a very large collection of psalms. Hence we say that it is not the prayer coming from the spirit of Judaism which is the element, but the indestructible element is the psalmody of the people . . . . It is evident that song is the main thing and therefore I would be in favor, even if it cost a few dollars more, to print it, to have all that the Hebrew mind has produced in the way of song united in one volume, with the understanding that whenever, next year, or two years, or in three years, or in ten years, new productions are made in that line, that every Conference, year after year, will add to them. Thus it will be a hymn-book for the American Israelite, and it will not only be a hymn-book for the American Israelite, but will also go into a great many American churches, as I have the evidence in my hand here that a great many Jewish hymns have made their way into the various churches. So much for the text. Now in regard to the music our Brother Gutman has said well, the music is the language of the heart in notes, as poetry is the language of the heart in words. And language is the expression of ideal sentiment and feeling, and in the Jewish Synagogue we ought by all means to have the Jewish expression of feeling and sentiment and thought. Secondly, we ought to have Jewish music. . . . There ought to be original Jewish music and Jewish hymns. And as the brother has said, that the Cantors' Association is capable and willing and desirous of undertaking that task, we certainly ought to give them an opportunity. But I would insist that all American productions shall be compiled, even if the hymn-book cost a few dollars more, with the understanding that in future when anything new is produced, and it is important that there should be new productions, they should be added to this book, or they should replace other productions not any longer fit for the time.

President Wise then took the chair and the Rev. Dr. Kohler was granted the privilege of the floor, speaking as follows:

I want to express my sincere thanks to our President for having here to-day, for the first time, touched my soul, my heart, in regard to praying and devotion which was the subject to-day. In this former discussion of yours I purposely refrained from taking part. Here I shall, and I also wish to refer to Dr. Talmage.* I heard him once state, I believe, to one of our members who is not here, that he owed the success of his attendance of his church to the singing. And I say we might learn indeed from our fellow-citizens and our brethren in other churches that we should cultivate that more, because here we can all join. When it comes to Hebrew, when it comes to a question of Reform or Conservatism or any part of the old or the new prayer-book, there we are always born critics, more or less occupying ourselves with roots or the far-fetched meaning of the words we meet or the interpretation or translation of the words we recite. But with the prayer the soul is seldom touched unless the song unites. Music is the language of all languages, is the language of humanity, and we have as yet been in the formation, in the composition, in the making up of our prayer-books too intellectual and too little emotional. We need not become Methodists or Moody and Sankey men,* but we should touch the soul, make people what they seldom do in our synagogues, cry. And the music, the song, can wrest fears [*sic!* It probably should read "tears."] even from those who come without any desire to pray, without any devo-

---

*[Ed. note: Probably Thomas DeWitt Talmage (1832–1902), Presbyterian minister in Brooklyn from 1869–1894.]
*[Ed. note: The reference is to Dwight Lyman Moody (1837–1899) and Ira David Sankey (1840–1908), two Christian evangelists who published the "Sankey and Moody Hymn Book" in 1873.]

tion. I heartily endorse the idea of giving greater care and attention to a hymn-book, and such a hymn-book as is offered to us whenever we enter any church where over the text the notes are given to make the people sing. . . .

. . . I want to call your attention to one thing more before I close. I have felt the need of music and song and have even felt like changing and have been prompted to change my own Friday evening service in view of the fact often overlooked by Reform prayer-book composers or writers that the text must be written with a view to make it singable, so to say, to make it resonant, rhythmical and apt to be sung . . .

The Rev. Dr. Harris* then spoke as follows: I feel with the previous speakers that the hymn-book is perhaps more important for our work than the prayer-book, partly because the prayer-book is written and we have only to revise the old prayer-book, and the hymn-book is not. I believe I voice the sentiment of every minister, whether progressive or not, that the need of congregational singing is the need of the hour. We have had a great many hymns and we have had some very fine music. We have not so far been able to get those simple airs that could be taken up by the congregation, and we have been even compelled sometimes to mistrust our cantors, anxious to give us rather elaborate music, music that a choir is able to sing, but music that can not be taken up by the people. Dr. Kohler has referred to the great strength of Christianity, their hymns. And here is the importance of uniformity. Whether you go to the country, in the farm house where you are stopping among a large number of Christians, or whether you are on board a ship or over in England, you will find they have the same hymns and the same music. And it does not matter what strangers they are; they may have never met before. Some may be Congregationalists, and some Methodists, and some Episcopalians, but they have the same airs, and without any preparation all can join. Therefore, the most important point, the vital point for a hymn-book, is first, that it must be uniform. It must be adopted by all or by none. We must in the first place find out what hymns there are (I am talking of the music of the old service) that could still be appropriated for our use to-day—some of the old Hebrew melodies that we all know, the old Yigdal and the old Adonolom. And while we are all ministers and can all write prayers, we can not write hymns. Hymns are poems, and only poets can write them. If we prepare a hymn-book at all it must be classical. Rather compile real

---

*[Ed. note: Maurice H. Harris (1859–1930), rabbi in New York City from 1882 until his death.]

poems, even if they be not written by Jews, provided the spirit is Jewish, if they be written by the standard poets of England and America. Rather take the best poetic thought suitable for hymnology than rhymy verse. Let us be modest enough to know that we are not poets—that we can not write hymns. And in the preparation of the music let us consider not the choir. We have been considering the choir too long. The choir has driven the congregation out as far as the worship of praise is concerned. It is time that the congregation be given a hearing before God; it is time that we give them a service of praise so simple that after it has been sung once or twice they can all join in it—simple melodies, simple airs. And I hope that the committee appointed on this question give due consideration to these two facts: the simplicity of the music and the poetry of the hymns. In my own congregation, to speak of a personal experience, wishing to introduce congregational singing, which we all wish to introduce, I was compelled even to go to the Christian hymn-books to select therefrom some of the old hymns that you all know and that have been introduced in some cases into the Jewish congregations. Therefore, let me beg of you to go slow in this work and not produce something of which we may be afterward ashamed. Let it be classic. Let it be simple, something that will last, and let us use all of the old that we possibly can.

NOTES

1 Ready biographical data can be found in A. Z. Idelsohn, *Jewish Music* (New York: Henry Holt and Co., 1929), pp. 246–260; 269–284; Adolph Guttman, "The Life of Salomon Sulzer," *CCAR Yearbook* 14 (1904): 227–237; and Alois Kaiser, "Sulzer's Music," *CCAR Yearbook* 14 (1904): 237–245.

2 Alois Kaiser, "Sulzer's Music," *CCAR Yearbook* 14 (1904): 239. His allusions to "Schreien" and "Nachsagen" refer, literally, to "shrieking" and "repetition." In context, they are derogatory descriptions of traditional cantorial practice in European synagogues. Cf. citations from Isaac M. Wise's German journal, *Die Deborah*, summarized in Joseph Gutmann, "Watchman on an American Rhine: New Light on Isaac M. Wise," *American Jewish Archives* 10:1 (1958), p. 140.

3 *CCAR Yearbook* 6 (1896): 33.

4 *CCAR Yearbook* 6 (1896): 31.

5 *CCAR Yearbook* 19 (1909): 83.

6 *CCAR Yearbook* 22 (1912): 334.

7 *CCAR Yearbook* 23 (1913): 149.

8 See A. Z. Idelsohn, "Synagogue Music Past and Present," *CCAR Yearbook* 33 (1923): 344–355.

9 I am grateful to Malcolm Stern and Jeffrey Stiffman, not only for this observation, but also for data on the *Union Songster*.

An 1854 Service*

On August 11, 1854, the following report appeared in Isaac M. Wise's English weekly, *The American Israelite.* Such journals abounded during the last century both in Germany and in the United States. Their editors used them not simply as newspapers, but as educational vehicles to chart the progress of Jewish enlightenment. Actual news coverage in *The Israelite,* in fact, is often relegated to second place, while lead stories tend to be lessons in Jewish history or practice. Since the general press had little interest in specifically Jewish news, and since travel was time-consuming and difficult, these journals functioned also to keep Jews abreast of what was happening to their correligionists in both Europe and America. Our article describes the introduction of the choir in services at the original Lodge Street site of what is now Isaac M. Wise Temple, K. K. B'nai Yeshurun. (Wise had assumed the rabbinate there in April.) The style of service described here, though revolutionary in 1854, later came to typify Reform worship. The concern for devotion, decorum, and dignity is reported with pride.

The Choir

Last Friday evening, August 4th, the choir performed for the first time the singing part of divine service in the Lodge Street Synagogue. The large concourse of worshippers on that occasion is a fair demonstration, that this reform was desired by the vast majority of the members of that synagogue, and is approved of by the members of the other congregations.

The choir consists of thirty-two persons, viz: fifteen young ladies, nine lads, seven young men and their leader, Mr. Hess. The choruses sung were:

---

*From *The American Israelite,* August 11, 1854; under the heading of "Communicated," it is entitled, "The Choir."

Mizmor Shir Lijom Hashabboth, and Adonoi Moloc,	S. Sulzer.
Borechu and Shema,	S. Sulzer.
Mi Chomocho,	S. Naumburg.
Ki El Shomerenu,	S. Naumburg.
Adon Olam,	S. Sulzer.

with a baritone solo by Thomas Lloyd.

The delivery of these somewhat difficult pieces of vocal music, does much honor to both the performers and the leader, convincing us of their diligence and musical taste.

The auditory appeared to us perfectly delighted with the truly Jewish melodies of ancient times, beautifully arranged in quarto-choruses, and tastefully delivered. The parents of the singers looked especially delighted. There was an eminent devotion, and notwithstanding the numerous congregation of both sexes the decorum was very good. The Hazan, Mr. Moses, performed his part to the entire satisfaction of all present.

Upon us those songs made an indescribable impression. We felt once more the beauty and sublimity of Hebrew poetry, which are so masterly re-produced by the compositions of S. Sulzer. When the passage was sung in Adon Olom, "He is my God, the Redeemer of my life," etc., tears filled our eyes, feeling once more the truth of these words. They appeared to us as a persecuted, maltreated and tortured queen, now restored to her dignity. If our divine service will be reformed in this beautiful and truly Jewish manner, we will have again a service worthy of the name.

Part Two

What We Believe

The Language of Debate and the Language of Prayer*

Abraham Cronbach

When Abraham Cronbach died (1965), his son-in-law and devoted pupil, Maurice Davis, wrote of him, "He glittered with greatness, greatness of soul. . . . What we preached, he practiced. What we dreamed, he did." And Jacob Marcus prefaced the publication of Cronbach's autobiography by noting,

> It would have been possible and appropriate, to entitle this memoir, "The Autobiography of a Saint." Such a title might have embarrassed the memorialist; if so, it would have been one of the few times in his life that the truth served to embarrass Abraham Cronbach.

Cronbach, Professor of Jewish Social Studies at the Hebrew Union College for twenty-eight years, was indeed a passionate devotee of the saintly, the spirituality implicit in religious experience; and a tenacious advocate of truth and social justice. His stand on issues was not always popular. Utterly opposed to the rule of brute force and power, he maintained an unshakable faith in pacifism—even during World War II. Similarly, unwilling to see the Jewish people become an armed nation like all others, he remained opposed to political Zionism. And when almost no one dared speak out on behalf of Julius and Ethel Rosenberg, it was Abraham Cronbach who petitioned President Eisenhower for clemency.

Though Cronbach was never convinced of the value of ritual, he experienced personally the efficacy of prayer in bringing about the nearness of God. How was it, he wondered, that the reality of God's presence could be so immediately obvious in worship, yet be the subject

---

*Part of a paper originally entitled "The Personal Aspects of Prayer," *CCAR Yearbook* 57 (1947): 379–388.

of debate in academic discussion? The answer to this dilemma came to him from his studies in linguistic philosophy: the language of prayer is not the language of debate. The following is Cronbach's own explanation, taken from a paper delivered to the CCAR convention in 1947.

The great stumbling block for religious thought throughout the ages has been the unsuspected assumption that language performs no other function than that of transmitting information. Semantics, which is the study of the way in which language actually operates, has disclosed that information is not the only office filled by human speech. Language can be designative or evaluative or dramatistic.

Language is designative when it supplies things with their names. Examples of designative language are: wall, curtain, platform, bulb, street, sky, and hosts of other nouns. There are also designative verbs as when one says: The man walks, the boy runs, the bell sounds.

Language can also be evaluative. When language is evaluative, it does not provide things with their names. Evaluative language divulges our *feelings* with reference to things. It voices our likes and our dislikes, our desires and our aversions. Examples of evaluative language are: beautiful, ugly, good, bad, splendid, wretched, glorious, miserable, and the like. There are also evaluative nouns like: saint, sinner, hero, coward, villain, progress, thief, aggressor, and the like.

Sometimes a word which is designative in one context can be evaluative in another. If one says: "I hired a man to sweep the floor," the word "man" is designative. How strikingly different is the purport of the word "man" in the passage from Shakespeare:

> His life was gentle; and the elements
> So mix'd in him that Nature might stand up
> And say to all the world, *This was a man!*

This time "man" is obviously evaluative.

Sometimes a word which is designative when used literally becomes evaluative when taken metaphorically. If one says: "The buttercup is yellow," the word "yellow" is designative. But if one accuses a newspaper of being yellow, "yellow" becomes evaluative. In the Bible, the word "angel" is designative; but if one lauds a man or a woman of today as being an "angel," then "angel" is evaluative. It is designative to say that the sun shines. It is evaluative when one remarks that a certain person leads a "shining" life.

Besides being designative or evaluative, language can also be dramatistic. Dramatization occurs when something easily pictured is substi-

tuted as a token for something intricate, complex, involved, compli-
cated, abstruse, far-reaching, and difficult to understand. Thus, Uncle
Sam dramatizes our federal government. The Wandering Jew dramatizes the tribulations of Jewish history. Freedom on her mountain
height dramatizes American ardor for American institutions. Every
cartoon is a dramatization.

Also science resorts to dramatizations. Science notes that water seeks
the lowest level, though water has no eyes that it should seek anything.
That is but a dramatistic way of speaking. Astronomy reports that the
sun attracts the earth, although the sun is not a glamorous female nor
the earth a responsive male. That is a dramatistic mode of expression.

Amid the personal aspects of prayer, the word "God" is evaluative
and dramatistic. In prayer, the word "God" personifies and acclaims
the redemptive phases of experience.

The world in which we live abounds in distress and anguish. There
are, in this universe, no unplumbed depths of agony. Every extreme of
pain, both physical and mental, has been endured and is being
endured. None of us has ever questioned Job's lament: "Man, born of
woman, is few of days and full of trouble." Those debating rabbis in
Talmud *Erubin* (13b) concluded that man's non-existence were better
than his existence. None of us has ever taken issue with Tennyson who,
in the modern age, observed:

> Never morn to evening wore
> But some heart did break.

And none of us has ever challenged Thoreau's remark: "The mass of
mankind lead lives of quiet desperation."

Yes, our world brims with woe and tribulation. And yet that is not the
entire story. The universe produces not only pain. It also offers sur-
cease of pain, deliverance from pain. The world generates not only
frustration but also an occasional triumph, not only defeat but also an
occasional victory. That is what we mean by the redemptive phases of
experience. The redemptive phases of experience are far and above
the most significant phases of experience. When we wish to designate
the universe, we say "universe." But amidst the personal aspects of
prayer we do not designate the universe. Amidst the personal aspects
of prayer, we dramatize and evaluate the infinite reaches of adversity
and deliverance which constitute the universe. Therefore, when we
pray, we do not say "universe." Appropriating a word hallowed by the
ages, when we pray, we say: "God."

However, people do not spend the entire of their lives at prayer.

Even the devoutest allot to prayer only a meager portion of their time. The Talmud mentions those ancient saints who devoted nine hours a day to the Eighteen Benedictions, but the Talmud betrays, at the same time, some misgiving as to the suitability of such an extreme. We have other needs in addition to the need for prayer. We must eat and sleep and work. We must go forth and meet people and deal with people and converse with people. No sooner do we consort with people than we encounter difference of opinion. If we favor the practice of prayer, we have to face those who oppose the practice. If we oppose the practice, we have to reckon with those who favor it. The result is controversy, debate, argument. Our entire orientation of mind and emotional tone in the midst of argument is so utterly and totally different from what it is amid the personal aspects of prayer that, when we argue, the word "God" ceases to be dramatistic and evaluative. When we argue, the word "God" becomes designative.

The outcome is that, not when we pray but when we dispute, do we confront those ancient and gruelling perplexities: "How do you know that there is a God?" "How can you prove that there is a God?" "How can there be a God of mercy in a world so replete with misery?" Not when people worship but when they argue, do they wrangle *pro* and *con* regarding a First Cause. Not when people pray but when they debate, does religion become identified with believing: if you believe a certain proposition, you are religious; if you believe something else, you are not religious. In German, the word for religion is *Glaube* which is also the word for belief. To believe means to regard a given statement as valid. But the statement is always a designative statement. The stressing of belief identifies language with designative language. It is unaware of evaluative and dramatistic language. The emphasis on belief equates religion with the argumentative side of religion. It ignores the devotional side of religion. It overlooks the personal aspects of prayer.

Not when we pray but when we argue, does there emerge the conflict between religion and science; inevitably so, because the propositions of science are preponderantly designative, and any designative proposition outside of science is likely to dissent from and to collide with science.

Not when we pray but when we argue, does there arise the issue of objectivity versus subjectivity and the assumption that prayer is discredited unless the suppliant's God is what the arguer calls an "objective God." Amid the personal aspects of prayer, objective and subjective are as irrelevant as the distinction between hot and cold is irrelevant when one discusses noises or the difference between sweet and sour is irrelevant when one treats of geometric figures. Objectivity refers to the fact that some of our experiences are shared with other people. Subjectivity refers to the fact that some of our experiences are unshared, are uniquely our own. We similarly speak of outward experiences and inward experiences, the outward being the socially shared and the inward being the unshared.

There are indeed situations in which the distinction between objective and subjective is one of great moment. But among those situations, we need not include that of prayer. Amid the personal aspects of prayer, the towering issue is not that of objective or subjective. The dominant issue is that of frustration or victory, defeat or triumph. We can be victorious either among our outward (that is, our socially shared) experiences or among our inward (that is, our unshared) experiences. Defeat also can prevail in either set of experiences. And yet, by and large, our defeats and our victories seem to pertain more extensively to our unshared experiences than to our shared experiences. We are not really defeated until we are inwardly defeated, nor are we truly victorious until we are victorious within. The quandary about objective and subjective belongs not to prayer but to controversy.

Not when we worship but when we argue do we detail the question about the efficacy of prayer, forgetting how prayer can be its own fulfillment:

> "Whom have I in heaven but Thee . . . the nearness of God is good unto me." "The Lord is my portion, saith my soul." "I have no good beyond Thee." "Thy love it is my heart desires." "Thou art all my soul's delight." "So panteth my soul after Thee, O God."

Three Paths to the Holy*

Samuel S. Cohon

Samuel S. Cohon (1888–1959) was a leading theologian at the Hebrew Union College, and a spiritual mentor to several generations of rabbis. The period of his influence coincided with Reform Judaism's integration of eastern European Jews (like Cohon himself) into its ranks. Their rise to prominence—hastened by events of the thirties—forced a reevaluation of the movement's very foundations. Cohon became an advocate of what can be described as a reassertion of Jewish peoplehood, and a positive approach to Jewish tradition. He was a principal author of the official statement of these views, the 1937 Columbus Platform, which, among other things, affirmed "the rehabilitation of Palestine," and "the obligation of all Jewry to aid in its upbuilding as a Jewish homeland." He delivered a major address to the 1928 CCAR Convention on "The Theology of the Union Prayer Book," and was a leading contributor to the 1940 edition. He edited the 1923 *Union Haggadah* and the 1928 *Rabbis' Manual*.

The following selection is part of a paper given at the 1930 CCAR Convention. Having dealt (in his 1928 address) with the theology of the prayerbook as it actually existed, Cohon now turned to "the religious ideas that must form the basis of a Union Prayer Book of the future." He spoke eloquently of three traditionally Jewish paths to God: the mystical, the halachic, and the philosophical. The reader may consider what each of these paths entails, the extent to which each may become dominant in our own day; and how the services of *Shaarei Tefillah* represent any or all of them.

I. Religion and Judaism

The simplest analysis of the older Judaism presents it as a three-fold path to the holy. Its primary path was mystical. It stressed the immedi-

---

*From an address published in the *CCAR Yearbook* 40 (1930): pp. 276-294; originally entitled, "Religious Ideas of a Union Prayer Book."

acy and the nearness of God. The wings of the *Shechina* touched the souls of the believers. The way to know God was to love Him, to trust in Him, to cleave unto Him, and to rejoice in Him. All of life was a revelation of the Divine. With Him is the fountain of life, in His light men see light. The world, despite its hardships and evils, is made radiant by the splendor of God. Faith thus becomes the atmosphere of the soul. To behold the beauty and the pleasantness of the Lord constitutes the highest wish of the enraptured soul. From the pages of Hosea and Jeremiah, of the hortatory sections of Deuteronomy and of the Psalms, to the Haggadah and Kabbalah and to the popular movement of Chasidism, this mystic path runs unbroken and gives the prayers, hymns and meditations of Israel their richness and their glow.

By the side of mysticism runs the path of *Halacha*. The love of God spells duties for man. It teaches him the way to live in the conscious presence of God, how to avoid evil, iniquity and sin. Under the ancient conceptions of revelation the manifold duties of man appeared as the direct commandments of God. In the Pentateuch the rabbis found 613 *mitzvot,* which in turn served as the foundations for all other laws of Judaism. The halacha in its entirety was thus conceived as God-derived. As a divinely revealed legislation it was not only binding upon all the children of Israel, but it showed the special love of God for His people. The halacha itself is thus permeated with mystic fervor. Whenever the danger of excess legalism appeared in Jewish life, mysticism manifested itself as a corrective. The Law was consequently ever revered both as the manifestation of the will of God and as the means of communion with Him.

Out of the mystic and halachic paths there branched the rational way to the holy. Inherent in both mysticism and law, rationalism developed as a separate discipline in response to the questioning mind and to the frequent need of defense of Judaism against the attacks of hostile systems of belief and thought. Through its own insights and with the aid of Greek and Arabic philosophy and science the Jewish mind interrogated reality in order to strengthen the Torah. The intellect came to the aid of the heart. Reason hastened to justify the dictates of the will and the cravings of the emotions. Science was invoked to fortify conscience. Though occasionally clashing with mysticism and the halacha, Jewish philosophy ultimately reinforced their fundamental aims through its clear analysis of the thought contents of Judaism. By bringing the religious ideas of Judaism into the open light, philosophy endowed them with new strength. By the side of the *mitzvot,* or the ethical and ceremonial laws, philosophy placed the *ikkarim,* or fundamental principles which explain and justify them. These mystic, halachic and philosophical elements represent the warp and woof of the historical liturgy.

II. Changed Outlooks and Values

In consequence of the revolutionary changes in the world of thought, all three paths to the holy which constitute Judaism have been considerably damaged. The phantastic forms in which mysticism was cloaked have been completely outgrown. The Platonic and Aristotelian foundations of Jewish philosophy and theology have likewise been discarded. However, their underlying motives remain unimpaired by the onslaught of modern knowledge. The heart and mind of man still function. Intuition and reason, in varying degrees and ways, still unlock the doors of life's sanctuary.

It is the path of the Halacha that has suffered most through the changed outlook of the present. In the light of the historical sciences it has become impossible for considerable numbers of men to regard the Pentateuchal legislation as directly given by God to Israel at Sinai. It rather appears as the product of long centuries of national development in Palestine. While many of its provisions, inspired by prophetic idealism, possess eternal value, others are plainly of transient character.

The unimpeachable spokesman of halachic Judaism, Aaron Halevi of Barcelona, in the thirteenth century calculated that out of the 613 Pentateuchal commandments only 270 are in actual observance. His mathematics rests not so much on actuality as on a midrashic interpretation of verse 2:5 of Song of Songs: "Though I sleep my heart is awake," which suggested to him that though the people of Israel is in *galut,* away from the Holy Land and the Temple, its heart is still awake to the Divine commandments. And the Hebrew word for "awake" is the numerical equivalent of 270.* The late Professor Schechter** was not so ambitious as Aaron Halevi. He was of the opinion that no more than a hundred *mitzvot* are still in force in present-day Orthodoxy. The waves of time have washed away even the impregnable rock of the Law.

Under these considerations it becomes increasingly embarrassing to speak of the Torah as binding upon us because of its direct delivery to our forefathers through Moses, or even to regard Judaism as Jewish life under the Law. The occasional references to the "laws and com-

---

*Ed. note: Each Hebrew letter has a mathematical equivalent. "Awake" is composed of an *ayin* = 70 and a *resh* = 200. Thus: 270.
**Solomon Schechter (1894-1936), scholar, and President of the Jewish Theological Seminary from 1902 until his death.

mandments, statutes and ordinances" entrusted to us can only be made in a historical and figurative sense. Modern Jewry no longer bows its head before the majesty of the Law. This may be a cause for rejoicing to many, but to others it may bring deep cause for concern. A Judaism that knows no Law is doomed to sterility. Laws may pass, but Law must abide. If Judaism is to be a force in our lives, it must continue to speak to us with a voice of authority. It may no longer speak in the name of God with regard to ceremonial matters that have lost their appeal to some moderns, but it still can and must inspire and stimulate to ethical and spiritual behavior by virtue of its inner truth and excellence. The beauty of holiness has an intrinsic appeal to the hearts of men. In an age that lays so much stress upon experimentation as the means to knowledge and to conduct, the rich historic experience of the Jewish people in the ways of holiness cannot be ignored with impunity. Out of the Jewish past there emerge the luminous ideals of religious culture, of pure family relationships and home life, of individual and social responsibility, and of the sanctification of personal and national joys and sorrows through holy days and seasons and through communion with God in prayer. These ideals have been the means of our self-preservation as the *Keneset Yisrael,* and they still hold out to us the promise of life and length of days. They must, therefore, be voiced in our prayer book in no hesitating manner. The art of the poet and the refined fervor of the mystic must be invoked to endow them with life, with power, and with beauty.

III. Use of Religious Ideas in Prayers

In our books of prayer, as in our general religious thought, the relation of finite man to the Infinite God must continue to be placed in the forefront. As in the past, religion must ever be for us a *Shir Hamaalot,* a song of ascents, an uplifting of heart and mind unto the heights, a mysterious inner consecration of man to God, an enthusiastic exultation in all that is good, pure and holy. Adequately expressed in words, the direction of the human spirit Godward becomes living prayer, lifting us to higher planes of feeling, thinking and doing, and enriching our lives with a new quality.

Here a practical problem confronts us. How shall we speak of God in our prayers? Two ways are open to us. Halevi* may be cited as the representative of one way. He takes the position that expressions

---

*Ed. note: Judah Halevi, twelfth century Spanish philosopher and poet.

savoring of anthropomorphism should not be excluded from our presentations of the conception of God, because they serve a useful purpose of making the idea of God real for the people and of cultivating in them the sense of reverence for the Divine.[1] Man needs symbolic presentations of truth in order to grasp its meaning.

The danger of such a procedure is evident from the past history of religion. With the least removal of restraint and care the symbol is mistaken for reality. Thus idolatry is born. Hence another way of presenting the idea of God suggests itself. Maimonides* may be taken as its representative. In his judgment the greatest caution must be exercised even with ignorant folk and with children to refer to God only in such terms as are absolutely free from anthropomorphisms and anthropopathisms. Negative attributes are best suited for this purpose. They do more justice to the nature of God than positive attributes. To be strictly consistent in relation to the idea of God, silence would be most appropriate.[2] Had not the Torah applied certain attributes to God, and had these not been utilized by the prophets and the men of the Great Synagogue in prayer, it would have been best to avoid them.[3]

Obviously the second alternative, while commendable for metaphysical speculation, is wholly unsuitable to religious devotion. Even philosophically minded men like Maimonides himself fall back, though with reservations, upon the way recommended by Halevi. We are told that Pascal, in a night full of anguish in which he struggled for the last time with the fancies of the world—the troubles of his heart and thought— and was soothed and charmed by mystic visions, invoked God, his true and only comforter, in these words, which he inscribed on the scapular and wore near his heart until his death: "God of Abraham, Isaac, and Jacob, not of scholars and philosophers."[4] Though inclined to rationalism, we cannot always live in abstractions. Sometimes we consciously take refuge in mysticism. And mysticism is exuberant and luxuriant by nature. It abounds in bold symbols and concrete figures, which must be taken as mystic license. The lover does not always pause to discriminate between the terms of endearment he addresses to his beloved.

Prayer is the expression of man's love for God. Being mystical in character and akin to poetry, it resorts to the pictorial and symbolic. Abstract ideas are clothed in live and pulsating forms. It appeals not alone to the critical philosopher and theologian but also to the humble worshipper. It is predicated upon the conviction that as sunlight shines

---

*Ed. note: Moses Maimonides (1135-1204) was both an outstanding *halachist*, and philosopher; born in Spain, but lived most of his life in Egypt. For a further discussion of his views on prayer see remarks by Reines, below, pp. 92–94.

for the layman as well as for the physicist, so the presence of God is near unto all who reach out after Him. He may be known through the heart and will as through the mind, and through love and devotion as through intellectual acumen.

The prayer book must, therefore, speak to the hearts of all worshippers. It achieves its purpose best when it utilizes past religious experience. A survey of attributes of God shows them to be the products of varied economic and political as well as of intellectual conditions. From patriarchal society we have the tender concept of *Divine Fatherhood,* so rich in its appeal to the heart of the worshipper. From tribal times we have the attribute of *Judgeship.* Monarchic conditions contributed the *King* idea, symbol of the sovereignty of law in the relations of the world and of men. Reflective thought yielded the striking figures of *Mekor Chayim* and *Borei Umanhig*—Fountain of Life, Creator of the World, Providence, the All-seeing Eye, the All-hearing Ear, etc. Modern insights may furnish us with new attributes of the Divine.

What is the purpose of employing these attributes of God in our prayers? Superficial thinking inclines to the view that they are used with the object of flattering God. The barest glimpse into religious psychology should convince us that the continuous references to the attributes of God is a necessity of our spiritual being. In the very act of worship we seek to make clear to ourselves the idea of the holy. Out of the region of emotion we strive to lift it into that of thought. We verbalize our religious feeling and thereby seek to render it capable of stimulating and of organizing our personalities and of strengthening our wills to moral and spiritual action. A catalog of attributes, arranged alphabetically, may fall short of its purpose with most of us. They must, therefore, be presented in more attractive and convincing manner. But no religious service may neglect this phase of devotion. Declarations like that of the *Shema,* of the *Kedusha* and of the thirteen attributes (*Adonai, Adonai, El rachum vechanun,* etc.) are charged with spiritual electricity. They give content to our nebulous notions and they kindle a holy flame within our souls. From the world of brass and of jazz, from the clatter of wheels and the noise of machines, from the realities of sense and matter, they recall us to the reality of the ideal of Holiness, whose essence is goodness, justice and truth. The proper recitation of the attributes of God in prayer and song uplift our whole selves, our wills, desires, passions, emotions, minds, convictions to the divine source of life and of reason. In the light of the Divine, we come to look upon ourselves *sub specie aeternitatis* [under the aspect of eternity]. We examine and search our hearts, we probe our purposes, we reawaken our dormant spirituality, and we reconsecrate ourselves to the holy life.

Our moral idealism becomes tinged with a fervent emotion, for we have enriched it with the motive of *Kiddush Hashem*. [Sanctification of (God's) name]. . . .

To rejoice in our faith and to draw strength from it we must follow courageously the threefold Jewish way to God. Our prayers, like our thoughts and our deeds, must help us as individuals and as a people to realize our full spiritual possibilities. We must learn to recapture the feeling so superbly articulated by Fleg:*

> We are the heartbeat of a world that wills
> To find its noblest self and to fulfill
> The law of Justice which it seeks to know;
> We are God's people, for we will it so,
> The stars our quest and truth our watchword still. [5]

---

*Ed. note: French poet and author (1874-1963).

NOTES

1 Kusari IV, 3, end.

2 A play upon Psalm 65:2: *Lecha dumiyah tehilah.*

3 Moreh Nevukhim I, chs. 35 and 59.

4 Cousin, Victor M., in *The Thoughts, Letters, and Opuscules of Blaise Pascal,* translated by O. W. Wight, p. 108.

5 Fleg, *Why I am a Jew.*

The Individual and the Community in Jewish Prayer*

Eugene B. Borowitz

Eugene B. Borowitz, Professor of Education and Jewish Religious Thought at the Hebrew Union College-Jewish Institute of Religion in New York, is probably today's primary spokesman for the theological position which he himself has labeled Covenant Theology. Standing in the existentialist tradition of Martin Buber and Franz Rosenzweig, he lays stress upon establishing a direct relationship with God rather than attempting to objectify any specific cognition of Him. Borowitz sees us relating to God not only as individuals, but as members of Israel, the people of the Sinai covenant.

With his usual display of clarity and logic, Borowitz spells out the consequences of this approach with regard to prayer, in the following essay, "The Individual and the Community in Jewish Prayer." His concern is the specifically Jewish form of worship which reflects the covenantal reality of addressing God both from the perspective of individual person and of member of the people, Israel. Beginning with a consideration of the place of Jewish prayer in the spectrum of worship possibilities representative of other faiths, he explores the tension between our personal and our communal selves, as we confront a God who demands that we address Him. Particularly enlightening is Borowitz's analysis of the contemporary American milieu, with its assumption that religion must be essentially a private matter, its "distant, detached, defensive, modern" individualism, and its "consumer mentality."

The forms of communal prayer vary greatly among the religions of mankind. From the formulas accompanying stylized dances to sponta-

---

*Originally published as a contribution to Arnold Jacob Wolf, ed., *Rediscovering Judaism* (Chicago: Quadrangle Books, 1965): pp. 109–131.

neous shouts and cheers, from quiet utterance at a local shrine to mass pilgrimage and recitation, the patterns differ almost without limit. Though Judaism and its daughter religions may hold similar, biblical views of God, man, and the worshipping community, yet the character of their divine services too may fall anywhere between widely placed poles. Thus the Quaker service has no set liturgy or ritual. The Friends meet at an appointed time and wait in silence for the Inner Light to move them to speak or pray. Whether much is said or little, whether emotion overflows or an unruffled calm is broken occasionally by a simple declaration, makes no difference. The meeting has served its function.

Near the other pole stands the Roman Catholic mass. Here all is ordered by God through the tradition of the church. The number, style and color of the vestments for this occasion, the specific psalms and prayers and their sequence, the very gestures of the officiant all are a fixed part of the only authorized pattern of formally required communal worship.

Each religious group shapes and justifies its service in terms of its faith. The Friends believe God works within the individual. For them, unless they are prompted by an active sense of God's presence within, all words are futile, all gestures in His direction meaningless. Better to sit silently and wait in openness for His stirrings in us than to assault Him or demand His gracious presence. Here, the group plays no special role in man's relation to Him. It is the useful instrument of mutual help and joint labor, but the Quakers have little doctrine of "the church." They work and pray together as little more than an aggregation of individuals faithful to the working of the Inner Light in each of them as in others of previous generations.

The Roman Catholic church, in substantial contrast, knows and encourages personal piety, but it knows, too, that this must be channeled through the church. The church is no human invention, no mere social instrumentality. God established the church. He did so that through it men might receive His grace and serve His will. The mass is the service He founded, the medium of His love and the honoring of His will. No private service of the heart, as valuable as it may be, can take the place of the church's celebration of the mass, nor is the worshipper's personal participation required for its effect. The mass is God's sacrament and fulfils its function not because of its subjective effect on those attending or on those performing it, but from God's action in it.

Where, within the broad spectrum of the possibilities of communal prayer, does Jewish worship fall? And what are the religious commitments which give it this form?

Jewish faith affirms the existence of a living relationship between God and all men, not just the Jews. The covenant God made with Noah and his descendants after the flood is its classic expression. Noah stands for Everyman, since with him God begins history once again. With the previous wickedness washed away, man receives another opportunity and mandate to serve God in righteousness. In the covenant relationship, God gives man some commandments by which to live (most versions say seven) and God, in turn, promises never to bring another flood to destroy mankind. Since that day men may have wilfully rejected or quietly ignored that pact. No matter; the Noahide covenant remains and, the Jew believes, provides a continuing possibility that non-Jews like Jethro or Balaam may truly know God, that there may be righteous men among the nations who will share in the world to come.

What prayer may mean to all men, as a Jew sees it, can be derived from this fundamental understanding. The covenant with Noah established the reality of man's relation to the one, true God. This gives man the basis, perhaps the right, to worship God. More, a real relationship between man, the creature, and God, the creator, would of itself require man to serve God in worship. So the Jewish tradition regularly understood that one of the Noahide commandments was the worship of God, not of idols. (Not without significance is the fact that the covenant with Noah is made when Noah offers a sacrifice.) It may perhaps be unfair to see in the prohibition against idolatry a mandate to worship God, or in the practice of sacrifice the beginnings of prayer. Whether the act of sacrifice was or was not early accompanied by private prayer is not relevant here. In Noah, Melchizedek, Jethro, and Balaam there is an early biblical tradition that non-Jews might truly worship God, a tradition which the rabbis centuries later formalized and symbolized in their concept of the covenant of Noah. As prayer accompanied sacrifice in biblical time and gradually established itself as a separate and legitimate means of Jewish worship, so it is safe to assume a similar legitimacy for the righteous non-Jew. (Solomon's dedication prayer beseeching God's attention to such non-Jewish prayers is a unique biblical indication. There are a number of positive rabbinic expressions.)

Another aspect of the general view may be derived from the view that all men, not just Jews, were created in the image of God. Man is enough like God to know God exists, to understand what God wants of him, to stand in a covenant with Him, and, thus, to worship Him. Man, because he is in essence like God, can and should communicate with his Creator, the Master of the universe in which man lives.

This is a belief about all men and, at the same time, about each man individually. From it, as prayer becomes ever more significant in Judaism, follows an emphasis on the individual. Our earliest information about Jewish prayer services (again foregoing hypotheses concerning the Temple sacrifices and the personal prayers mentioned in the Bible) comes from the first century of the Common Era. In these sources the Jewish prayer service is already determinedly individualistic. Nothing happens in the service which the man who has come to pray does not himself bring about. The fixed order of the prayers, the leadership of respected figures, the communion with neighbors, the special room devoted to the worship of God—all these may help. They may be invaluable to the individual, even humanly indispensable. They remain means, instruments, accessories. They cannot take the place of the individual's own action, his turning to God in attentive respect.

The rabbis called this indispensable personal element of prayer *kavanah*. They debated to what extent the unlearned and the ill-at-ease, the simple-minded and the confused, must have *kavanah* if their service was to fulfil the commandment to pray. Realistic as always, they might reduce the requirement to a heartfelt "Amen" ("so be it" or even "that is what I too mean to say") to the leader's prayer; or to the first sentence of the Shema; or perhaps even to its last word," . . . One!" Still, these were the *limits*. They were the extremes to which they were willing to go to make regular prayer possible for real men in real history. But beyond this minimum of individual devotion even their realism could not force them to go. Ultimately the Jewish view of prayer involves an act of the will, a turning of the self. Normally, *kavanah*, personal involvement and projection, was the standard and the hope of Jewish worship.

Thus, the Jewish service, unlike the Catholic mass, is never sacramental. God does not so much work through the proper recitation of liturgy as in free response to it. The Jewish service is precisely a prayer service, an order of petitions, praises, thanksgivings, and acknowledgements which men created for God. Its essential characteristic is address, not persons, acts, or places. Anyone may lead a Jewish service, and Jewish ordination is not required to qualify or consecrate one for this role. No objects are used in the service, though a prayer book will help one to remember the order and wording of the prayers. The service may be held in any reasonably appropriate place. While ten men are required for the full form of worship, the multiplication of one by ten does not suddenly alter their religious significance as individuals; it only makes them formally representative of their community. As far as their worship is concerned, they still depend upon the personal efforts of those present. Unless the congregants pray, regardless of rabbi, cantor, synagogue, or the number present, they have not achieved Judaism's purpose in directing them to assemble for prayer.

The point is important not only as a matter of comparison, but because it is vital in understanding the contemporary ineffectiveness of Jewish worship. The contemporary synagogue in its eagerness to have aesthetically appealing services has largely forgotten the role of the individual worshipper.

Nineteenth century Jewry, as it emerged from the ghetto into western culture, properly saw the need for a change in the atmosphere of congregational prayer. Jews could not accept the aesthetic and social conventions of their neighbors in their daily lives without similarly modifying the style and tone of their worship services.

Such cultural adaptation was not new in the history of Jewish prayer. The elegant structures and exalted stance of Spanish Jewish poetry had displaced the intricate word play and learned allusions of the original poets of the Holy Land, only in turn to be succeeded in central and eastern Europe by a more fervent, free-flowing diction. Now modern Europe approached things spiritual with dignity, reserve, quiet, and solemnity, and so these qualities, under the heading of "decorum," were transferred to the synagogue. As against its ghetto forebear, today's synagogue displays the sobriety and reserve that are the contemporary conventions of attention. In this tone, the modern Jew recognized cultural clues to what is important and significant. Thus the decorous style of the modern service does indeed prepare him as a citizen of this culture for the worship of God. And if personal attention and concentration are crucial to Jewish worship, then surely such an emotional setting will eliminate what modern men consider distracting. This much, and it is important, may be said for the movement to dignify Jewish worship.

After decades of experience, the time has surely come to acknowledge that there has been a loss as well. Insistence on an orderly service has nearly eliminated the active role of the individual worshipper, largely by concentrating the effective conduct of the service in the hands of professional prayer-leaders, the rabbi or the cantor. Worshippers are expected to be quiet about their prayer. They must not disturb those around them by raising their voices, crying their grief, or otherwise putting their deeply felt emotion into expression. Rather, they must conform their needs to the congregation's volume, velocity, and emotional level. They are expected to be self-contained—the exact opposite of prayer, which is honest expression from man out to God.

The rabbi and cantor, without anyone's saying a word but with that firmness that culture knows how to impose, are set different limits. They are expected to be more emotional, more personal, as they lead and interpret the prayers. In part, this is because in a group searching for dignity, they can be counted on to do so more effectively. That is to say, the reading of the rabbi and the singing of the cantor will have few, if any, mistakes. They will not hesitate, mispronounce, change keys, lose tone, or become confused. Rather, their renditions can be relied on to be pleasing to the ear, to add beauty to the service. They are aesthetically dependable.

The trained officiant is emotionally dependable as well. True, the range of expression he is permitted is far greater than the congregation's. His knowledge and experience have equipped him not only to show feeling but, more important, never while doing so, to transgress the proper social limits. With the worshipper repressed, the beautiful, safe release provided by the rabbi or the cantor now dominates the service.

What began as a necessary, useful alteration of Jewish worship has therefore created its own evils, undermining the very foundations of Jewish prayer. Under the guise of decorum the worshipper has been aesthetically cowed and emotionally neutralized. This is not to say that beautiful music, meaningfully rendered, cannot uplift and exalt the individual congregant. The long tradition of Jewish song and chant, going back further than that of the prayer texts themselves, speaks eloquently of music's religious value. Likewise the hoary record of men valued as leaders of congregational prayer, men who for their ability to express their fellows' will in prayer were highly honored, testifies to the virtue of pious and consecrated leadership in worship. The problem is not what good leadership can add, but what it has tended to supplant.

Without individuals investing their thoughts and emotions, their full attention, their devoted selves, in prayer, the Jewish service has lost its meaning. Whenever one "listens to" the rabbi or cantor, more in peaceful enjoyment than in identification and common meaning, the crucial distinction between the synagogue and the recital hall has been transgressed. Once started on this passive way, the congregation will always find it easier to shift its prayer responsibilities to those whom it has hired to pray for it. They do it so nicely, so dependably. They should really be allowed to do it all—which is but one step from having them do it alone, without benefit of congregants, not just participating but even attending. The rabbi and the cantor must be masters of their craft if they are to lead their congregants, yet they must use their talents to stimulate, not replace individual participation if they are to keep their services Jewish at their core.

Jewish worship is by belief and practice uncompromisingly individualistic, and its future depends upon the increasing ability of individual Jews to participate in the service and fulfil its expectations.

These general views of prayer in Judaism should not blind us to the fact that the Jewish service is far from a Quaker meeting. Judaism may base its understanding of prayer on the individual man's relation to God, but it refuses to stop there. Judaism does not think of man abstracted from his relation to mankind. It does appreciate the meaning of the individual in isolation, but holds him, the single one, in unremitting importance, against a background of society and history. For the Jew, man is a social and historical creature. Hence his prayer should properly be a communal, comradely affair. Public worship is a universal human need and, also, a specifically Jewish requirement.

A religion which denied the worth of history might well consider private prayer superior to group prayer. But Judaism's basic view of the universe is historical. The Bible knows man almost from his creation as a child of history. Man's sin began and still powers the movement of events. But history is no senseless, chance succession. There is a God who rules over time. History has a purpose and a goal—that era when God's rule will be fully established by its manifestation in lives of justice, peace, and love. God's kingdom-to-be is not a private matter between one individual and God. It must be accomplished with all men and be manifest in all lives, or it is unworthy of the Lord of the universe. The individual man cannot understand himself, cannot properly know his own life's purpose unless he sees it within the context of all mankind and all of history. Isolated from his fellows, he isolates himself from God's social goals.

To want to pray, but only alone and only for oneself, seems therefore to make too much of self, too little of God. Judaism commends communal prayer because God cares for all as He cares for each one, because, while God is the God of each private individual, He is the God of *all* individuals as well. The single self is indispensable. Without any *one,* mankind is incomplete. So too, without *all other selves,* equally precious to God, the single self loses its context and hence its final significance. Man cannot find himself only in others, but he also cannot find himself without them. If prayer is supposed to open man to the truth of his existence it must begin with self but it must reach out to all mankind.

Judaism values communal worship not for its specific Jewish purposes alone, but for all men. Group prayer, by confronting us with others, by asking us to link our prayers to theirs, reminds us immediately and directly that it is never enough to pray for ourselves alone. Speaking as "we," the individual discovers, acknowledges, articulates the needs, desires, hopes, which he, though one man, shares with all men because he is not only a private self but a member of humanity. Besides, when we are conscious of those with whom we stand, what we may have wanted to pray by ourselves is generally made less selfish, more humble, and therefore more appropriate for utterance before God. There before us is the newly bereaved young widower with his three small children. Near him stand the white-haired man who, close to the age of retirement, suddenly faces bankruptcy; the beautiful young woman who has just come from the hospital after the removal of a breast; the quiet mother whose consultation with the school psychologist was deeply disturbing. When we join *them* in prayer, when we must, to say "we," link ourselves with them, we, and our prayer, are refined; and often exalted far beyond our own means, for *they are praying now*, lifting us, helping us, with their "we," even as they silently reach out to the congregation for compassion and understanding.

The joy of others similarly affects our worship. We are buoyed up by the happiness of the new grandparents offering their heartfelt thanks, the engaged couple who will be married this Sunday, the newly appointed vice-president of his firm, the recently honored community worker. Their joy infuses us so that what might have been a nagging, niggling, whine of prayer can as a proper "we" become worthy of God's attention. Indeed, the dynamism, the momentum, the upreach of a congregation truly at prayer, takes the individual from the commonplace, the humdrum, the depression of his daily routine, and projects him and his prayer far beyond himself. The joy of congregational worship is that together, by a mathematical miracle, individuals transcend the selves they were before the service began. And prayer does so, not against the worshipper's intimate individuality, but by calling him, on the most personal and private level, to do all he can, to lead and lift, to bear and support, all those with whom he stands.

Social worship is a sharp spur to ethical sensitivity as well as to enthusiasm. To stand together as equals before God with the man we dislike, the woman who has cut us, the boors who repel us, the intellects who snub us, the neighbors we do not trust, the fools we cannot bear, to say with them in some bond of unity, "we," is to shake our self-righteousness and expand the breadth of our conscience. Much of what we must pray to God is what we share with them in belief, thanksgiving, and petition. And He hears us as one with them. How can we now see them as enemies, adversaries? How can we prevent our prayer from charging us with a new sense of responsibility, not for our immediate synagogue neighbors alone, but for those of our city, our nation, and our world? Here, form and content join in happy harmony. The social context of praying makes immediately practical the ethical imperatives of the prayers themselves. Learning to pray the communal "we" is the first active step in fulfilling every prayer for righteousness and justice. The act of praying together itself commands us; therefore we know it to be commanded.

Nor should these general comments end without a practical word about personal frailty. The individual, when he is his own standard, will pray when he feels he needs to. Prayer then, finds its occasion and its value in response to his private moods and feelings. What happens under those circumstances to regular prayer with respect to frequency, intensity, and unselfish content is a commonplace of modern versions of religiosity. The man who objects that he cannot pray on schedule often does not pray at all. And when, in this hectic world, he finally allows a conscious desire to pray to take priority over all the important things he should be doing now, he finds he does not have the knack. Obviously prayer in response to the inspiration of a moment has a unique significance, one well worthy of cherishing. But it is a supplement to, not a substitute for, regular public worship—and the acquired habit of turning to God in prayer is readily transferred from the congregational to the private situation.

Where the individual operates by delicious surprise, the community prays by fixed rule. There are two reasons for this. The practical one is: everyone will know when to assemble. The theological one is equally simple. By virtue of devotion to its prophets and saints, the community is less concerned with man's momentary mood than with God's constant presence. If God is real, if He is truly God, men should speak to Him, seek Him, commune with Him regularly—anything less can only be considered folly. And as there is no time when He is not God, when the universe is free of His rule or when men are released from His commandments, so there is no time when men may ignore Him with impunity. On God's side, there is no time when prayer is undesirable. Prayer needs to be as regular, as continual, as much a part of living, as is man's continuing dependence on God. Individuals tend to forget or overlook this. Forgetting is their defense against God's ruling their lives. The community has a better memory.

Some religions have pressed this faith to its logical limit and encouraged their adherents to call on God at every moment, generally by ceaselessly repeating His name. Judaism has avoided this rather mechanical, inhuman pattern. God is always ready for prayer, but man is not. Jewish prayer is directed to God but springs from man. Hence Judaism, in characteristic practical fashion, has sought a rule appropriate to both the partners, one consistent not just with Jewish doctrine but with its goal, to live in history for God's sake. Congregational Jewish services each day are limited to three: morning, afternoon, and evening, with the latter two most often held at twilight and thus combined, as it were, into one service. These regular assemblies remind the Jew, particularly when he attends, but even when he does not, that he should be praying at least twice a day. Is it not true that, left to the promptings of his own heart, he will not arrive at even so modest a standard? Modest that is, if God is God . . .

Much of the conflict between private and group prayer is really that issue. The Synagogue, the Congregation of Israel, knows God is real. That knowledge is what created and sustains it. That is why it has prescribed appropriate regularity for its worship. The individual has his doubts and his weaknesses—besides, he is busy. When he believes, and when he remembers, and when he has strength, he will pray. Abraham Heschel's analysis is correct. The problem of prayer is not prayer. The problem of prayer is God. *If* God is real, men should pray—regularly. So says the distant, detached, defensive modern individual. The Synagogue says rather, *since* God is real, let us meet to worship Him at least twice each day.

Thus, the doctrine of God and man-in-general that inheres in Jewish faith leads it to command group prayer for religious, ethical, and practical reasons. That is a purely universal judgment, applicable to all men alike. Like much of Judaism's universal content, it is implicit in traditional sources and only rarely explicit. Still, it is part of Judaism and the background which sets off specifically Jewish needs for communal prayer.

The Jew as man, as sharer in the covenant of Noah, is, like all men, enjoined to worship with others. But the Jew shares in the Covenant of Sinai as well—that is what constitutes him a Jew, not just a man—and thus a special necessity for communal prayer acts upon him.

This distinction, being critical to the issue of private versus group prayer in Judaism, demands particular elucidation. To put it bluntly, can Jewishness ever adequately be defined in purely personal terms? (Secular or semi-secular but still non-theistic descriptions of the Jews are beyond discussion here. In discussing Jewish worship it is of course the Jew known to the synagogue and prayer book who alone is relevant.) Is being Jewish something that operates privately and so can be expressed in a life of relative isolation? Is Jewish faith only something between each single one and his God alone, so that living one's Judaism does not essentially involve a community?

In part, the answer to these questions must be "Yes." To deny the personal element in the Jew's relationship with God is to deny Judaism's fundamental view of man-in-general, that he is created in God's image, that he can and should know and serve God. But in larger part, to say that Judaism is merely a religion of individuals requires an emphatic "No." The Judaism of the Bible, the rabbis, the philosophers, the mystics, the Judaism of almost every modern Jewish thinker, and decisively the Judaism of every Jewish prayer book, avers that Judaism is the religion of a people, a folk, a community. "The Jews" are a social entity in their own right, not merely an aggregation of believers. The individual Jew shares in the religion called Judaism as a member of that people-folk-community. His Jewishness, as personally as he may and should feel it, as privately as he may believe and practice it, is not his by virtue of individual discovery or creation, but by his membership in the Household, the Congregation, the Children of Israel. He brings his will, his assent, his reinterpretation to a relationship which God established with this community. He participates in what may, for purposes of corrective exaggeration, be called a group faith, a social religion.

How strange that sounds in a day when men are accustomed to speak of religion as a highly private matter, something each person should decide for himself. This all-pervading personalism (akin to what sociologists have described as "privatism") stems from several sources. One is surely a reaction to the power of the state. Let it legislate in every area, but let it not require of good and faithful citizens any set religious practice or creed. Another motive derives from a rejection of intolerance and fanaticism. Which religion is truest, or what practices within that religion one should follow, should ultimately be a matter for each person to decide himself. Compulsion, lay or clerical, being told what one must do by friend or relative, seems an infringement of freedom and a denial of personal responsibility. For most Americans, the practical content of their religion is consciously regulated by selection and choice. In the end, they follow only their heart or conscience, a standard particularly precious to modern Jews since it legitimizes their deviation from traditional Jewish law.

Judaism, as the faith of a people, does not deny the individual's right to freedom and judgment. It grants extraordinary liberty to the individual in matters of belief. Today, even in practice, through several organized interpretations of Jewish observance, all of them dynamic, all seeking to make place for personal interpretation, the role of the individual has been safeguarded and amplified. And the practice and tradition of individuality, one Jew over against other Jews, is legendary.

Nonetheless, religion for the Jew, as the tradition understands it, is not primarily a personal but a communal matter. The Torah was not given to Moses as an individual possession to share with others of a similar mind, but to the Jewish people as a whole. Again and again Moses is commanded, "Speak to the Israelite people and say to them . . . ." The Bible is the history of this folk who found God and joined their destiny to Him. Its concern with individuals is almost exclusively for those who influenced the life and character of their folk. (The personal side cannot be absent, as the wondrous Book of Psalms, among other examples, makes clear.) The covenant of Noah was made with all mankind, and through it each man has a relation to God. The Covenant at Sinai was made with Israel, the Jewish people, and thus each Jew, as a Jew, shares this unique Jewish relation to God as an inheritor of his people's Covenant.

A religion founded on individual decision might one day find that, through laziness or inattention, few people cared. Where the individual is everything, history and its long-term movement means little or nothing; certainly little more than the history of the individual. Judaism takes the other view. Its God is the righteous Lord of creation who demands and assures that the history He made possible will end in free acceptance of His rule. The sweep is cosmic, the scope all-embracing. Judaism is primarily a religion of history, of God's will for mankind, of human destiny entire, and it envisions Israel's role and the individual's worth against that background. For it remains true, in all the grandeur of this purpose, that there is no history without individuals, no Kingdom of God among men unless He is acknowledged in single souls. Again the individual is indispensable—but against this measure not sufficient or ultimate.

Because its range stretches the limits of finitude, Judaism cannot be satisfied to be a religion whose continuity depends on private human decision. Without an endurance as patient and inexorable as time itself, Judaism's hope to transform and redeem history might be destroyed. As the religion of a people, Judaism counterpoises to the individual will-to-be-a-Jew social processes whereby the folk itself continues from generation to generation. History and literature, language and land, custom and folkways, all provide historical momentum. Thus too, the Jew enters the Covenant on entering the people, by birth, not by decision (though one not born a Jew may, paradoxically enough, take the latter route). One born a Jew may spurn or be indifferent to his people's historic character and toil—but his individual repudiation or indifference cannot change the record of history, nor the imperatives it creates for those born into the Jewish people. The Covenant of Sinai transcends the individual Jew, as it encompasses him. (The people, too, might as a whole deny its past. Today this is not hypothetical speculation. But Jewish faith includes faith in Israel as it is based on faith in God.)

Judaism is a folk religion because this best suits its religious goals. Jewish peoplehood is an indispensable part of Jewish religious thought and Jewish religious practice. A specifically *Jewish* religious life, as contrasted to that of Noahide man-in-general, means, therefore, life in and with the Jewish people, the Covenant community.

THE INDIVIDUAL AND THE COMMUNITY IN JEWISH PRAYER

Jewish worship is, classically, communal in character. Its Jewishness derives not from the external facts that Hebrew is used, traditional texts are recited, or Jewish symbols are displayed. It is Jewish because it is born out of the Covenant at Sinai and articulates Israel's bond with its God. The special language, texts, symbols all stem from this root relationship. Jewish worship, then, is the people of Israel, assembled before its God out of continuing loyalty to their Covenant, to acknowledge, praise, and petition Him. The group may be small; traditionally as few as ten are acceptable for a full public service. When at least ten Jews congregate to pray, they constitute the Covenant folk in miniature. They represent all Israel, past and present, here and everywhere. Not ten or more individuals, but the Covenant people itself now confronts its God. The man who prays in the synagogue prays as a participant in a Jewish history which continues into the living present, and his prayers, therefore, express the needs of the community in which he stands. Jewish law is clear. The individual Jew should seek to pray with a congregation. But if he cannot (that great phrase without which nothing could endure in history) then he may pray alone. Even alone, he should pray the congregational service (with some deletions), preferably at the time the congregation is praying. For a Jew, one's individuality is connected with being one (sic!) of the Jewish people, sharer in a mutual Covenant with God.

The Jewish prayerbook, the *Siddur*, speaks out of this particular situation of the people of Israel gathered yet again to meet its God, to renew their ancient pact and beseech His current help. That is why most of its prayers are in the plural. They speak of "us," of "our," of "we." This plural should be taken with full seriousness, in all its useful ambiguity. "We" may only mean "I," put in a rather formal, or editorial plural—important, since without "me" there is no meaningful prayer. "We" may mean "this group with whom I am now praying," and therefore I and my neighbors. It surely also means "this congregation or community," those who should be here but may not be, those with whom we share our Jewish hopes, labors, and anxieties. It means all of these—but including these, and embracing them, it means primarily "We, the people of Israel, the folk of the Covenant. . . ." Now what might have been a tiny, almost selfish, "we" has risen from our cosy group in its familiar associations to embrace all of history in loyalty and obedience to its Master. Through this great Jewish "we" the individual "I" has found an incomparable dignity and an immeasurable worth. This is the boon which worship as a member of the Covenant people freely bestows.

And this too is the source of the special problem of Jewish prayer today. With some good fortune, modern man may be able to admit that he has faith, that he believes in God. He may even be able to overcome his embarrassment enough to learn to pray to Him. But this is personal religion, *his* God, met on *his* terms and in response to *his* needs. These prayers are intimate indeed, else they could not arise. The *Siddur* asks him to pray to Israel's God of the Covenant—and to make Israel's Covenant-based prayers his prayers. What a gap to bridge, what a chasm to cross! If the problem of prayer-in-general is God, then the problem of *Jewish* prayer is *Israel*. To pray as one of this historic people, identifying oneself with its membership and its mission, that is the demand made of modern Jewish man by the *Siddur*.

Contrast this challenge with the tone of much else of today's society. Modern America is unthinkable without the thoroughgoing commitment to please the consumer and satisfy his individual needs. Banks say they will be his friend; automobile companies seek to give him status; cigarette makers almost openly promise to enhance his sexuality; politicians mold themselves to the image he desires. Millions of dollars and countless hours of creative research are expended each year in an effort to lay bare the individual's current dissatisfactions, to reach him on a level he can enjoy, and to fulfil his remaining unfulfilments. Moreover, many now promise him that there are no risks involved; no charge will be made until he has received the first gratifications, or, if not satisfied, he may have his money back, or even double. Modern man is trained to the consumer role. He waits patiently, even in boredom. The seller must please him—or else.

Many a religious institution has sought to meet modern man on this level, to "sell" its wares, to appeal to the religious "market" in terms of the benefits its services provide. Attending group worship keeps families together, soothes housewives' nerves, and decreases managerial ulcers or coronaries. Religion permeates deeper, affects distressed areas speedier, brings longer lasting comfort.

These claims are not unwarranted. Religion can and has changed men's lives for the good, and what it offers is so poorly known that it needs the techniques of public relations to reach the unaffiliated. That is not the issue here. When a religious institution renounces its knowledge and tradition of the holy as its basic criterion of activity, particularly its worship, when consciously or unconsciously its new goal is the American pattern of pleasing the consumer, it has begun its own self-destruction. It has made the congregant/consumer, not God, the focus of its concern—and while the service of God does not require ignoring man's desires, it is clear where the real priorities lie. The worship of the synagogue and the content of the prayer book reflect *God's* pre-eminence and see the needs of the individual fused with those of his religious community, the Jewish people.

The gap between Jewish prayer and American consumer logic as it applies to religion can be clarified by noting its effects. A man finally decides to come to a service. He has been told for so long that it will be good for him that he decides to give it a try. He waits for something to happen. Perhaps the music soothes him a little, the quiet is assuaging, the prayers are comforting, and the sermon is not only understandable but even somewhat inspiring. Some consumers are satisfied with such rewards. Most are not, which is why attendance at worship is poor. They frankly find more than an occasional visit, for reasons of sociability or habit, unsatisfying. As they say, they don't "feel anything special." Nothing unique "happens" to them that cannot be duplicated in more palpable or less demanding form. Religion really does not "do anything" for them. It doesn't "produce" when given a try.

From this general experience, the consumer-logic inevitably concludes: the fault is with the institution, in this case the synagogue, and its prayer book in particular. To get people to services today, the deduction follows, they must have a religion which fits in with their immediate way of life. Thus it is foolish to use a prayer book written centuries ago, in a remote poetic style, about vague generalities that largely fail to express contemporary experience. A few of the old prayers or practices should be retained for emotional or symbolic reasons (the new modernity knows that emotions are important), but the only successful service today would be one that embodied and articulated the very present needs of those praying.

This suggestion runs into great difficulty whenever men seek to put it into practice. Most free and unregimented liturgies (Methodist, Baptist—even the patterns of Quaker meetings or Jewish youths' "creative" services), when they continue from week to week and month to month, fall into a standard format and a regular style. Spontaneity is not easily regularized. Moreover, the personal needs of the congregants are not easy to discover in depth nor to express in a fresh and appealing way. As a result, attempts at a personalized service generally end up a mixture of the customary and the creative, with both the traditionalists and the individualists unhappy with the results.

Why not, however, utilize modern technology to follow this theory to its logical conclusion? No rabbi or committee, regardless of assistance or library resources, could be as effective in identifying the inner needs of worshippers at one given moment and creating a service from modern and ancient materials, verbal and musical, to express them, as a properly stocked and programed computer. The possibilities both in diagnosing needs and responding to them in varied format are exhilarating. A check list of moods and emotions could be provided to each prospective worshipper to determine his individual situation or, if that is too superficial, some sort of religious inkblots which would allow him to project his depth desires. Each Friday before sundown, the worshipper phones the computer and, according to a prearranged code, feeds it his need-data as of the present moment. Thus he knows that tonight's service will reflect his personal situation, and, having also participated in its creation, is very likely to attend. On its part, the computer is a model of rabbinic openness, gratefully and patiently accepting all calls with understanding; perhaps, by simple wiring modifications, even several at one time!

The creation of the service is speedy but to the highest standards. Experts in religious worship have previously programed the machine with the most varied possible patterns of effective religious services, as well as a feedback device which limits the frequency of their repetition. At a given time before the service, to keep the need-data as current as possible, the computer devises the evening's service. First, it mathematically determines the exact proportion of moods which will be present. Then it draws from its memory section from the entire range of literature, perhaps worldwide as well as Jewish, selections appropriate to the needs. These, according to a pattern effective for the night's goal, it structures into a service. The next chore is typing and duplicating (printing, in more affluent congregations), the computer efficiently making only as many copies as there have been calls, plus extras based on experience at this time of the year, with this weather, with such and such competitive activities going on, as to how many others will come. A truly sophisticated installation would provide for evaluation, registering the congregation's response to this service and including such responses as part of its guidance for the future. Thus, so to speak, the computer could *learn to create* ever more effective services.

One more of the many other values of this system must be mentioned: help with preaching. Surely the sermon, too, should speak to authentic congregational situations. Hence the computer might guide the preacher in his choice of text or approach. Better yet, the energetic preacher will stock his computer with a variety of sermons (again based on the computer's memory and analysis of previous congregational need patterns and reactions), and the computer, while selecting materials for this service, could also select the sermon most appropriate to it. What is more, the electronic brain could be relied upon to keep the manuscript, if not the delivery, down to a length carefully adjusted to the congregation's, not the preacher's, needs.

What is satire here will one day be attempted in all seriousness. Those who are committed to the religion of individual needs should obviously do what they can to make their faith function better.

Judaism has traditionally sought the standard of its practice and the chief guide of its observance in another direction. What it cannot do, what it believes no religion can hope to do and still be worthy of ultimate concern, is to make the individual worshipper the final measure of the value of the synagogue in general or the Jewish service in particular. When every judgment is based on whether the prayer book moves him personally, whether the ceremonies satisfy his intimate longings, the question must inevitably also arise whether God also adequately serves him. Now, the essential blasphemy of this position becomes clear. When religion abandons itself to consumers and makes them its judge, it has created a new and false god in place of the One and Only God. And this false and fickle god of the public will betray its "religious" leaders and institutions today as in its various guises it has in the past.

This does not mean that religion cannot *in part* be evaluated by how it responds to the human situation or to deny that every religion must in significant *part* meet man on his own level. The sin lies in making this the exclusive or even dominant goal. Man does have needs but, if one may dare to say it, so does God—rather man's needs are best met in terms of God's will, His law, His purposes. Religion is more God's commands than man's desires, God's goals than man's dreams, God's presence than man's existence, though both are critical. Man fulfils himself in serving God, not in pursuit of anything he ever was or in his imperfection might, without God, imagine himself to be. This is what Jewish tradition implicitly understood as it sought to relate each man through the community and its discipline to God, and thus to his fullest self. The synagogue and its communal worship are built on that premise. If the modern Jew is to learn to pray as a Jew, and not just as man-in-general, he does not need a better prayer book but a better theology, not a different form of worship but a deeper belief.

Or, perhaps, he needs to be helped to realize what in the depths of his soul he somehow still does believe, that he is both individual *and* Jew, single one *and* member of the Covenant folk. Then perhaps he can reach beyond the shallow self-centeredness that characterizes so much of modern man's life and that is responsible for its pervasive subsurface anxiety, and learn to say ever more wholeheartedly the "we" that must always begin with and lead back to the self, the "we" that reaches out beyond the individual, beyond neighbors, beyond the congregation, to embrace all the people of Israel (and through the people of Israel, all mankind), and to affirm with such a "we" this one Jew's place among his people before its God. Then, in sum, he will pray *as a Jew,* and praying as a Jew will know what his life of prayer can mean to him as a private self.

It is a paradoxical faith that produces the pattern and structures of Jewish worship. Each individual can and should pray for himself—but a Jew prays as one of the Covenant people. Jewish prayer is simultaneously individual and communal, and the *Siddur* is Judaism's living response to the demands of this faith.

Prayer and a Growing God*

Henry Slonimsky

There was something eruptive about him ... At any
moment an idea or the juxtaposition of mental associations
would catapult him out of his chair, and, evidently propelled
by some demonic force, he would, in one or two strides,
come physically within inches of a student in the front row.
Then—grabbing his hearer's wrist or coat lapel, and crying
"Listen!"—he would pour out his thoughts as though he
were buttonholing the collective audience, to make it stay
until it saw things his way.

Thus did Julius Kravetz eulogize Dean Henry Slonimsky, who died in
1970, after devoting nearly half a century to Stephen Wise's Jewish
Institute of Religion in New York. "He spoke books better than most
people wrote them," said his friend Richard Aldington. He was a
teacher who could quote Blake, Shelley, Pascal, Plato, Dostoevski,
Nietsche, Melville, and the Midrash—in one single lecture; who
imparted great ideas as if his life depended on it.

He was at home in world literature, but had a passion for the
spiritual expression of his own people, which he found particularly in
the Midrash and the *Siddur*. This article on prayer is illustrative of his
gift for poetry, and his preoccupation with both the tragic and the
heroic aspects of life. His personal philosophy was a radical one,
postulating no perfect all-powerful divinity, such as the tradition took
for granted; but a growing God who needs man quite as much as man
needs God. Is prayer answered? What are the roles which a struggling
God and a heroic humanity must play in the tragic arena of life?
"Prayer and a Growing God" is one of the most moving and thought-
provoking essays on these questions.

---

*Published originally under the title "Prayer," in *The Jewish Teacher* 33:3 (February, 1965):
pp. 3–7, and reprinted in Henry Slonimsky, *Essays* (Cincinnati: Hebrew Union College
Press, 1967), pp. 118–128.

71

Prayer is the expression of man's needs and aspirations, addressed to a great source of help—to the Friend whom we suppose to exist behind the phenomena, the Friend who is concerned for man's needs and for his high aspirations, and who is resolved to help.

What are those needs? First and foremost, health and food and life itself, without which there is nothing; then, on a higher plane, the need for forgiveness of sin and wrongdoing; and finally the need that all the great and good causes of the human heart shall be brought to victory, that the poor and oppressed shall be comforted, and wrong righted, and justice done and goodness prevail.

And these prayers are addressed to a God who is accessible to prayer, not just a Power but a Power who is a *Shomeia Tefillah,* one who listens to prayers. A "First Cause" (the philosopher's God) is not enough, and cosmic emotion evoked by the grandeur of the universe (the poet's God) is likewise not enough. In religion we need a God who values what the good man values;[1] i.e., a God who besides being the "King of the Universe," the great God of nature, is also "a Power making for righteousness" (Matthew Arnold)—one "who comes to judge the earth, to judge the world with righteousness" (in the Psalms for Friday evening, Ps. 96:13 and 98:9) [*GOP,* p. 121]. *And because God is concerned for the values which the good man values, He is open to the good man's prayers and appeal for help.*

And so in the great daily recital of petition and prayer, the "Shemoneh Esreh" (the Eighteen Benedictions), which is a staple of our Prayer Book, the Jew specifically includes this aspect of God. "Hear our voice O Lord our God . . . and accept our prayer in mercy and favor, for Thou art a God who hearkenest unto prayer and supplications . . . Blessed art Thou, O Lord, *who hearkenest unto prayer*" [*GOP,* p. 42].

And in the same spirit this God is conceived as supporting the fallen, healing the sick, freeing the prisoners [*GOP,* p. 135], as bringing justice to those who are robbed, as giving bread to the hungry, as opening the eyes of the blind, as loving the righteous [*GOP,* pp. 112-113].

These are the demands of the human heart: how tragically inadequate the response! But, mark you: despite repeated and recurrent and constant failures to receive adequate reply to these cries for help, man is so convinced of their utter rightness, of the imperiousness of these claims which he makes upon the universe and therefore upon the God whom he imputes to that universe as its heart, that he will not take no for an answer. No failure can discourage or refute him. That is, prayer issues from depths which our philosophy dreams not of, and cannot plumb, and therefore cannot invalidate. The things man prays for, his life, his ideals of justice and goodness, are felt to be so supremely important that the very stars in their courses are expected to fight for their realization and preservation.

Here then we are clearly in the presence of one of those aboriginal and basic acts of the human soul which must give us pause. Prayer is what Goethe would call an *Urphaenomen,* an aboriginal and basic event rooted in the very character of the human spirit, a kind of archetype of the human mind.

And hence it is that the prayerbooks of people are their most significant books, certainly their most characteristic books; and wherever they are authentic and sincere, deriving from deep enough and earnest enough moods (as is the case with the great classic prayer-liturgies), they are also the most important and most indispensable of their books.

And so I regard our old Jewish *Siddur* as the most important single Jewish book, a more personal expression, a closer record, of Jewish sufferings, Jewish needs, Jewish hopes and aspirations, than the Bible itself; which for one thing is too grand and universal to be exclusively Jewish (as Shakespeare is not the typical Englishman), and for another, whatever is quintessentially needed for daily use has been squeezed out of it into the prayerbook and so made our daily own. And if you want to know what Judaism is—the question which has no answer if debated on the plane of intellectual argument—you can find out by absorbing that book. The Jewish soul is mirrored there as nowhere else, mirrored or rather embodied there; the *individual's* soul in his private sorrows, and the *people's* soul in its historic burdens, its heroic passion and suffering, its unfaltering faith, through the ages.

A while back I spoke of unanswered prayers, and that the failure to receive an answer does not wither the urge to pray in mankind, nor dry up the deep source or well-spring from which prayers surge up.

Nevertheless, in spite of this unfailing well-spring, we must raise the question of the validity of prayer, and pass in review the strongest that can be said against it. If prayer, if religion which stands and falls with prayer, cannot withstand the utmost that can be urged against them, they are not worth having.

Leaving out the many who are merely indifferent, or who touch prayer and religion only at the merest tangent or thinnest surface, there are those who reject prayer with deliberate intent and express reasoning. There are those who do not need to pray; or who disdain to pray; or who regard prayer as a pathetic human fallacy, a childlike anthropomorphism in a world of iron necessities, an attempt to impose human values on a universe which is alien to them and which has no concern or regard for man's needs.

There are some who really don't need to pray: the few lonely and strong, the rare souls who are sufficient unto themselves, gods in their own right, of whom the poet Henley speaks:

> In the fell clutch of circumstance
> I have not winced or cried aloud,
> Under the bludgeonings of chance
> My head is bloody but unbowed.
> It matters not how strait the gate,
> How charged with punishment the scroll,
> I am the master of my fate:
> I am the captain of my soul.

But however we may exclaim in admiration of the heroism of the man, it is a lonely cry and an unhopeful, a hopeless cry; it is at bottom a counsel of despair, heroic but enveloped in gloom; above all it can never become a philosophy for mankind because it is so utterly individualistic and self-centered—it leaves out of account altogether and says nothing of the great hopes and dreams of *mankind,* for which cooperative effort, and faith in the future, are a prime essential, cooperative effort between men, and between man and God.

Another mood of refusal to pray to a god is embodied in the great Greek myth of Prometheus. Prometheus is the Titan who stole fire from heaven and proposes to make men independent of the envious gods. Zeus chains him to a rock in the Caucasus and has a vulture or eagle eat out his heart or liver every day anew as it grows again, until he is delivered by another Titan and hero called Herakles.

The greatness of the myth is to indicate the grandeur of man. The weakness of the myth is to regard God as envious. Man is grand but not self-sufficient. He has to do the actual work, but he is rooted in a background which feeds and nourishes him, and which is not envious but on the contrary is the divine support and soil and source of his strength.

A third and the most ominous type of refusal to address ourselves to "a Friend behind the Phenomena," to a "Power-not-ourselves making for righteousness," is the scientific viewpoint if carried out to the extreme that the world universe is a system of rigid necessity—that the world cannot be cajoled or *changed*— that things have to be as they are;

and that it is therefore a childish fantasy to think we can budge or refashion them. The name which best sums up this viewpoint of rigid necessity is a Jewish name: Spinoza.

As against this necessitarian viewpoint and at the opposite pole, prayer is the expression of the religious view, of the religious outlook, that the world is not a rigid system of ironclad and heartless necessity fixed to all eternity, but with an open future which we can help make or mar, and above all, proceeding with a purpose and towards a goal no matter how falteringly or dimly, and which it is our task to help achieve—that it is not devoid of direction, or of concern for values such as men cherish: justice, goodness, love—but on the contrary finds its whole meaning and aboriginal intention in the emergence and flowering of these ultimate goals.

"Last in production but first in thought, first in intention:" this expression used by the poet of the *Lecha Dodi* concerning the Sabbath [*GOP,* p. 124], is also a good expression of the religious outlook generally. Jeremiah and Bach, the life of love and beauty, are the last to appear in the cosmic scheme, but the first in intention; when the starry nebulae first began to shape themselves into solar systems, it was in order to eventually culminate in man and his advance. And Bergson's *élan vital,* the creative urge which strives towards ever and ever greater perfection, is more Jewish and more religious than the fixed and finished and unchangeable necessity of Spinoza.

Who can prove these things? Who can decide the rightness of the religious viewpoint? There is enough design in the universe to make atheism look silly: there is enough heartlessness in the universe to make religion Heartbreak House.

But if your heart does not already urge you, urge you so strongly that no frustration can refute it, so that with the Hebrew religious seer you can utter the most heroic and the most religious of all words, "Though He slay me yet will I trust in Him" (Job 13:15)—no mere intellectual demonstration would have the slightest avail. It is the deepest intuition of the best of the race at all times and among all peoples: an intuition, an anticipation, an act of faith: the faith that what our heart wants the universe also wants, and God wants.

I give as an example of that intuition the culminating cry at the end of Beethoven's Ninth Symphony, where the human voices suddenly emerge above the instruments. That cry expresses this jubilant and triumphant assurance: Be embraced ye millions (*seid umschlungen Millionen*), take this kiss for the whole world (*diesen Kuss der ganzen Welt*), above the stars a loving father must be present (*Brüder, über'm Sternenzelt muss ein lieber Vater wohnen).* Musician and poet (Beethoven and Schiller) unite in this religious act of faith.

And if it be not true in the sense of literal empirical verification here and now around us—if this deepest hunch, this hunch without which life seems shabby and worthless, is merely a hunch, we have got to be good sports and take a chance on it. Or rather, if it is not fully true we have got to try and make it true. *Maybe that is the secret.* If it is not true maybe it is not yet true and waiting to be made fully true. Maybe it is our task as human beings to be helpers and co-creators with a God who is still in process of gradual realization, who needs our strength to carry out His designs as we need His strength to hearten us. *Maybe God and perfection are at the end and not at the beginning.* Maybe it is a growing world and a growing mankind and a growing God, and perfection is to be achieved, and not something to start with.

Our own prophets and prayer books seem to have had an inkling of this fact. At culminating points in our liturgy we say in a phrase borrowed from one of the last of the prophets (Zechariah 14:9): "On that day He shall be one and His name shall be one." On *that* day, not as yet alas, but surely on that day He shall be one *as He is not yet one.* For how can God be called one, i.e., real, if mankind is rent asunder in misery and poverty and hate and war? When mankind has achieved its own reality and unity, it will thereby have achieved God's reality and unity. Till then God is merely an idea, an ideal: the world's history consists in making that ideal real. In simple religious earnestness it can be said that God does not exist. Till now He merely subsists in the vision of a few great men's hearts, *and exists only in part, and is slowly being translated into reality.*

And that is our answer: the world is in the making; and man is a protagonist in that great drama; and prayer, which is the communion of the soul with the great reservoir of power, is an irreplaceable element in human life and advance.

But let us not make things too easy for ourselves. Why is it that not all prayers are answered? And why can't all people pray, but have to use other people's prayers printed in books? And why should we have to pray at all, since God presumably must know what we want and therefore should not need to be reminded?

These are tragic questions, and all of them are involved and inevitable in a world constituted like ours, where the spiritual power is only part of the universe; a world which is in process of growth, a world which is struggling from lower to higher planes, from the unperfected to the more and more perfected.

We can't all pray from our own creative resources because we are not all of us religious geniuses, and prayer and religion are as truly a form of genius, a gift from God, as poetry or music or any high endowment. We can't all write Shakespeare's poetry or Bach's music but we can still make it our own: we can open our hearts to it, and enrich and expand ourselves by sharing and appropriating it. And so in prayer we must turn to the great religious geniuses, the Isaiahs and Jeremiahs and Psalmists, and make our own the visions they have seen, the communion they have established, the messages they have brought back, the words they have spoken as having been spoken for us because truly spoken for all men. And by an act of sympathetic fervor, of loving contagion, to achieve their glow, and to fan the spark which is present in all of us at the fire which they have lighted.

This does not mean that all the deepest prayers and all the best poetry and all the highest music have all already been written, and that there is an end to inspiration. The future is open, there is no limitation on the wonder of insight and creation. But we each of us in our time and place have to husband the resources available and to warm our hands at the fires already lighted.

So much for one question. Another graver question is why most prayers seem to go unheeded and unanswered. The answer to that is that this is not true. True prayers never go unanswered. But what is true prayer? We shall see later that it is a prayer which God Himself puts into our hearts to give back to Him enriched by our fervor, our power. That is true of all inspiration and so of religious communion with the Godhead. And the answer to such true prayer is always a gift of power, a gift from the great reservoir of power.

And if in the supremely tragic case in which it happens that man prays, and God gives, and still both together go down in apparent defeat, that defeat is inevitable in a world slowly growing, and where the forces of darkness, of blindness, opaqueness, indifference or even malice, against which God and man are together leagued and arrayed, are still in the ascendant. Moreover, that defeat itself is a spiritual victory, because it is an heroic effort, which pushes back the domain of darkness and suffuses with light and spirit the opaqueness and indifference of the lower order, and adds stature to God and man. That heroic effort on the part of man aided by God is the supreme act of spiritual creation, the creation of a new order of being.

And finally, the smart question is why we should have to pray at all to a God who should know us and who therefore should supply our wants without our troubling Him.

Our theory of the correlation of God and Man, whereby they

mutually re-enforce each other in a mystic life-giving circle, growing together through each other's gift and enrichment, holds for religion as for all the major creative efforts of man—for music and poetry and the arts of beauty, as for the visions of justice and government and character and love. God is the source of inspiration, but man must do the work and give it back to Him enriched—fashioned, articulated, built. "In Thy light we see light" is the simple literal truth: inspiration is from God. But it is we who must weave that light into a fabric and utterance. God hands a chalice to mankind which mankind must hand back to Him at the end of days, foaming with its own inner saps and juices, its own sweat and blood and wine, its own infinite experience. Not the alternative of Christian theology, God's grace or man's works, but the two together is the subtle and profound position of Jewish religious thinking. Thus Akiba, the greatest of the rabbis, tells us at the end of the Mishna tractate on Yom Kippur, as the consummating thought of that tractate, "Happy are you O Israel: before whom do you cleanse yourselves, and who cleanses you? Your Father which is in heaven." Not man alone, not God alone, but the two together confront a world which is mere material for being made divine.

And the same profound idea is embodied in the death of Akiba as contrasted with the death of Jesus. Both seem to be forsaken by God, by the God for whom they have given their lives. But Jesus cries out in his despair the agonizing words of the Psalmist, "My God, my God, why hast Thou forsaken me?" (Ps. 22:2)—and that seems to be his final utterance. Whereas Akiba, though likewise forsaken, and left to be flayed alive by the same Roman executioners, and with a similar mood of despair echoing in his ears from his disciples who stand around him and who ask, "Can this be the reward for the saint and hero?" nevertheless rises to supreme heroism, and in a world in which God seems to be woefully lacking he proclaims his belief and his companionship with God. "Hear, O Israel, the Lord our God, the Lord is One" are his last words as he breathes out his great soul. That is true religion: to insist on God in a Godforsaken world, or rather in a world not yet dominated by God, and thus to call Him into being.

As similarly on an earlier plane the pagan hero Prometheus defies the god who will not help, whereas Job, though cruelly and unjustly tried, still utters the sublime words, "Though He slay me yet will I trust Him." Again the insistence on a God who as yet is sadly wanting, a God who by such faith is made to emerge. Again not God alone, not man alone, but the two together, for man gets his faith subterraneously from the hidden God.

We invoke in conclusion the name of that great rabbi who seems to us the supreme embodiment of the Jewish type. Akiba quotes and makes his own the concluding words of an utterance which occurs repeatedly in our Rabbinic writings (Yoma 23a, Gittin 36b, Shabbat 88b), and in which not merely is Jewish religiosity expressed sublimely, but which I regard as the full expression of the mood and attitude of the heroic man as such, the mood and attitude of the tragic hero in a growing world like ours: "Our rabbis have taught: those who are persecuted and do not persecute in turn, those who listen to contemptuous insults and do not reply, *those who act out of love and are glad of sufferings*, concerning them Scripture says, They that love God are like the sun going forth in its strength" (Jud. 5:31).

To act out of love and to be willing to bear the suffering which the good and true man must inevitably bear in a world like ours, in a world which is only partly divine and which must be won for God through the efforts of man—that is the deepest utterance of the rabbis and the culminating idea of Jewish religiosity and of Jewish prayer.

NOTES

1   "A First Cause is not enough," from Montague, "Belief Unbound," pp. 6– 7. "Religion is not merely a belief in an ultimate reality or in an ultimate ideal. These beliefs are worse than false; they are platitudes, truisms, that nobody will dispute. Religion is a momentous possibility, the possibility namely that what is highest in spirit is also deepest in nature— that there is something at the heart of nature, something akin to us, a conserver and increaser of values . . . that the things that matter most are not at the mercy of the things that matter least."

No Retreat From Reason!*

Roland B. Gittelsohn

In 1963, the Central Conference of American Rabbis convened for a colloquium on Jewish theology. One position absent from the program was that of religious naturalism, and the following year, Rabbi Roland B. Gittelsohn, an outspoken advocate of the naturalist position, requested and received the privilege of addressing the convention and restoring the theological balance.

The naturalist perspective Gittelsohn presented is predicated on the thought of Mordecai Kaplan who has contended for over half a century now that a supernaturalistic conception of God is not essential to Judaism. Gittelsohn was drawn to Kaplan's philosophy because, in his own words,

> I have come to believe through the years—with increasing firmness of conviction—that the greatest spiritual need of our generation is a new vocabulary for ancient and eternal truths, a concept of religion and God which will really function in our lives and the lives of our children.

In 1961, he wrote *Man's Best Hope* (from which the above quotation is taken), in which he explicated his own system of religious naturalism, a position to which he has subsequently committed himself in several other books and articles.

How can a Jew remain true to his faith, yet deny the supernaturalism inherent in so much of his traditional talk about God? What

---

*Part of a longer essay that appeared in the *CCAR Yearbook* 74 (1964): pp. 191–203. Reprinted in its entirety in Joseph L. Blau, ed., *Reform Judaism: A Historical Perspective* (New York: Ktav, 1973), pp. 186–203.

does it mean to claim that God can be envisioned as a power or force within nature? And, if God is not a supernatural being who "hears prayer," how can the Jew pray "to Him?" These are some of the questions to which Gittelsohn poses answers.

What . . . is the position of the religious naturalist in Judaism? That God is to be found within nature, not acting upon it from outside itself. This involves, to be sure, a much deeper and broader understanding of nature than may formerly have been the case. Men once thought of nature as being only physical. Acting on that premise, it became necessary for the religious among them to assume the existence of a spiritual entity outside nature to account for that in human life which is manifestly extra-physical. Today it is possible to think of nature as encompassing in itself both the physical and the spiritual.

Perhaps the most wondrous accomplishment of science in our time is its increasing propensity to see existence as unified and whole. The old boundary lines have been breached. George Russell Harrison, Dean of the School of Science at M.I.T., writes: " . . . the more closely one examines the borderline between living and nonliving matter, the more is one forced to conclude that there is no boundary that is definite, no place where a breath of life comes sharply to inform matter."[1] As it is with the organic and the inorganic, so is it with matter and energy, with unconsciousness and consciousness, with the physical and the spiritual. They are aspects of each other. Where one preceded the other in time, the ultimate eventuality was potentially present at the inception.

What glorious overtones modern science has added to the watchword of our faith! As God is one, so the universe is one, life is one, man is one! That which is spiritual in man—his soul—has evolved out of his protozoal beginnings no less than his spine or hand or brain. And such evolutionary development was possible because there was Soul in the universe from its beginning. The religious naturalist neither denies God nor diminishes Him. He simply enlarges his concept of nature enough to include Him.

The religious naturalist believes in natural law which manifests itself both physically and spiritually. He believes that God is the Creative Reality responsible for that law. He sees God no less in the inevitable collapse of corrupt societies than in the fall of a dead weight in response to the force of gravity. He is only now beginning to perceive how even our noblest and loftiest ethical ideals are also rooted in reality. . . .

. . . Evolution has tended in five significant directions: from chaos to order, from competition to cooperation, from conformity to individualization, from mechanism to freedom, from the purely physical to the spiritual. If this insight is valid, it bespeaks an inner thrust in the evolutionary process, something more than just a combination of random mutations plus natural selection.

When we act in accord with that thrust, our behavior is ethical. When we ignore or defy it, we are unethical. The Ten Commandments are authentic not because they were supernaturally revealed to Moses, but because they correspond with the inherent law of the universe, which is both physical and spiritual. Ethical conduct is rewarded and unethical conduct punished, not because a supernatural God is jealous of His prerogatives but because in the long run only conduct which is consistent with the nature of the universe can succeed. This, to the religious naturalist, is the meaning of the rabbinic comment: "When Israel does His will He fights for them . . . and when Israel does not do His will He fights, as it were, against them."[2]

Here is one of the crucial and exciting junctures at which the creative partnership between faith and science holds so much hope for the future. It was the geologist, Kirtley Mather, who wrote: " . . . Biologists and paleontologists have been increasingly impressed by the importance of the role played by mutual aid and co-operation in evolutionary development. . . . Especially with respect to man's lineage, evolution tends toward the development of ethical behavior in complete harmony with the high principles of the best religious traditions."[3]

From the theological side of the equation, Mordecai Kaplan has said almost the same thing: " . . . Moral laws come from the same source as the laws of gravity, light, electricity. . . . They reveal a side to nature which is not only materialistic, nor only subject to the law of physical cause and effect, but also purposive, spiritual or divine. Moral and spiritual values are as much a part of nature as are our pains and pleasures."[4] To my knowledge, Robert Gordis has not identified himself as a religious naturalist. Yet it would be difficult to state the naturalistic creed more succinctly than has he: " . . . The moral order is rooted in the universe and the natural order is the matrix of morality."[5]

Some Objections

There are some among us who will protest—in fact, who have already protested—that this seems to eliminate the transcendency of God, to make Him only immanent. Indeed it does. But let us not too hastily reject the naturalistic interpretation of God for this reason. Our ancestors needed a transcendent view of God because they had so limited a view of the universe. A cosy, self-contained little universe—consisting of earth, sun, moon and a sprinkling of stars—is too small to encompass the divine.

But ours is an incomparably different kind of universe. Where our fathers knew of only one sun, we are aware of millions. Where they believed the light which emanated from the sun reached us almost immediately, we know that it takes eight billion years for light waves to travel from one end of the universe to the other, assuming that the universe has ends. We know that if our earth were reduced to the size of a period punctuating this sentence—which means to say, to a diameter measuring one-fiftieth of an inch—our sun would be nineteen and a half feet away; the nearest star would be removed by 1,005 miles; the farthest known galaxy would be 81,830,000,000 miles away! Is it really an affront to God to suggest that perhaps today heaven and the heaven of heavens can contain Him? God is transcendent to humanity, yes. He is transcendent to our galaxy, yes. But I am not so sure that it remains necessary to think of Him as transcendent to the entire universe of nature, as we know it today and will know it even better tomorrow.

Some scientists have suggested that perhaps the universe itself is infinite. If this should prove in time to be true, will it then be insisted by some among us that there are degrees of infinity—that an infinite God is more infinite than an infinite universe? Or will it not then be necessary, in the spirit of Maimonides, to understand the Torah differently?

Is there room for revelation in a naturalistic understanding of Judaism? Of course there is, though this too must eschew supernaturalism. Last year* Steven Schwarzschild objected to our striving after divine truth "by applying entirely human tools to entirely human material." Aside from the fact that our material of inquiry and speculation, in my interpretation as in his, goes far beyond the entirely human, let me ask in the name of common sense and reality: what kind of tools can we possibly have that are not human? What tools other than human ones were used by the authors of Scripture and Talmud? When a man says "God said to me," or "God told me," or "God revealed Himself to me," he is expressing with a human tongue affirmations reached by a human heart or intuition or mind. And being human, he may be mistaken at least as often as he is correct.

At the moment when any human being claims to be the recipient of divine revelation, the content of his message can be tested only by the

---

*Ed. note: The author alludes here to the debate in the CCAR Convention of 1963, referred to in my introduction to this article. Steven Schwarzschild, then a rabbi in Lynn, Massachusetts, now a professor in the Department of Philosophy at Washington University, St. Louis, was one of the speakers.

judgment of the most spiritually sensitive men of that generation on the degree to which this new affirmation squares with what they know about the nature of reality. Where there is no basis for such judgment in previous knowledge and insight, the only test is time.

In short, God reveals Himself to men through men. Such revelation can take place in the laboratory or the space capsule, at the artist's easel or the composer's desk, as often as on the mountain top or in the sanctuary. It can come through mystic speculation, through intuition, through reason, through the study of empirical data or through a combination of these. It can be—whatever its source—a promising truth or a painful delusion. Whenever a human being, in contact with the Ultimate Essence of Reality, rises to a level of creativity or comprehension never reached before in the pursuit of truth, beauty, or moral excellence, then and there the Divine has revealed itself to man again. Dr. William Etkin, biologist and anatomist, spoke a truth in his own field of competence which I would apply more generally: "When we learn to comprehend a new geometry, a new chemical concept of gene structures, a new statistical analysis of the evolutionary process, a new theory of instinct, or any other of the great theoretic triumphs of contemporary science, we recognize that somehow we are in tune with the Creator and His Creation."[6]

More Questions

A wide variety of additional questions has been raised about religious naturalism, mostly by men and women of good will for whom this relatively new way of understanding faith represents, precisely because of its newness, a threat to the very existence of religion. Though I cannot hope to do even half-justice to them in the short time which remains, neither have I the right or the desire to evade them. One such persistent question has been: does a naturalistic view of Jewish theology rule out the mystic approach to God? Though I must confess in all honesty that my disposition and metabolism are such as to allow for only a minimum of mysticism in my own religious experience, I do not see why this has to be true of others.

Arrogance is surely not a component of religious naturalism. All the knowledge we have or are for a long time likely to have will not eliminate the mysterious and the unknown from the universe. We shall be fortunate at best just to nibble away successfully at the outer edges of our ignorance. Even as there are some among us who are more sensitive to the reality of God through reason or scientific investigation, so others may have a special capacity for the mystic experience. As yet we have no naturalistic explanation for such talent; we just don't know enough about it yet. Many a phenomenon which our ancestors could understand only as supernatural, we today perceive to be the expression of natural processes. Perhaps the same thing will be true one day of the mystic experience.

Naturalism does not necessarily mean that mysticism is either irrelevant or spurious. Neither does it mean, however, that every mystic intuition of God is authentic or the content of every alleged mystic revelation of His will accurate. Some day we may know enough to explain this kind of sensitivity, too, by natural means. Meanwhile, let us listen to the mystic respectfully, reverently, but always with an awareness that he could be wrong.

It has been said that the religious rationalist deals with a concept of God, not with God Himself. Permit me to confess that I find this line of argument extremely difficult to follow. All of us have concepts of many things. When these concepts square with reality, they are valid. When they are at variance with reality, they are illusions. How can a rational human being, whose endowment includes a mind, not struggle for a concept of God? Whether he be rationalist, mystic, naturalist, supernaturalist—whatever his disposition or inclination, so long as he is a thinking human being he will have to deal with God and with his concept of God. At best the concept will coincide with the reality. Even at worst, however, both will exist.

Perhaps the crux of the matter here is a suspicion that the rationalist worships a God of his own creation. If he does, he is no longer a *religious* rationalist. The fact that I have a concept of God does not mean that God is therefore a construct of my own mind. I have a concept of gravity, of chemical reactions, of protons and electrons and atoms. This does not mean that I have invented all these; only that I have been able to conceptualize that which objectively exists in nature. Even so—though, of course, with far less certainty or precision—my ability in part to project a concept of God in no way diminishes His reality in the universe. When my heart and my mind both lead me in the same direction, why should I deliberately spurn the promptings of either? I am convinced that God exists in the universe, that He preexisted mortal man, and will survive any possible demise of man. We do not differ here on the existence of God as a reality. We differ only on the means best calculated to help us understand God and follow His will.

It strikes me as odd that the rationalist and naturalist should be accused, so to speak, of "inventing" God, when it is precisely he who has striven most zealously to find tangible evidence of God outside himself. If there is in fact a danger that men will harbor concepts of God which are products of their own imaginations, which do not correspond to objective reality, it seems to me that such danger is greater by far among those who rely exclusively on mystic intuition than among those who attempt to correlate the products of intuition, of reason, and of science into a unified and balanced whole.

Closely connected to the foregoing is the suspicion that the partnership between science and reason can lead only to a God of cold abstraction. This need not be true in religion, any more than it is in marriage. Both are—and forever will be—for the most part emotional experiences. There is no more danger of emotion being dethroned in religion than in the love relationship between husband and wife. There is danger in both, however, of emotion taking over so completely that reason and fact are evicted. When that happens, we are in trouble.

When a man and woman wed on the basis of a purely emotional and physical infatuation, without stopping to evaluate, logically and factually, whether their personalities and values are compatible, the probability of success in their marriage is minimized. There are, of course— and should be—non-rational factors in every marriage. If the union is to bring happiness to its partners, there should not be irrational factors. A proper admixture of reason and fact, far from diminishing or endangering the emotional commitment of marriage, enhances it.

Even so, religion is to a large and necessary degree an emotional commitment. Here too, however, there are times when the microscope and the mind must say "no" to the heart. The intelligent man can be emotionally committed only to that which is an aspect of truth. His commitment must be rational and realistic. If not, he flirts with illusion and runs the risk of becoming spiritually psychotic.

One more question begs for consideration. . . . Is there room in a naturalistic and rationalistic theology for prayer? Will it help toward an answer if I attest that here is one naturalistic, rationalistic, religious Jew who prays every day of his life? Who prays, moreover, out of deep conviction that his prayers can have major consequences. Who believes that within the natural order of things there is something in the universe which is responsive to his prayers.

I resort to analogy once more, aware of the fact that all analogies are imperfect. The main difficulty with this one is that it makes God seem impossibly mechanical and cold. Yet perhaps it will nonetheless clarify what prayer can mean to a naturalist. At various locations in my home, as in yours, there are faucets. Each of these is the terminal point of a pipe, which leads back to a water main, which in turn is connected to a pumping station. When I in my thirst seek a drink of water, does the engineer in that pumping station respond to my need? Not in the sense that I petition him for water and he, on the basis of my past conduct or of his affection for me, decides to grant my request. Not even in the sense that he is directly aware at that moment of my thirst. But in a larger and more significant way, the engineer does respond to my need; in fact, he has responded to it even before I myself was aware of it. He has created a system which makes it possible for my need to be met provided that (a) I understand the nature of the system, and (b) I understand the nature of myself and my relationship to the system, and (c) I assume my share of responsibility to activate the system. Lacking these three requisites, I can stand before the faucet all day long, piteously begging for water, and my thirst will not be slaked.

With all its admitted imperfections, this comes close to expressing a naturalistic concept of prayer. It holds that God is a spiritual Force or Power—throughout the universe and in each of us—which makes it possible for us to rise above our ordinary understandings and accomplishments. God is there, whether we pray or not. God performs His necessary work in sustaining and operating the universe, whether we pray or not. Our words of worship in no way alter God or change His course of conduct. They can, however, alter us. They can make us aware of spiritual potential of which we are otherwise oblivious. And by helping us—if you will forgive the commercial terminology—by helping us to capitalize on that potential, they can change our lives immeasurably. In short, prayer too can be understood as a natural phenomenon, as a meaningful relationship between nature and the individual, as a natural bridge between Ultimate Reality and myself.

Conclusion

Let me return now at the end to the place where I began. I would not pretend that this kind of religious orientation will be adequate for all of us, nor would I make any effort to force it upon any who resist it. But I would insist, with all the vigor of which I am capable, that this is an authentic, legitimate, Jewish religious view which can bring enrichment and value into the lives of many. For me there is no need for the supernatural, no dichotomy between religion and science, no requirement that I divide my life into separate categories or compartments. I refuse to surrender the insights of science or to retreat from reason or to abandon my faith.

Thus far, thank God, that faith has been firm and enduring enough to sustain me in the most shattering crises of my life. But this has been true precisely because my faith has never been insulated from the rest of my experience as a human being, has never made claim to a province or domain where it is inviolate.

WHAT WE BELIEVE

Within nature itself, consistent with reason and the findings of science, my faith gives me anchorage in the universe, shows me where I belong in the cosmic scheme of things, convinces me that in my moments of disappointment and grief no less than in those of exultation and ecstasy, I can contribute to God's universal plan. Though my connotations may not be exactly the same, it enables me to say, with as much deep conviction and commitment as anyone:

> He is my God, my living Redeemer,
> My Rock in time of trouble and distress.*

NOTES

1 *What Man May Be*, p. 65.

2 *Sifre* 59b.

3 H. Shapley (ed.): *Science Ponders Religion*, p. 39.

4 *Jewish Frontier*, March, 1962, p. 27.

5 *The Root and the Branch*, p. 164.

6 *Judaism*, Spring 1963, pp. 179 ff.

---

*Ed. note: The author's original citation in Hebrew is rendered here in the translation of *Gates of Prayer*, p. 729.

Polydoxy and the Equivocal Service*

Alvin J. Reines

In the opinion of Alvin J. Reines (Professor of Jewish Philosophy at the
Hebrew Union College-Jewish Institute of Religion), a sharp dichotomy exists between Judaism as it was understood before the dawn of
modernity, and thereafter. Before the nineteenth century, one could
correctly speak of an Orthodox interpretation of Jewish tradition; a
monolithic homogeneous whole which was regarded as authoritative.
One hundred years later, however, such a situation was no longer the
norm. The very possibility of commonly accepted, objective evidence
on which Orthodoxy's case for absolute truth depended could no
longer be taken for granted. Orthodoxy's opposite, which Reines labels
Polydoxy, was born.

Polydoxy, for Reines, is the essence of Reform Judaism. It is religious
pluralism, marked by radical freedom. Reform Jews recognize that
with the demise of objective evidence on which the surety of Orthodoxy
could be predicated, there emerged, necessarily, an age in which
subjective evidence would have to suffice for the religious quest.

The Reform Jewish community, then, "is an association of persons
who affirm the radical freedom of one another and who pursue a
dialogue on the ultimate nature of existence." Given the subjectivity of
the evidence underlying their religious affirmations, there is no reason
to believe that they will all agree on any particular religious question
(other than their right to freedom, of course). If this is indeed the
essence of the Reform religious community, one must ask how a group
of such potentially diverse individuals can meet for common prayer,
and what form their prayer book might take.

These are the questions which motivated the following essay. In it
Reines defines what he means by polydoxy, levels a critique against the
Union Prayer Book, and suggests that the key to a common service for
Reform Jews is equivocal language, language which may be subjectively

---

*From the *CCAR Journal* 14:1 (January, 1967): pp. 29–41; originally entitled, "Shabbath
as a State of Being."

understood by each worshipper according to his or her own theological predilection.

What does Reform Judaism require of a book of *Shabbat* service?[1] The outstanding and essential characteristic of Reform Judaism is that it is a polydoxy, an open or liberal religion allowing for theological pluralism. Reform Jews can and do subscribe to different meanings of the term God as well as to diverse concepts of the essential religious act or act of salvation that the different meanings of God entail. It is self-evident that the *Shabbat* service should reflect and represent this free essence of Reform if it is to be a common book of service, the Reform Jewish book of service. The Reform service clearly should strive to serve the religious needs and interests of all who are Reform Jews. The *Union Prayer Book* does not serve the common need. Its concepts and language literally and unequivocally represent only one of the possible Reform Jewish theological positions. The question now enters whether the *Union Prayer Book* is inconsistent or incoherent with the Reform Jewish movement.[2] Our answer is dependent upon the aura and implications of the *Union Prayer Book* rather than upon its contents themselves. It is clear that inasmuch as the *Union Prayer Book* does represent one of several possible Reform theological positions that in itself it is consistent with Reform Judaism. To the degree, however, that it presents this position as the only Reform position it is inconsistent with the free essence of Reform Judaism. In other words, the *Union Prayer Book* is inconsistent with Reform Judaism if its concepts and principles are set forth as the dogma, creed, and orthodoxy of Reform Judaism. On the other hand, the *Union Prayer Book* is incoherent with Reform Judaism when it exists as the sole and common Reform Jewish service. Occupying this lofty station, it commands for itself and the theological position it represents all possible expressions of Reform Jewish service. This is particularly so since the absolute and unequivocal language of the *Union Prayer Book* suggests little depth or mystery, and consequently, leaves scant room for interpretation and private meaning. A great burden, therefore, is placed upon those Reform Jews who do not agree with its literal significance, and many are estranged and alienated from the divine service.

To illustrate the diversity that exists within Reform Judaism, let us examine briefly the theological and soteriological principles that underlie the service of the *Union Prayer Book* and compare these principles with those of three other Jewish positions. To emphasize that the *Union Prayer Book* does not allow expression to positions that are properly Reform Jewish—even by a narrow standard, let alone a polydoxy—the positions selected are those of three Jews whose views are respected and even honored in the Reform Jewish movement. Furthermore, to indicate that the *Union Prayer Book* service does not adequately reflect the full theological spectrum of the historical Jewish continuum, as well as contemporary views, the positions chosen come respectively from the Biblical period, the Middle Ages, and the present age. These three positions are those of Amos, Maimonides, and Martin Buber.

The theology underlying the *Union Prayer Book* may be characterized as a form of theistic absolutism which may be termed conversation theism.[3]* (This qualification is important since not every theism, not even every theistic absolutism, is a conversation theism.) Anthropomorphism and anthropopathism give competent knowledge of the Godhead; positive attributes are unqualifiedly and properly affirmed of God. Accordingly, we know that God is a person, the absolute creator of the universe, omnipotent, omniscient (conscious of the world as well as Himself), and all-merciful.[4] We know, too, that He relates directly to the individual, that He exercises complete providence over every person and thing,[5] and that He reveals His will with certainty and clarity in a perfect revelation, the Torah.[6] God arbitrarily has elected the Jews to be His chosen people, and He has charged them with the mission of informing all men that theistic absolutism as depicted in the *Union Prayer Book* is the only true concept of God.[7] Since God is "the Father of all men,"[8] all men are brothers, and should live together in harmony.[9] In this way, the Messianic Age will be realized, willed by God as the inevitable end of history.[10] God has established an unconditional and irrevocable covenant with the Jews: they are His people and He exercises over them forever a special providence. This covenant holds forever no matter what the Jews may do.[11] Man himself has no worth of his own;[12] his rational capacity is of no value;[13] his power is meaningless.[14] God receives, is directly influenced by, and responds to the prayers of men much as a human person receives, is influenced by, and responds to conversation.[15] Prayer is direct conversation with God. Such conversation is not only possible, but is the primary means of salvation.[16] This distinguishes conversation theism from other concepts of theism, as the concept that man may engage in direct conversation with the Deity, and that such conversation brings special favor in this world and immortal expectation for the next.[17]

---

*Ed. note: Since this article was written as a critique of the *Union Prayer Book,* before *Gates of Prayer* was composed, the author refers exclusively to prayers in the *UPB.* Readers will have no difficulty identifying similar instances of language typical of "Conversation Theism" in those *GOP* services which are not predicated on the philosophy espoused here by Reines.

Amos' concept of God is also a theism, but it is not a conversation theism and, for all practical purposes, not a theistic absolutism.[18] Positive attributes may be affirmed of God; God's nature and ways as they relate to man and history are known to the prophet, but what is known to the prophet is not that which is depicted in conversation theism. God, according to Amos, does not extend providence to the individual; the national society is the unit of providence. Unlike the providence of theistic absolutism, there is no individual retribution, only collective responsibility. The just man living in the unjust society must undergo the fate of his society. The righteous individual, therefore, may suffer destruction for the sins of others. Neither is God all-merciful. He has made a covenant with Israel, but this covenant is neither unconditional nor irrevocable. Israel can break this covenant and lose irretrievably the divine favor. The terms of the covenant are that the Jews as a community practice social justice and common humanity toward one another or lose irretrievably God's favor. This loss entails the destruction of the people as an organic national community and perhaps their extinction. Israel has no mission to preach to the world of the nature and truth of God; her task is to establish justice within her own gates. The chosen character of Israel is that she had made a special covenant with Deity promising morality for the collective divine providence. The same moral law, however, holds true for other peoples, and the same covenant can be made with other peoples. There is no intrinsic merit to the Jewish people assuring eternal survival, nor is there eternal survival for the individual, since there is no immortality. Amos does not subscribe to conversation theism; prayer is not the essential religious act, or, apparently, a religious act at all. Although God enters into conversation with the prophet, prayer is neither asked for as religious duty nor responded to as having fulfilled a religious obligation. What God requires of man is moral social conduct; this is the act that influences the Godhead. It is possible that sacrifices are included in the essential act, but however this may be, it is clear that social justice is the *sine qua non* of salvation—social justice that has to come within the limited time stipulated by the God finite in mercy. As the prophet says, "I hate, I spurn your feasts/I take no pleasure in your festal gatherings . . . /Take away from me the noise of your songs/ And to the melody of your lyres I will not listen/ But let justice roll down like waters/ And righteousness like a perennial stream . . . / So I will carry you into exile beyond Damascus/ Says the Lord, whose name is the God of hosts."[19]

Maimonides' theology, as presented in the *Moreh Nevukhim*,[20] is not a theistic absolutism if by theistic absolutism is meant a God who does all that is ascribed to him in conversation theism. Unlike conversation theism and Amos' theology, Maimonides claims that positive attributes cannot be affirmed of God. Aside from the fact that His existence cannot be denied, nothing is known of God except what He is not. God is thus absolutely transcendent; negative attributes provide the only precise way of speaking about Him. Leaving aside precise formulation for the moment, there are certain general things about God that may be said. God cannot do the impossible, and interfering with the established laws of nature or of reason is included in the impossible.[21] Thus there is no supernatural providence exercised. Neither is there individual providence for the world, mankind, or the Jews. Only select members of the human species achieve providence. This providence comes through their own act; by realizing their intellects to an extraordinary degree, they come to the knowledge that gives them mastery over natural causation and frees them from its inexorable consequences. Persons who do not reach this state of intellectual perfection, even though they may follow the rituals and ceremonies of Pharisaic Judaism, including prayer, do not come under the aegis of providence.[22] Neither the notion of the Jews as a chosen people nor the concept of mission plays a role in Maimonides' religious philosophy. Providence comes to the Jews as it would to anyone else, with the realization of intellectual being. It is this same act of intellectual realization that is the essential religious act for Maimonides. There is no relation possible between God and man;[23] salvation comes only through personal realization. Whatever there is of immortality comes about in the same manner. Since there is no God-man relation, conversation-prayer is impossible and exists only as phantasy. As Friedlander remarks, "According to Maimonides it is not by sacrifices or prayers that we truly approach God."[24] Conversation theism is not only untrue for Maimonides, it can be akin to idolatry. Maimonides' opposition to prayer and conversation are explicitly expressed. After apologizing for the language of the traditional prayerbook, and explaining that it was written for the masses but is not to be taken literally, Maimonides writes:

> We cannot approve of what those foolish persons do who are extravagant in praise, fluent and prolix in the prayers they compose, and in the hymns they make in the desire to approach the Creator. They describe God in attributes which would be an offence if applied to a human being; for those persons have no knowledge of these great and important principles, which are not accessible to the ordinary intelligence of man. Treating the Creator as a familiar object, they describe

Him and speak of Him in any expressions they think proper; they eloquently continue to praise Him in that manner, and believe that they can thereby influence Him and produce an effect on Him. If they find some phrase suited to their object in the words of the Prophets, they are still more inclined to consider that they are free to make use of such texts—which should at least be explained—to employ them in their literal sense, to derive new expressions from them, to form from them numerous variations, and to found whole compositions on them. This license is frequently met with in the compositions of the singers, preachers, and others who imagine themselves to be able to compose a poem. Such authors write things which partly are real heresy, partly contain such folly and absurdity that they naturally cause those who hear them to laugh, but also to feel grieved at the thought that such things can be uttered in reference to God. . . . You must consider it, and think thus: If slander and libel is a great sin, how much greater is the sin of those who speak with looseness of tongue in reference to God, and describe Him by attributes which are far below Him; and I declare that they not only commit an ordinary sin, but unconsciously at least incur the guilt of profanity and blasphemy. This applies both to the multitude that listens to such prayers, and to the foolish man that recites them. Men, however, who understand the fault of such composition, and, nevertheless, recite them, may be classed, according to my opinion, among those to whom the following words are applied: "And the children of Israel used words that were not right against the Lord their God" (2 Kings 17:9); and "utter error against the Lord" (Isa. 32:6). If you are one of those who regard the honour of their Creator, do not listen in any way to them, much less utter what they say, and still less compose such prayers, knowing how great is the offence of one who hurls aspersions against the Supreme Being.[25]

In an earlier passage, Maimonides summarizes his position thusly:

The most apt phrase concerning this subject is the dictum occurring in the Psalms, Silence is praise to Thee, which interpreted signifies: silence with regard to You is praise. This is a most perfectly put phrase regarding this matter. For of whatever we say intending to magnify and exalt, on the one hand we find that it can have some application to Him, may He be exalted, and on the other we perceive in it some deficiency. Accordingly, silence and limiting oneself to the apprehensions of the intellects are more appropriate—just as the perfect ones have enjoined when they said: Commune with your own heart upon your bed, and be still. Selah. (Ps. 4:5).[26]

While it would appear upon superficial acquaintance with the language of Martin Buber's theology that he is a conversation theist, this is not the case. Indeed, he is not a theist at all, but a panentheist whose God contains as well as transcends the universe.[27] Buber is in close agreement with Maimonides that God is not an object of knowledge; He does not, in fact, exist for us as an object at all. Unlike Maimonides, however, Buber believes man can enter into a direction relation with God. This comes about either through an I—Thou relation with some particular Thou or with that which is met as the eternal Thou. He writes:

> Every particular Thou is a glimpse through to the eternal Thou; by means of every particular Thou the primary word addresses the eternal Thou. Through the mediation of the Thou of all beings, fulfilment and non-fulfilment of relations comes to them: the inborn Thou is realised in each relation and consummated in none. It is consummated only in the direct relation with the Thou that by its nature cannot become It.[28]

Despite the difficulty present in talking about the God that "cannot become It," there are certain things that God clearly does not do. God does not exercise providence over man in any theistic sense of the term. He does not interrupt the natural order, and consequently, man is dependent upon the natural causation of the world of I—It and his own resources. There is no immortality. Neither does God reveal himself explicitly to man: the supposed literal revelations are the words of men who are reacting to and expressing an I—Thou happening. Yet the fact that there is an eternal Thou does have essential significance for man. The quality of person[29] as an attribute of God is the reason man can enter into an I—Thou relation, and through this relation or meeting realize authentic existence, "I become through my relation to the Thou; as I become I, I say Thou. All real living is meeting."[30] The I—Thou relation is the essential religious act, the act of salvation. Is the I—Thou relation prayer in the conversation sense of the term, or, in fact, in any sense of the term? The answer must be no. For one thing, the eternal Thou who is addressed is either powerless to answer the petitions of prayer or beyond them. Moreover, prayers, at least in part, are verbal and addressed to an object of conversation. The I—Thou relation (since it can take place with a tree,[31]) is not at all a verbal relation between two consciousnesses, but an existential relation in which there is a "flowing" of "being" and the penetration of an "I" that makes it full. Prayer, then, as theistically understood, is meaningless for Buber. Only if the words of prayer, no matter how heartfelt, are accompanied by an I—Thou relation is there any value to the experience, but then, it is not necessary to have the words of prayer at all, for it is the I—Thou happening alone that makes the words valuable. The superfluity of the prayer of conversation theism for Buber is clearly seen in the following passage:

> Many men wish to reject the word God as a legitimate usage, because it is so misused. It is indeed the most heavily laden of all the words used by men. For that very reason it is the most imperishable and most indispensable. What does all mistaken talk about God's being and works (though there has been, and can be, no other talk about these) matter in comparison with the one truth that all men who have addressed God had God Himself in mind? For he who speaks the word God and really has Thou in mind (whatever the illusion by which he is held), addresses the true Thou of his life, which cannot be limited by another Thou, and to which he stands in a relation that gathers up and includes all others. But when he, too, who abhors the name, and believes himself to be godless, gives his whole being to addressing the Thou of his life, as a Thou that cannot be limited by another, he addresses God.[32]

Generalizing the four positions enumerated above, we find they represent four major classes of religious systems: Those in which the divine is open to prayer, and prayer, at least in part, constitutes the essential act of religion; those in which the divine is unmoved by prayer, and the essential religious act is moral social action; those in which the divine is not open to prayer, and the essential religious act is the realization of personal being; those in which the divine is not open to prayer, and the essential religious act is some mode of non-verbal existential relation. (In addition, there are, of course, the eclectic systems that combine elements from the various positions.) These systems not only represent important theological themes of the Jewish continuum, but, in substantial measure also represent the basic positions taken in Reform Judaism today. Yet, for three of these four systems, the *Shabbat* service of the *Union Prayer Book* is inappropriate. Based on a narrow conversation theism expressed in rigidly univocal terms, its thoughts and words are largely inconsistent with other Reform theologies. Moreover, even though this paper is not intended to be a critique of the merits of the theological position expressed in the *Union Prayer Book,* but rather an effort to show that the latter is not competent for Reform Judaism, still some observations concerning the incoherence of several of its notions with general as well as Reform experience may be in order. For one thing, the denigration of human reason in the prayerbook of a movement founded on Biblical science is contradictory and almost frivolous. Moreover, who in the present age cannot help but stand in awe of man's rational and scientific achievements! Furthermore, in a movement founded on study that demonstrates the human and fallible origins of the Bible, and the primitive nature of large portions of its content, how can it be said the Torah is perfect? How can the Scriptural "commandments" be spoken of as if it is institutionally accepted that they were explicitly and in fact revealed, when it is clear that in Reform Judaism no certainty exists as to the origin of the "commandments," and each Reform Jew decides personally and arbitrarily what the "commandments" are to be? Finally, the unqualified optimistic emphasis upon an all-powerful, all-merciful providence carrying through an unconditional, irrevocable Messianic covenant with Israel strikes a hollow sound in the generation of the holocaust, with its steadily diminishing Jewry, and ever increasing nuclear capability.

The question now before us is a difficult one: Is it possible to create a *Shabbat* service, and a book of *Shabbat* service, that will meet the demands of both the Jewish continuum and Reform Judaism for diverse theological expression? If the answer to this question is that it is not possible, that more than one book of service will be required, we need not retreat from this step. There is no reason alternative books of service or elements from two books of service should not be employed to enrich and vary the *Shabbat* experience. More than one congregation has already created for itself alternative services to those of the *Union Prayer Book.* However, before we answer this question in the negative, I believe that every effort should be made to produce a common book of service that will have the capacity to serve all Reform Jews. Where congregations prefer their privately created services, such a common service would coexist as an acceptable alternative. The benefits of a common book of service are evident: it serves as a unifying symbol pointing to shared goals and a single community; it serves the congregation whose own members are too divided in their theological views to agree on an individual service; and above all, there is concrete ethical instruction as well as moral discipline in employing a book whose very existence implies the mutual affirmation of one another's authenticity and being despite diverse theological commitments.

In approaching a common book of service, I believe the following general requirements, inferred from the foregoing analysis should be borne in mind.

1) The book of service cannot be a prayerbook alone. Since there are those Reform Jews who take the word God to refer to that which is either beyond prayer or otherwise not open to personal address, the book of service must lend itself to other meanings than that of divine conversation.

2) The book of service, accordingly, must be written in consciously equivocal language allowing private interpretation and meaning. This requirement was often satisfied in the past by the fact that the worshipper did not understand the Hebrew he was reading, which enabled him to accommodate the public verbalization to his private religious needs. The *Kol Nidre* provides a classic example of this.

3) The book of service obviously will demand personal creative activity on the part of the one who uses it. Thus in a polydox religious community, the temple service has at the same time a private and public dimension. It is a private experience conditioned by a public setting.

4) The book of service should be understood as not necessarily constituting in whole or in part the essential religious act of every Reform Jewish system. For those who are conversation theists, the book of service may well constitute such an act; for others the service will not be, but rather point to or evoke, the essential religious act.

5) The book of service is not to be taken as a statement of the necessary beliefs or dogmas of Reform Judaism. To identify a liberal religion with any of its services is to confuse an ocean with one of its waves.*

One further point remains to be considered in connection with the *Shabbat* service of the *Union Prayer Book;* this is the *Shabbat* itself. Not only should the Prayerbook become a Common Book of Service, but it seems to me that the concept of the *Shabbat* in Reform Judaism should be rethought as well. The nature of the *Shabbat,* as it is presented in the

---

*Ed. note: Plainly *Gates of Prayer* is intended as just such a book of common service, largely for the reasons expressed by Reines. But it attempts to be so in a different way. Service Six for *Shabbat.* Eve adheres to Reines' formula: not addressing God in the English sections; and employing Hebrew passages that have lost their literal meaning, to become symbolic and equivocal expressions for the modern Jew. The other services in *Gates of Prayer,* however, represent different theological positions, so that in sum the book affirms the freedom of choice inherent in Reform Judaism, and is thus consistent with it.

Union Prayer Book, is inappropriate to a polydoxy. It is intimately, if not intrinsically, related to conversation theism, so that if the latter is rejected there is little meaning left to the former. The *Shabbat* in the *Union Prayer Book* is essentially a "day," a temporal and physical occasion, whose special significance is revealed to us in explicit "commandments," in obedience to which certain kinds of activities are to be pursued or avoided. I will omit the objections that can be brought against this concept of the *Shabbat,* both those implicit in our own earlier remarks and others, and simply describe the concept of *Shabbat* to which I subscribe, which, I propose, is a more appropriate concept for the Reform Jewish community. This concept may be termed the "*Shabbat* as a state of being." It involves the following analysis.

The meanings of the following terms are to be distinguished: symbol, vehicle symbol, and symboland.

A symbol is that which refers or points to some state or thing.

A vehicle symbol not only refers or points to some state or thing; it is a vehicle or direct means of realizing the state or producing the thing as well.

A symboland is the state or thing pointed to; or the state or thing realized or produced.

Applying this classification to the term *Shabbat,* we find that it can be analysed into three distinct elements: the *Shabbat* as symbol; the *Shabbat* as vehicle symbol, and the *Shabbat* as symboland.

The *Shabbat* as symbol, as it appears in the literature and liturgy of the Jewish continuum, refers indiscriminately both to the *Shabbat* as vehicle symbol and the *Shabbat* as a state of being. I take the former to be a means of realizing the latter, which is the essence of the *Shabbat.*

The *Shabbat* as vehicle symbol can refer to a "day"; a sacrificial, prayer or ritual procedure; or to any number of similar things organized into a complex; as is the case, e.g., in Pharisaism.

The *Shabbat* as symboland refers to the essence of the *Shabbat,* a state of being that may be characterized as a state of intrinsically meaningful personal being. Phenomenologically this state is experienced as "full" being; the state in which the self cannot ask as though it does not know—"Why do I exist?; Why being, why not nothingness?"—since the state of the self at the moment of the question is itself the reason and the answer.

This analysis of the *Shabbat* provides us with the framework for a polydox *Shabbat* service. We can assume that no matter the theology to which an individual Reform Jew subscribes, he will desire, and the essential religious act of his theology as an act of salvation will entail, plenary being—the state of *Shabbat* being. Hence we have here a common goal aspired to by all members of the Reform community, and a meaning of *Shabbat* that can be universally accepted. The problem of a common vehicle symbolism is that the vehicle symbol reflects or constitutes the essential religious act of a theology, and when theologies differ their essential religious acts differ as well. This problem is resolved by the five requirements laid down earlier for a polydox service, particularly by the point that the service must be written equivocally so that private meaning can be poured into its words and language. For some the service will constitute a relation with the infinite; for others, an occasion for ethical commitment; still others will engage in acts of self-realization; and others will find in it ultimate existential relation. All will find the beginning realization of plenary being in the concrete, public, and mutual affirmation of their integrity and existence.

Perhaps it should be pointed out in conclusion that I do not believe that the larger problem of the loss of meaning of the *Shabbat* in our time has been resolved with the resolution of the theoretical difficulties of the *Shabbat* service. This paper has not been directed to that problem. Yet I feel that with the concept of *Shabbat* as a state of being, a step has been taken in the proper direction. It is important to understand that it is not the essence of the *Shabbat* that has lost value, but a particular vehicle that has for many become an impotent symbol for realizing this essence. It is not Reform Judaism that is rejected when temples are empty on a Friday night, nor the *Shabbat* as a state of being, but a particular vehicle symbolism. Conversation theism rituals, "seventh-days" that do not fit real-life calendars, and other traditional vehicle symbols, no longer serve for many to realize the state of *Shabbat* being. Let us not despair at the impotence of the old; we require all our energies to create the new, to meet the challenge of discovering potent symbols and effective modes of *Shabbat* realization for our times and future times. A new age is upon us, and we must think in as radically different terms as its radical novelty requires; only in this way will we have the forms prepared to receive its force in an orderly and productive manner.

NOTES

1 The term service is used advisedly. A "book of service" is broader in meaning than a "prayerbook." The former expresses and includes religious activity that is not necessarily conversation-prayer, the sense that prayer commonly has, and which, for argument's sake, it will have in this paper. For many, however, prayer does not have the connotation of conversation-prayer.

2 The distinction between consistent and coherent as employed here is this: that which is coherent with a totality of things will enjoy a higher degree of integration with that totality than that which is only consistent. Thus while a totalitarian political party can be consistent with a democratic society, it is, nonetheless, incoherent with such a society.

3 This occurs on almost every page, e.g., "With a father's tender care Thou rememberest me every day and every hour;" *UPB*, p. 35.

4 "Infinite as is Thy power, even so is Thy love;" *ibid.*, p. 12, *et. al.*

5 *Ibid.*, p. 18; *et. al.*

6 "The law (Torah) of the Lord is perfect. . . ;" *ibid.*, p. 149. Also, "This is the Torah, the pillar of right and truth;" *ibid.*, p. 94; *et. al.*

7 *Ibid.*, pp. 34, 71.

8 *Ibid.*, p. 34.

9 *Ibid.*, p. 71.

10 *Ibid.*, pp. 71f.

11 *Ibid.*, pp. 42 and 44.

12 "*All* goodness and truth are Thine;" *Ibid.*, p. 29. Also, cf. p. 101.

13 " . . . lean not upon thine own understanding;" *ibid.*, p. 53. Also, n. 10, *supra*.

14 *Ibid.*, p. 101, *et. al.*

15 This is the premise of practically every page.

16 This, too, is implied throughout.

17 E.g., the third reading, p. 73; but also implied throughout.

18 I will discontinue references at this point except for special instances. It was necessary to annotate precisely the references to the *Union Prayer Book* since it was the primary subject of inquiry.

19 Amos 5:21, 23, 24, 27.

20 The *Moreh Nevukhim* is Maimonides' basic work. It is the key to his other writings.

21 III, 15.

22 III, 17, 18.

23 I, 52.

23 *Moreh Nevukhim*, I, 52.

24 M. Friedlander, *Guide of the Perplexed*, III, 294, n. 1.

25 *Ibid.*, I, pp. 218f.

26 S. Pines, *The Guide of the Perplexed,* pp. 139f.

27 That Buber takes his system to be comparable to that of Spinoza indicates even pantheistic sympathies, M. Buber, *I and Thou,* 1958 [2nd ed.], p. 135.

28 *Ibid.,* pp. 75f.

29 I.e., *"Thouness."*

30 *Ibid.,* p. 11.

31 *Ibid.,* p. 7.

32 *Ibid.,* pp. 75f.

Part Three

How We Worship

Stumbling Blocks to Prayer*

Ely E. Pilchik

A truly basic question is whether modern man, steeped in secularity, and sophisticated beyond measure, is even capable of experiencing the holy any more. Though the question of the possibility of prayer is not new, it has received considerable attention, particularly in recent times. Certainly, a ubiquitous urge to pray was not immediately evident in most Americans, a fact readily admitted and mourned over with almost predictable regularity.

Our selection is by a distinguished rabbi, Ely Pilchik, who has eschewed dry scholarly debate in favor of poetic and literary allusion. He presents three specific dilemmas of modernity with which the reader will surely identify. His illustrations are poignant, and his conclusions thought-provoking. Are the stumbling blocks he mentions still at work in our community? And if so, how do we overcome them?

Prayer is the communication between man and God. It is premised on the existence of man and the existence of God. God, in Jewish tradition and experience, encompasses many things, has a multiplicity of attributes; among the foremost—compassion, concern about the life and well-being of man. To Him man communicates his deepest needs in an ingratiating form: he expresses adoration, thanks, and finally asks petitions—grant life, grant health, grant livelihood, grant peace.

I

The first stumbling block to prayer in our lifetime is the utterly unbelievable Holocaust. One of the most searing outcries of that break

---

*From the *CCAR Journal* 14:1 (January, 1967): pp. 65–70

is "Requiem" by the distinguished English writer Lionel Davidson:

Gottenu, Du, they used to say.
He will help, they used to say.
Perhaps they said it as they waited for the shower.
Perhaps they believed it as they trembled in the shower.
(It was only a jokey shower.
They dirtied themselves in the shower.
You dirtied yourself in the shower.)
   Open Thou my lips and I will praise
   The loving mercy of Thy ways.
Who made the shower, *Gottenu?*
Who made the shower?

It had happened of course many times before.
It had happened to them plenty of times before.
But always it was possible for them before
To explain it:
In terms of an act of faith,
Or one of your measured rebukes,
Or some kind of purgative pill.
   He doeth according to His will. *(Selah)*
   He doeth according to His will.
What kind of an answer was that? *(Selah)*
What kind of an answer was it?

But this time it was different.
This time nobody asked.
(To nearly kill the lot, as a test, a rebuke, a pill
Or some similar incoherence connected with His will?)
Who could ever believe it?
Who could bring himself to believe it?
Who could blaspheme so to believe it?
   Oh guard my tongue from evil
   And my lips from speaking guile.
So most just stopped believing.
Most just stopped.

(Between me und *Du,* they'd had you
But wouldn't say so. How could they say so?
After creating you, the perfect Jew?
No, they couldn't say so.
But they knew. All the ones who

Thought about it really knew.
Kept up observance and forms, perhaps: but knew.
  With this thong to Thee I bind me,
  I betroth me, yea I bind me.
Of our bond, our vow, our due,
Tonight absolve us, *Gottenu*.)

And is it over, the entertainment of the ages,
The perfect entertainment of the ages,
That had so occupied the finest;
Is it over? One act at least.
We couldn't sustain the fantasy
Of the invisible hero and his inaudible words
And are left in saddest intermission.
  And now what shall we say to Thee?
  And who can stand in place of Thee?
We can't go on with You now.
Can't go on.

(If You're finished, we must face it
And we'll have to do without.
We'll have to do without. We'll have to do.
We couldn't live on in that way
And we can't die here in this way
And we don't yet know of ways excluding You.
Having made You, we must make You, *Gottenu*.
  It was evening, it was morning
  And He saw that it was good.
We must make anew the play now.
Make anew.)

We need a stand-in for the true one, for the alien unknown
That has made what it has made as it has made.
(The milky way and battery hens,
The dinosaur, carcinogens.)
No dialogue with that one—how with that?
But we couldn't do without one so the teacher dreamed us *Du*
And he made you in your image and he wrote the play for you.
  A tree of life to them that grasp it,
  Endless life for them that grasp it.
But You fluffed Your lines and faded,
Oh You faded, *Gottenu*.

So now we gather to atone
For Your transgressions with our own.
(We made You.)
And our vows shall not be vows.
And our bonds shall not be bonds.
And our oaths shall not be oaths.
(We made You.)
But our hopes shall be new hopes
And our dreams shall be new dreams
And our lives shall be real lives.
(We will make You.)
So we think of You tonight
As You were before this night,
Our perpetual delight,
Our first-born.
We will dream You yet again.
Will conceive You yet again.
But the earlier dream is dreamed now.
Earlier bonds have been redeemed now.
Soll Er liegen in sein ruh.
Requiescat in pace, *Du.*
Shalom, Shalom, *Gottenu.*

II

The second stumbling block to prayer—is our seeming needlessness, our fatness. It was expressed by Henry Slonimsky:*

> American Jewry has become in the course of my life-time almost entirely middle class with a middle class mentality. When I was a boy some sixty odd years ago the great majority of the Jewish population in this land was working class, proletarian, trade union, left wing radical in character and outlook. They have all made the economic and social advance. But with the conquest of poverty something fine has also departed; there has been a loss of a certain precious spirit. The very placidity and contentment that mark the golden mean so-called, exclude the virtues both of the high and of the dispossessed low. William Butler Yeats once said of the aspiring Ireland of his day that only those who had risen above or had

---

*Ed. note: See above: Henry Slonimsky, "Prayer and a Growing God," pp. 71–79.

fallen below the conventions of education, i.e., only the rare few chosen ones or the illiterate peasantry, would have a heart for the great things of the spirit. The middle class mentality everywhere and among all peoples is unreceptive to any deeper spiritual experience, and on the whole incapable of any profound metaphysical conviction. And for us Jews this bourgeoisement of the Jewish people in America has a special poignancy. For while our friends and neighbors have a middle class we are a middle class. So that in our case, Judaism, the Jewish religion, with its millennial pathos of harassment and suffering, and insistent leadership towards a messianic goal, seems to be threatened with a loss of function. And our very leaders, the rabbis, as beneficiaries of the system, often receiving the salaries of high industrial executives, are almost bound to succumb unconsciously to the seduction of thinking with that type of mentality. What now becomes of religion, of Judaism?

III

The third stumbling block to prayer—is the new God who knows not and cares not about man—science: listen to George Wald, Professor of Biology and Researcher in Biochemistry at Harvard University:

> I find no encouragement as a scientist for the belief in an external being or agency that answers prayers. It seems to me that the act or habit of prayer may have other sanctions. It may indeed be a most valuable activity. By praying, one formulates one's needs and desires, and that in itself is a good thing. To an extent, one objectifies and experiences the catharsis of voicing one's desires; and perhaps that is even a step toward realizing them. But all those effects are internal. In that view of prayer, one is not praying to oneself, yet then perhaps to what one conceives as one's higher self, as all that one might be able to conceive oneself to be?—Question: How indispensable in theology is the belief in one who answers prayers?

Some scientists and a vast host of their followers put it more harshly: how indispensable to life is the belief in one who hears prayers?

IV

These are a few of the stumbling blocks, some mountainous, some no more than a pebble.

For men of Job-like faith, like the famed survivors of the inquisition and shipwreck celebrated by Solomon Ibn Verga, or the old Rabbi in Budapest I met this summer who lived through the Holocaust and still recites *Ani Maamin** because "My thoughts are not your thoughts, neither are your ways My ways, says the Lord" (Is. 55:8), the first block can be overcome, but I suspect the Rabbis of Budapest are few indeed in our generation. Those few, perhaps for us all, cling to the conviction in T. B. Yebamot 64a: "The prayer of the righteous overturns the attribute of anger in favor of the attribute of mercy."

For men who cling to the teaching in T. B. Hagiga 9b: "The Holy One blessed be He surveyed every virtue that must be given to Israel, but found only poverty," the second block can be conquered. How many be such in our age?

The third block, science, I believe to be the great challenge to us today.

In his Hibbert lectures delivered in 1892, Claude G. Montefiore, touching on prayer in Judaism, quoted the exhortation from Exodus Rabbah XXII, 3: "Before a man prays let him purify his heart." Then he added: "And there was surely never a religious community to whom prayer was a more real satisfaction and comfort, and who were, if I may say so, more happy and at home in their houses of prayer, than the Jews."

The saving remnant of that community lives here, now, and calls upon us to call Israel to prayer.

---

*Ed. note: See *Gates of Prayer,* pp. 411, 575, and notes thereto; as well as comments in "The Liturgical Message," pp. 153/4.

Affirmation and Study*

Israel Bettan

The instructional or didactic element in Jewish prayer is well known. The Torah and Haftarah readings, the numerous biblical and rabbinic passages that are recited daily, and the *Shema* itself are examples. So study as a licit form of prayer, though a foreign concept to many religions, has long been accepted by Judaism.

Reform Judaism, with its accent on prophetic ethics, and its optimistic vision of bringing the promise of the Enlightenment to its messianic fruition, was quick to include those theological and ethical readings which accorded with its conception of Judaism as a set of highly developed moral teachings. To these were added a goodly number of additional selections drawn generally from the prophets or similar hortatory sources. The result was that parts of the *Union Prayer Book* came to resemble congregational sermonics in which worshippers recited prophetic readings about justice, righteousness and so on, addressing their remarks to each other rather than to God.

In this, Reform Judaism mirrored American religion generally. Within Christian circles the social gospel became fashionable, while non-theists abounded, proclaiming that religion's task is basically a social one: the curing of society's ills. Many Reform Jews wondered aloud whether their liturgy ought not to include more reflections on and admonitions toward social justice.

This is the setting for the following remarks by Israel Bettan, Professor of Midrash and Homiletics at the Hebrew Union College. They constitute the first section of an address given in 1930, regarding the wisdom of newly revising the *Union Prayer Book*. Bettan spoke against such a revision, addressing his remarks to those who would, in his opinion, confuse the prayerbook with the pulpit, mixing moral instruc-

---

*Part of a longer essay that appeared in the *CCAR Yearbook* 40 (1930): pp. 260–275. Reprinted in its entirety in Joseph L. Blau, ed., *Reform Judaism: A Historical Perspective* (New York: Ktav, 1973), pp. 285–301. Originally entitled "The Function of the Prayer Book."

111

tion with worship. In so doing, he raised the issue of the extent to which the prayerbook ought to reflect statements of belief generally. Is it the task of a prayerbook to stake out brave new claims of truth and ethical certitude? Or should it resist the temptation to tamper with time-honored claims which are necessarily more meager in purview, but which the entire Jewish community can accept? Is it the function of prayer to spur its worshippers on to ever more moral behavior? If so, should the latest ethical cause find expression in the prayerbook? Or should we avoid mixing preaching with praying, lest we polarize our community into opposing camps over issues which appear earthshattering at the time, but pale into relative insignificance later? As this lengthy introduction may indicate, the issue is still very much with us today. Those who would like to see the cutting edge of social reform reflected in the liturgy will label the general principles to which everyone assents as too modest or even irrelevant. Bettan represented the opposite position in his usual eloquent way.

The function of a new institution or project can be described solely in terms of its future accomplishments; an ancestral creation like our prayer book, whose history is coeval with the history of Judaism itself, affords a more dependable basis for the determination of its function. Its aims are clearly written in its results, which still abide with us. What it has done is an earnest of what it will continue to do. Its design reflects its age-long purpose. Its development in the past bespeaks its destiny in the future.

The first thing that strikes our attention when we carefully examine the structure and content of our liturgy is the familiar fact, so rarely stressed, that our prayer book is not a book of prayers but a manual of divine worship. It comprises many prayers of adoration, of thanksgiving and petition, but it abounds likewise in vital religious instruction. Impressive recitals of the salient facts of our sacred history and solemn reiterations of the fundamental principles of our faith find their place, alongside of the purely devotional elements, in the service. The *Shema*, with its accompanying paragraphs, occupies as central a position in the liturgy as do the Eighteen Benedictions; and the reading from the Scroll, with the subsequent interpretation of the passage read, is as much a part of our worship as are the prayers and meditations. The oft-repeated witticism that the Jew prays philosophy owes its origin to an unconscious confusion in terms. Prayer, though an essential element of worship, forms but one of its component parts. Instruction in the Law, knowledge of the faith, complement prayer in the order of the service. Worship, Jewishly conceived, is the service of the heart, which is prayer (Taan. 2a) supplemented by the joy of the heart, which is Torah (Cant. R. 3). The Jew does not pray philosophy; he worships his

God in a prayerful spirit and in a philosophic temper. He worships with his mind as well as with his heart, intellectually as well as emotionally.

This function of the prayer book, to enlighten as well as to renew and sanctify, the molders of our liturgy controlled with admirable skill and foresight. It was a comparatively easy matter to define the attitude in which the worshipper should make known the needs of his soul. For the primary needs of man are more or less static and universal, varying only in the degree of their urgency at any given moment. We all want life and health, clearness of vision and strength of will, faith, courage, peace, happiness. It is quite otherwise with that attitude in which the soul reaches out for a larger truth. For truth is broad, many-sided, and ever-changing. Knowledge is subject to numerous classifications and widely-varying estimates. To determine the nature of the instruction that might best be crystallized in a manual of common worship called for sureness of insight and soundness of judgment. Above all, it called for the wise and careful formulation of some guiding principle by which the process of selection might be conducted with the utmost objectivity. And as we scan the non-intercessory parts of our daily ritual we cannot fail to discern the principle that must have governed the choice of material. For whether the lesson taught is theological, historical, or ethical in character, it is always the cardinal doctrine, the memorable event, the simplest of moral guidance, that claims the attention. There is nothing in these selections, derived from biblical or rabbinic sources, that attempts to do anything more than to confirm the people in a faith that is already theirs, to recall providential acts with which they have long been familiar, to rehearse religious or moral precepts from which no believing, right-thinking Jew could well dissent. Take, for example, the passage dealing with the things the fruits of which a man enjoys in this world and whose stock is reserved for him in the world to come, in which are enumerated such rudimentary practices as honoring father and mother, dispensing charity, attending the house of study promptly and regularly, extending hospitality to wayfarers, visiting the sick, dowering the bride, attending the dead to the grave, exercising devotion in prayer, making peace between man and his fellow [GOP, pp. 52–53]. Or, take the brief prelude to one of our most beautiful and moving liturgical utterances: "At all times, let a man fear God, secretly or openly; let him acknowledge the truth, and speak the truth in his heart; and let him rise early and say: Lord of all worlds!" and so forth [GOP, p. 288]. These, and others too numerous to mention, are all simple and well-known rules of conduct that require no special demonstration to win popular assent. It is quite evident that those who first organized the material of our services held to the view that it was not the function of a manual of common worship to inculcate new doctrines, to impart new truths and facts, or even to make novel applications of old truths. They must have felt, and felt rightly, that instruction of a more minute and complex nature, subtler analyses of the truth, broader and more far-reaching applications of fundamental principles, should come from the teachers and preachers in Israel. In short, the character of the selections made points to a definitely fixed policy, not to allow the prayer book to usurp the place of the pulpit in Synagogal worship.

The Environment of Prayer*

Joseph Gutmann

Joseph Gutmann, Professor of Art History at Wayne State University in Detroit, is an outstanding authority on Jewish art. His studies include numerous articles and books on synagogue architecture, ceremonial art objects, and illustrated manuscripts. He has argued vociferously against the popular misconception that Jewish law has forbidden and thus retarded any significant artistic expression of the sacred by Jews.

Perhaps the most noticeable corollary of this unfounded presumption is the supposition that pictures have never been used in Jewish prayerbooks. The frequent illustrations in medieval illuminated Haggadahs are often mistakenly viewed as exceptions to the rule. In fact, as Gutmann argues here, prayerbooks of the past have contained art; and prayerbooks of the present suffer from a lack of aesthetic sensitivity.

The essay reproduced here deals with the *Union Prayer Book,* and was written as one of a series of articles by various authors proposing criteria which should guide those commissioned with the task of liturgical reform. Whether Gutmann's criticism is equally valid for *Gates of Prayer,* and whether further editions of Reform liturgy should give greater consideration to Gutmann's critique are serious questions deserving our attention.

There should be *batei ha-midrash,* beautiful and pleasing in structure, for this increases the love of learning and the desire for it and also improves the memory. Furthermore, the viewing and contemplating of pleasing forms, beautiful engravings and drawings broadens and stimulates the mind and strengthens its faculties . . . It further seems to me that it is necessary and obligatory to adorn sacred books and to pay special heed to the beauty, splendor and loveliness in them. As with God, who

*From the *CCAR Journal* 14:1 (January, 1967): pp. 53–58.

wanted to beautify His Holy Place with gold, silver, jewels and precious stones, so it should be with His holy books.[1]

The advice of a Catholic theologian? Not at all, but the recommendation of a Spanish Jew, the fourteenth-century grammarian and philosopher Profiat Duran. I am at pains to cite this opinion of a leading Jewish thinker, since it is still all too common to read and hear it repeated that the Jews have a congenital incapacity for artistic achievement; as the people of the Book, that since they considered Torah the only worthwhile intellectual pursuit; their overriding ethical concerns and demands left no room for the realm of aesthetics. It might be asked: Was the Orthodox Jew of yesteryear aesthetically sensitive? Did he heed the advice of Profiat Duran? If the answer is no—if Duran's opinion was eccentric—how, then, are we to account for the rather abundant existence of beautifully produced medieval prayer books from Germany, Spain and Italy? But what can we say of our Reform prayer books? I submit in evidence a book which is quite familiar to you—a book which in its format, its layout, and its total lack of artistic sensitivity makes us wonder whether the Orthodox Jew of the Middle Ages has not a great deal to teach us about aesthetic sensibilities in worship—the *Union Prayer Book.*

Closely related to the traditionalist Jew's putative aesthetic blindness is the notion that art played no role within the traditional Jewish worship service. This standard fiction or hobbyhorse, again, is grounded in no Jewish historical reality. As early as the third century, in the synagogue of Dura-Europos, art was used didactically in a series of wall frescoes to convey the central ideas of rabbinic Judaism with its stress on resurrection, messianic redemption and salvation in the world to come. These paintings, incidentally, are the forerunners of popular illustrated Christian texts like the medieval Biblia Pauperum intended for believers who were ill-educated and too poor in worldly goods to afford expensive texts.

Medieval Jewish prayer books graphically spelled out the prime concern of orthodox-rabbinic Judaism—salvation of the righteous in the world to come. In Germany, for instance, the worshipper found himself confronted with such symbols as Leviathan, the fish, and Behemoth or *shor ha-bar,* the wild ox. The primeval beasts were expected to delight the palates of the righteous at the messianic banquet in the world to come, for rabbinic tradition held that the righteous would witness "Behemoth, which with its horns will pull Leviathan down and rend it, and Leviathan will, with its fins, pull Behemoth down and pierce it through."[2] The struggle of the beasts is depicted in connection with the Sukkot morning liturgy since it was further believed that God would use Leviathan's skin to construct a sukkah for the banquet of the righteous in messianic times.

The Spanish Jew of the Middle Ages inserted representations of the Jerusalem Temple appurtenances into the opening pages of his Hebrew Bible. Why did he do so except to fortify his daily liturgical petition for a speedy restoration of the Temple in the messianic future? In this, of course, he followed Maimonides, who scorned naive messianic notions like eternal eating and drinking in the Garden of Eden. Maimonides preferred to dwell on the reestablishment of the Jewish kingdom under a king-messiah, who would unite the Jews into a nation, rebuild the Temple, and reintroduce Jewish law.

The illuminations in medieval Jewish prayerbooks and the images painted on the walls of early synagogues had a common goal—to convey vividly, meaningfully and aesthetically the collective and shared Jewish thoughts, feelings and symbols of specific and diverse Jewish communities in the long span of Jewish history.

Our task in using art, whether in prayerbooks or in the synagogue proper should be, ideally speaking, no different from the task of our forefathers. We, too, through art wish to convey meaningfully and aesthetically the collective Jewish thoughts, feelings and symbols of our 20th-century Reform Jewish communities. Yet, however fervent, wishes do not necessarily advance goals. The self-contained religious community with its own microcosmic universe of discourse and symbolism exists no more. The images in the art of early synagogues and medieval Hebrew prayerbooks needed no explanation—no lengthy lectures, no pamphlets, no learned papers—they were understood by all, because they communicated the shared ideas, feelings and aspirations of a specific Jewish community.*

Emancipation, separation of Church and State, a highly industrialized society with its stress on science, these are only a few of the factors which have shattered the secure, self-contained world of faith and the symbolism ministering to it.

As Hegel said so aptly: "In an age of piety one does not have to be religious in order to create a truly religious work of art, whereas today the most deeply pious artist is incapable of producing it."[3]

Some of the more liberal Christian thinkers in our own day are very cognizant of the dynamic changes which have taken place. Says Canon

---

*Ed. note: Compare the discussion of symbolism in the concluding essay, "The Liturgical Message," pp. 135–9.

C. Parks Streete: "The old ways of communicating just don't communicate any more."[4] The Dominican Father Couturier stated that ideally Christian art should be resurrected by geniuses who happen also to be saints, "but under actual conditions, since men of this kind do not exist . . . it would be safer to turn to geniuses without faith than to believers without talent."[5] And Father Régamey writes: "To expect a truly sacred art of a society of our materialistic type, and especially a Christian art of nations once again become practically pagan, seems to me a chimera."[6]

As Hegel and Christian thinkers have realized, the creation of a truly religious art in a predominantly secular society is most difficult, if not impossible. Similarly, the search for common and shared institutional religious symbols in a non-religious society runs counter to the deepest affirmation of our own day—the exploration of the unique personal self. Our age which has focused on individual search rather than on collective faith and salvation, not only has called into being a variety of theological responses—witness the diversity of responses in our movement—humanistic, agnostic, reconstructionist, neo-orthodox, existentialist. It has also, and naturally, elicited a great variety of individual affirmations in terms of artistic responses. Rabbis can appreciate theological problems, they are aware of the desperate need to explore the theological realm for answers. But no such need is felt for the arts, and the result is that Jewish leaders have lagged far behind their Christian counterparts in experiments to incorporate the arts into worship.

This diffidence about art is hardly surprising in view of the much misunderstood traditional taboo against art that lingers on even in enlightened Reform circles. An age of specialization, furthermore, where no one can hope to keep up with developments in every field, is an additional restraining factor—and still another is the common human tendency to conceal ignorance by dismissing perplexing fields like contemporary art as totally irrelevant to our searches.

Since many rabbis prefer Freud to Israel Baal Shem Tov, or appear to see more relevance in Whitehead and feel more at home with him than they do with Maimonides, why then should they choose for their synagogues and homes so-called antique mezuzot, omer calendars, and spice boxes over products of contemporary art? Why should some Reform rabbis champion the creation of a distinctly 'Jewish Art,' despite the fact that such an art has never existed?[7] The art of Dura-Europos, for instance, is firmly rooted in late Roman and Parthian art, and the medieval Hebrew manuscripts stylistically are indistinguishable from medieval Gothic art. The sterile, academic depictions of a bearded sage and yeshiva *bachur* to be seen on the walls of Reform rabbinic studies and homes constitute not Jewish art, as mistakenly believed, but represent a style of art that embodies the bourgeois values and taste of the nineteenth century. Even so, such paintings, linked as they are to ghetto nostalgia and sentimentality, comfort and soothe their owners. Paintings of this type require, moreover, little genuine emotional engagement. They are relics of an age of faith and may at best evoke a sense of religious security; they are pious anchors in rapidly changing and puzzling times. This art may remind us of the warmth of our Orthodox childhood; it may recall the certainties of a long superseded Orthodox faith, but ought we not to question—and most seriously question—whether nostalgia, reverence, security, and yearnings for yesteryear should be the prime motivating factors in our confrontations with art in worship?

Some Reform congregations, it must be pointed out in all fairness, have made attempts to use contemporary art. Yet how uneasy this alliance between art and Reform Judaism is manifests itself all too often. Shows featuring contemporary art within the synagogue are more often flashy gimmicks than genuine searches, and not uncommonly they enhance neither religion nor art. The architecture of the synagogue, made daringly and strikingly modern by leading architects with the great attention they have paid to soft-tilting seats, good lighting, plumbing, acoustics, ventilation, and with special arrangements for expansion on the Holydays, frequently have as an afterthought a few traditional symbols plastered to the walls or some dubious antiques placed within the ark, all in order to make a utilitarian building distinctively Jewish and to set it apart from the nearby bank or Protestant church. At times, an embarrassing opulence within the synagogue echoes "not a quiet harmony calling for an examination of the life one leads, but the market-place taste of congregational leaders, who create a 'sanctuary' which reflects, affirms and sanctifies the commercial values by which they live."[8]*

I have stressed the negative aspects. What are the possibilities for positive achievement? There can be no doubt, it seems to me, that many symbols and artifacts once relevant to a Jewish community are today no longer meaningful—and all the pious nostalgia and reverence in the world will not make them so. Certainly it is true that conversations between the rabbi, ignorant in art, and the artist, ignorant in theological matters, are difficult. Yet, bridges must be built, for as a recent article stated: "Young people are fed up with ways of worship, stifled by deadly decorum."[9]

---

*Ed. note: Compare Sharlin's comments regarding music, pp. 125–7.

Intelligent confrontation and dialogue must begin. Such a confrontation demands, of course, a creative search on the part of the rabbi to develop a meaningful theology and to communicate it to the artist, so that the artist can effectively translate abstract ideas into beautiful concrete forms—forms that will not offend the eye with crude cheapness or a harping on nostalgic pieties, but instead will stimulate awareness and discovery of a faith still very much alive.

As Meyer Schapiro has said, modern art forms can

> induce an attitude of communion and contemplation. They offer to many an equivalent of what is regarded as part of the religious life: a sincere and humble submission to a spiritual object, an experience which is not given automatically, but requires preparations and purity of spirit. It is primarily in modern painting and sculpture that such contemplativeness and communion with the work of another human being, the sensing of another's perfected feeling and imagination, becomes possible.[10]

Clarity in the theological realm is a *sine qua non* for intelligent integration of the arts within the Jewish worship service, for the very dimensions of the synagogue, its use of space, forms, colors, materials, lights and symbols, should reflect the theological aspirations to which a Reform rabbi and his congregation subscribe. Asking the right questions is at this juncture perhaps more important than getting pat answers. "Israeli art . . . Jewish art . . . does it really matter?" asks Mordecai Ardon, the leading Israeli painter. "When you look at a work of art, ask yourself only if it is original, interesting and well handled. If it is, fine. And only then, ask if it has any Jewish content. If it has, *mach shabbes!*"[11] Art has played a role in the Jewish past—it can and should play a role in the Reform Judaism of the future. It can help us in our probing and searching of Jewish tradition, in our seeking to convey spiritual meaning in modern terms.

The Midrash tells us that even Moses, who excelled most men in nearly every respect, was seen as inferior to Bezalel in the realm of art. According to the Midrash, Moses had great difficulty with the construction of the menorah.

> Twice he ascended Mt. Sinai to receive instructions from God, and twice he forgot the instructions on his descent. The third time, God took a menorah of fire and showed him every detail of it. And yet Moses found it hard to form a clear conception of the menorah. Finally God told him: "Go to Bezalel, he will make it." When Bezalel had no difficulty in executing it, Moses

cried in amazement: "To me it was shown many times by the Holy One, blessed be He, yet I found it hard to grasp, but you without seeing it, could fashion it with your intelligence. Surely you must have been standing in the shadow of God *(bzel-el)*, while the Holy One was showing me its construction.[12]

Moses' example of deferring to the artist in matters of aesthetic judgment could well be followed by religious leaders today. The Midrash implies that the artist is God-directed and God-inspired. Man, through the artist, can share in the divine gift, for the artist is the final arbiter of what beauty is. Only by understanding the intention of the human artist can we grasp some of the beauty of the Divine Artist and carry out the Commandment to worship God in the "Beauty of Holiness."

NOTES

1 *Ma'ase Efod.*, p. 19.

2 *Lev. R.* 13:3.

3 W. S. Rubin, *Modern Sacred Art and the Church of Asssy,* New York, 1961, p. 73.

4 *Life* [*Magazine*], Oct. 21, 1966, p. 63.

5 *Rubin,* op. cit., pp. 68-69.

6 *Ibid.*, p. 54.

7 See J. Gutmann, "Jewish Art: Fact or Fiction?" *CCAR Journal,* XII (April, 1964), pp. 49–54.

8 A. Kampf, *Contemporary Synagogue Art,* New York, 1966, p. 72.

9 *Life* [*Magazine*], Oct. 21, 1966, p. 72.

10 Kampf, *op. cit.,* p. 65.

11 M. Ronnen, "Art in Israel," *Midstream* (Sept. 1964), p. 54.

12 *Num. R.* 15:9.

Israel's Influence on American Liberal Synagogue Music

William Sharlin

William Sharlin is a respected cantor, composer and student of Jewish music. His studies are broadly based, ranging from Yeshiva University and Manhattan School of Music (New York) to the Jerusalem Conservatory of Music (Israel), and the Hebrew Union College-Jewish Institute of Religion (New York and Cincinnati). His compositions include the 1972 Inauguration Services of the College President, Alfred Gottschalk, and his Sabbath Suite, first performed at New York's Lincoln Center two years later. His particular scholarly interest, to which he refers in this article, is the Chasidic *nigun*.

The following remarks were made at an international conference on Jewish music, held in New York in November, 1975, as part of the Hebrew Union College's centennial celebration. Its original topic, "Israel's Influence on American Liberal Synagogue Music," attests to its contemporary relevance. But the author converted his topic of the moment into a discussion of more basic, perhaps even ultimate, concerns: a definition of "the worship entity," the nature of true musical influence, the impact of secularity on religious experience, and, for Sharlin personally, the essential characteristic of "religious intent."

The reader may wish to compare Sharlin's remarks with the 1892 rabbinic debate on music (above, pp. 30–34), and the editorial introduction thereto.

My first response to the title, "Israel's Influence on American Liberal Synagogue Music," was to frame it as a question, not as a declaration. Putting it into question form demanded a clarification of what precisely we mean by these words. Has Israel indeed influenced our music? That question in turn demanded a prior consideration of three others:

1. What exactly do we mean when we speak of musical "influence?"

2. What is the essential nature of the "worship entity" and how must it serve as a pre-condition for musical influence?

3. How does the phenomenon of secularism in the synagogue affect religious experience and, more important, how does the religious entity act upon the secular?

We will look into these three interrelating phenomena as they functioned both in our past synagogue history and in the present struggling process of change.

The concept of influence should not be considered as a simple cliché, for it is dependent on a profoundly sophisticated process. When an existing musical entity receives new elements into its body, it reacts either by passively permitting the new to function side by side with the old, and forcing no substantial change in either its character or original purpose; or it directs its energies upon the new elements, shaping and transforming them so that they will, in the end, serve the existent mainstream. Influence in this latter case implies a mutuality of purpose, by which the old *is* influenced by the new, but only while exercising its own influence in return. Which of these two processes takes place, or in what state of balance the two function, depends on the strength, the vitality, the acceptance of and the respect for the existing entity. The more the established entity still possesses its own vitality, the more it dominates the process. The more it loses its core force—its independence—the more it submits itself to domination by the new. I use the word domination, since, in this case, the mutual interplay of old and new which constitutes true influence does not actually take place.

Now, what do we mean by the worship entity? To my mind, its essence lies in its independence. While it serves, it does still exist in and of itself. It has its own life. We who participate in it do not create it but enter into it, submitting ourselves to its own stream and substance. Its potential is not only that it is there, but more important that we experience its presence and are able to submerge ourselves in its life. Though we may retain our individuality, we become subservient to the force and energy of the entity.

What actually constitutes "entity" is not easily recognized, for it is made up of both the tangible as well as the intangible—in different states of balance—in different situations. There are the obvious elements of form and continuity that for the most part are stable and predictable, having a logical flow of liturgy to which a musical content responds with seriousness and respect. But these tangible elements, important though they are, cannot produce a worship entity without the presence of the intangible. My own life's experience has led me to describe this more elusive element as religious intent: the desire, indeed, the need, to enter a spiritual experience, to elevate oneself, to surmount the ordinary. A transcendent God will be at the center of this religious intent for some; for others, God in man will suffice to motivate the act of elevation.

Our third preliminary question concerns the dichotomy between sacred and secular. But a precise definition of what is secular and what is sacred is not particularly pertinent to our theme. It is a fact of history that the secular has always been a major source from which both Synagogue and Church have drawn considerable raw material. This fact must be seen as constituting an integral condition of the sacred experience. For the sacred itself is not totally independent. It is the end result of the transformation of the ordinary into a state of elevatedness. Because of this process, one might say that the sacred is actually in need of and perhaps even dependent upon, the secular. I cannot resist turning to that great master of the Church, Johann Sebastian Bach, who sharply demonstrated the validity of this process. One of the remarkable aspects of Bach was his conscious openness to the newly developing musical idioms of his time. He borrowed from the French dance to the opera. Yet, his profound religious need enabled him to digest, assimilate actively and thus transform these secular elements into the greatest of sacred works. What is essential, then, is not the content of the secular, but the attitude imposed upon it. Similarly, our own amazingly rich and varied tradition has always been shaped by this crucial process of desecularization, or "religionizing."

With this in mind let us examine the traditional synagogue of the past to see how the dynamics of influence functioned. One of the concepts that has helped me understand the nature of synagogue musical development I owe to my respected teacher, Eric Werner. It is an appreciation of the difference between active and passive assimilation.

Active assimilation is a powerful process, by which the old absorbs the new, digesting it until its original character is virtually lost. Passive assimilation, on the other hand, receives new musical content but allows it to retain its original shape and form. Most crucial to my thinking, however, is the realization that even in the latter case, assimilation of the new into the old still occurs. The new tune or musical pattern, while objectively retaining its original external content, is transformed by the independent energy of the living worship entity, in an experiential way. The force of religious intent penetrates and overcomes the foreignness of such musical material, submerging it into its own stream by imbuing it with a serious and believable sense of the sacred. The alien is transcended by spiritual purpose.

With the dynamics of active assimilation in mind, we can examine the extent of Israel's influence on contemporary synagogue music. How much influence has there been, if indeed, there has been any at all?

In the past several years, a body of song material from Israel, particularly that of the so-called Chassidic Festival phenomenon, has been adopted by the American synagogue. Both the eagerness with which we have seized upon these songs and the manner in which we have used them, need to be seen as part of a growing and unconscious fundamental change in the direction of worship. At the heart of this change is a sliding into secularity. This is not the result of a conscious wish to secularize our worship experience; it derives from our being increasingly caught up in the breakdown of a worship entity and the weakening of its prime mover, religious intent. We have seen, after all, that the secular can contribute to the sacred, but if the sacralizing process itself diminishes, the secular is allowed not only to retain its own character but even to contribute to the further weakening of spiritual energies. As the ability to transcend the ordinary decreases, the secular necessarily exerts greater dominance. This music, therefore, has not "influenced" the mainstream of synagogue music in the dynamic sense of there being mutual reciprocity between old and new, because our weakening religious potential has stood passively by, incapable of asserting its influence over the secular elements of many of these songs.

So we use them as an end in themselves. To begin with, we lose a sense of discrimination in how we select these songs. We must, after all, acknowledge a certain difference in character among these materials. There are some tunes that approach the genuineness of the folk as well as the classical Chassidic quality (*Yedid Nefesh,* for example). There are others that attempt to achieve this end but result in a sad mixture of the contrived and the pop. And finally there are those tunes which are wholly permeated with the pop, totally commercial in character.

Selectivity, as I see it, means the desire to ferret out that which can be assimilated into a religious experience. Some tunes achieve this more easily because their basic elements derive from established sacred substance (and association) and in themselves can evoke the spiritual spark—if we would but recognize this substance. I say this, particularly, because we are first exposed to some of these more quality tunes via Israeli recordings which present them in a style and arrangement appropriate to the cabaret, not the synagogue. Such popularization deafens the listener to the presence of core quality and the potential seriousness of the tune. The danger here is the carrying over into the synagogue the commercial facade of the tune and not its inherent religious value.

Then, there are songs which defy all attempts to relate them to the sacred. The catchiness of such tunes is to be viewed with caution for it is very often this element that reveals its popular intent. These resist all efforts towards transformation and serve only the immediate needs of sensory stimulation.

We should consider as well the sustaining possibility of the melodies we use. I have often marvelled at how some of the old synagogue tunes, not extraordinary in their character, have been able to maintain themselves for long periods of time. Part of their lasting power must derive from the fact that they have not been experienced as independent songs as such. They have been so integrated into the total worship entity that an objective analysis of their musical virtue becomes irrelevant. I never tire of the old *Eitz Chayim* melody because it serves that least shakable liturgical rubric, the Torah Service. The reverence that still pervades this part of the service permits this simple, classically pure melody to sustain itself on and on. Conversely, how often have we become frustrated when we realized how eagerly we receive the newest composition only to find ourselves tiring of it in a relatively short time.

Another area to ponder is our placement of these tunes in the context of the service. A lively song with certain innate limitations may still function well at the close of the service. But were it to be substituted for the "May the words" at the end of the *Tefillah*, when quiet meditation is the mood of the moment, we would be guilty of total disregard for the integrity of the worship entity. Respect for the stable continuity of the service begs for a sensitivity to context.

Perhaps most crucial is the manner in which these melodies are presented. Tempo, for example, is critical. Many of these festival tunes do have spiritual potential, but only when sung in more moderate tempi. Here lies one of our greatest misconceptions about the classical Chassidic *nigun*. A *nigun* was never rushed! Space in time was considered an essential prerequisite for successful entry into the energy of the tune. The *nigun* sung in a frivolous haste betrays the singer's equally frivolous and shallow grasp of the tune. What more can one say about the manner of singing? Which direction shall one take the tune—out into the streets, or up into the heights? Does the externalness of the tune dominate the singer or does the singer control the tune's loftier essence? Where there is no religious intent we bring the ordinary into the synagogue, and, ultimately, drag the synagogue itself down to the ordinary.

Our growing submission to secularity affects our attitude to old songs too; specifically, the musical mainstream of the liberal synagogue, developed during the past century or so. We are dealing with a vicious cycle: the more the character of the pedestrian permeates the service, the less are we either able or willing to receive and respond to the more serious and potentially inspirational music of our past. Symptomatic of this process is the slow but steady diminution of choir participation, whereby a rich and valuable legacy is being left by the wayside. Secularization dulls our very perception. Unable to remain open to its inspirational value, we see this music, at worst, as cerebral—intellectual—or, at best, as merely aesthetic. The waning drive to ascend, clouds the soul level of much of this music, causing us not only to shy away from it, but even when we perform it, to replace inner conviction with an unconscious sense of apology, leaving only the externals to come forth. The spark of holiness is present somewhere, but seeking it out requires a persistent religious will, which flies in the face of the growing impact of the secular.

I can speak of this out of my own experience. In the past several years I have found myself avoiding some of this literature. I have now begun to revive it. But I do so with great deliberation, insisting that we sing only that music whose inherent spiritual essence we may rediscover and reexperience. When this occurs successfully, my belief in the validity of such serious music today, is once again reinforced.

So what, then, has been the influence of Israel on our synagogue music? Obviously, from my perspective, if we mean true influence, lasting influence, with both old and new interacting authentically to serve the worship entity, then such influence has not yet taken place. True, the secular thrust of Israeli culture may very well have cut into American synagogue life, reinforcing its own gravitation towards the secular. But we cannot consider Israel as having influenced our music in the critical sense. Perhaps such influence is yet to come. As we experience the inevitable transience of many of the Chassidic Festival tunes, we will either reject them or, hopefully, be moved to act selectively upon them, finding in ourselves newly discovered religious energy. Only time and history can answer the ultimate question, "Shall synagogue music submit, or shall it assert itself, once again?"

Part Four

The Liturgical Message

The Liturgical Message

Lawrence A. Hoffman

We have now traced Reform worship through its European origins and American foundations. We have analyzed the traditional liturgical themes, and looked at theologies, old and new. We have discovered that worship is more than just words, and an understanding of the worship experience more than textual analysis. We must now draw together the many topics of this book, and see how everything so far discussed, from the meaning of the prayers to the music of the choir, combines to provide a liturgical message. In this message lies the key to Jewish identity.

Our starting point is the realization that the prayerbook, unlike most other forms of rabbinic literature, is intended not for scholars but for the general community. This is not to say that prayerbooks may not, at times, be scholarly. But, generally speaking, if an author wants to write for his scholarly peers, he writes tracts on prayer, not prayerbooks. The great prayerbooks in Jewish history have frequently included synopses of such tracts, along with the prayers, but these have been intended as relative popularizations of scholarship distilled to the educational level of a Jewish community which was, on the whole, not highly versed in the technicalities of Jewish law and lore.

The first comprehensive prayerbook known to us, for example, was a ninth-century work composed as a letter to Spanish Jews who wanted to know the order of prayer. Its author, Rav Amram (858–871), was a preeminent Jewish scholar, entitled the Gaon, and residing in Babylonia. Though he included considerable scholarly discussion drawn from the Babylonian Talmud, his commentary could more accurately be described as a condensation of talmudic teaching for a community which did not know exactly what the Talmud said on the subject of prayer. The second such book, written roughly half a century later, was by another Gaon, Saadia by name (928–942), who wrote his instructions in the Arabic vernacular, since his readers did not even understand the technical jargon of talmudic Aramaic. Far from being ignorant, his readership was well acquainted with Arabic culture, poetry and philosophy; but such enlightened education did not include a thorough grounding in the legal bases of Jewish worship, and it was this information that the new prayerbook offered, in language and style designed to impress the specific community to whom it was addressed.

Similarly, throughout time, new prayerbooks made their appearance, each purporting to introduce prospective worshippers to some new aspect of Jewish lore. Each represented a relative popularization of a religious system whose original and highly abstruse formulation was being converted into prayerbook format for the use of the general community. Thus, Kabbalistic prayers whose mystical implications required volumes to define in detail were issued in prayerbook form with but a few summary lines or paragraphs. Philosophical doctrines which could be grasped fully only by the most acute intellect were summarized in poetic form for communal prayer. Reform prayerbooks which the outsider may mistakenly judge to be mere dilutions of the medieval *Siddur* which preceded them, were in reality shorthand accounts of a Jewish world view that took decades to be explicated. It is significant that no major Jewish movement, no schismatic sect of importance, contented itself with abstract theorizing. Maimonides wrote philosophy, but also a prayerbook. Sixteenth-century Lurianic Kabbala spawned its own mystical prayerbook; and it was worship patterns that divided eighteenth-century Chassidim from their opponents. The appearance of a prayerbook is tantamount to the dissemination of learning previously restricted to scholars, to the community at large.

The prayerbook thus becomes the community's major contact with primary Jewish sources. Despite romantic notions to the contrary, it simply is not true that whole generations of Jews in the past have habitually been at home in the vast literature of the rabbis. Before the invention of printing, how many people could afford to possess even a few of the goodly number of books upon which the elaborate structure of rabbinic Judaism was constructed? And even after the Gutenberg revolution in typesetting, how many people had the leisure time, the intellectual ability, or the economic freedom to undertake serious study of a literature that had grown by leaps and bounds to include not only the two Talmuds but responsa from around the world, commentaries, midrash, philosophy, and several schools of mysticism?

But the prayerbook was the property of every Jew. Before printing, people repeated prayers by rote, or at least listened to their recital daily. Wealthy patrons hired scribes to write personal copies of the *Siddur*. And after the sixteenth century, the prayerbook was the one volume which made a crystallization of the Jewish legacy readily available. True, the literal meaning of the Hebrew words was often beyond the linguistic competence of Jews whose education was not what they might have wished, but the "message" inherent in the prayerbook is transmitted by factors that go beyond comprehension of the prayers. (It is precisely these other factors which we are after here.) That the prayerbook owed its popularity to its unique capacity to carry such a vital message is beyond doubt.

That message is, as we have already said, the connecting link between the arcane Jewish theorizing amenable only to scholars, and the Jewish people as a whole. We have already dealt sufficiently with the scholarly half of this equation, pointing out how different prayerbooks contain the distillation of more complex theories; and how the prayerbook is the medium whereby scholars as would-be leaders in the community reach out to their constituency with a prayerbook version of their message. But the people to whom the scholars reach are not purely passive receptacles of that message. They have the critical option of accepting or rejecting the prayerbook they are handed, basing their decision on the degree to which the scholarly message of the prayerbook corresponds with their own intuitive image of what it means to be Jewish. In other words, the average Jew no less than the professional scholar necessarily confronts the existential task of living a Jewish life within a particular society. He differs, however, in that he probably has not formalized his intuitive sense of what Jewishness implies, except through his day to day behavior. In fact, it is that very overt definition of Jewish identity that the laity seeks from its leaders who are judged by the extent to which they can successfully apprehend the problems and tensions of their lay contemporaries. From a lay perspective, then, the prayerbook is the leadership's definition of Jewish identity. A political analogy would be the platform offered the constituents of the party. In liturgical terms, we would say that if the prayerbook's message (or platform) accords with the image the people (or party) have of themselves, they accept the book. If not, they reject it.

The process of prayerbook formation, then, is really synonymous with the evolution of the Jewish community. As long as the community remains relatively unaltered; that is, if the makeup of the community and the environment in which it acts remain relatively stable, the community retains its inherited prayerbook without question. If, however, the factors that make for Jewish identity change, the picture of

Jewish life contained in the prayerbook begins to appear outdated, and the community puts pressure on its leaders to prepare a book which will reflect the new reality of Jewish identity. If the changes behind the dissatisfaction are minor, the liturgical response can be minor too: a few new prayers are added; a new format for the old book is adopted; some minor alterations of custom are devised; and we say the prayerbook has been revised. At that point the basic book is the same, just as the people are the same, but minor adjustments in the people's life have been admitted into the official definition of Jewish community, and integrated into the same general view that prevailed previously.

But such revisions can occur only so long as Jewish life remains essentially intact. Suppose the social structure of the Jewish community undergoes really basic alterations: through massive social mobility, perhaps, or large-scale immigration. Or, suppose the external environment changes through wars or anti-Semitism; or through social causes like messianic movements, religious schism, and the like. At that point the old book simply appears to be hopelessly out of step with the times, and patchup attempts to amend its message will fail. A thorough reevaluation of Jewish identity is called for, and the result is a new prayerbook, which will be accepted if it is seen as an adequate response to the new environment.[1]

Prayerbooks, then, whatever else they may be theologically, are also social documents. New prayerbooks represent a new social context. If, to revert to our own time, the *Union Prayer Book* is now replaced in many congregations by *Gates of Prayer,* the reason is not to be sought in the relative merit of the two books. True, people will debate the two worship styles which they see the two books epitomizing; and, mistakenly, their argument will revolve about such emotionally laden issues as authentic or inauthentic Judaism, cold or warm services, lofty or prosaic language, passive or active congregants, and so on. Objective observers should recognize, however, that these adjectives (cold, warm, lofty, etc.) are without exception employed not as designative terms, descriptive of an objectively verifiable state of affairs, but as evaluative, even argumentative language.[2] What is at issue is different worship styles representing different conceptions of communal identity. Arguments over the prayerbook mask deeper differences over the definition of community which the books presuppose. Since the American Jewish community represents a vast spectrum of identity patterns, it is natural to find no total agreement on the merit of the books in question. But the problem lies less in the books than in the community itself.

We would do better, then, to understand how a prayerbook presents its message of Jewish identity, and to focus our attention on the two visions of Jewish communal identity contained in the *Union Prayer Book* and *Gates of Prayer*. We shall find them both to be meritorious from a liturgical or religious standpoint, though at odds over their interpretation of the essence of Jewish community.

II

There are three basic elements that present the liturgical message to the worshippers: prayer content, prayerbook structure (or design), and service choreography. The first of these, content, is actually a combination of two elements: the manifest content, that is, the overt meaning of the words themselves; and symbolic association, a far more amorphous entity which is very difficult to define clearly, let alone to ascertain in any particular case, yet which has enormous psychological and sociological ramifications. Let us take each of these in turn, beginning with the symbolic content.

Symbolism has been studied by philosophers, logicians, and social scientists of all bents. By and large, they agree on the existence of symbols, but on no single definition of what a symbol is or how it functions. Since all communication involves translating one's individual, and therefore private, experience into socially familiar language, some scholars define a symbol with reference to communication skills, generally.[3] Any word, for example, thus becomes a symbol, in that it is used by the speaker to point to the object it represents in such a way as to be understood by the listener. The same is true of gestures, like shrugging one's shoulders or shaking hands; and of objects, like red traffic lights which symbolize "Stop!" People are able to function together as a group because they can translate their experience as individuals into a common symbolic code.

Further reflection reveals that symbols may have different levels of meaning, each with its own psychological significance. A learned Christian may recognize the word "Talmud" as referring to a given set of Jewish books, but he remains ignorant of the psychological dimension that word has for a rabbi trained in a *yeshivah*. Similarly any Jew knows what a cross is, but has no way of knowing what it means to a religious Christian. Thus it becomes possible to differentiate symbols according to the level of psychological significance at which they function.

Perhaps the most outstanding attempt to explain this process of differentiation is that of Carl Jung. Though, for our purposes, we need not be concerned with—nor, for that matter, even accept—the reasons he gives for the differentiation, we shall find his basic dichotomy of symbols to be of great value.[4] His psychological investigations led him to suggest that sometimes people are fully aware of what things stand for, but at other times, their real meaning lies buried in the unconscious. He called the last category, symbols, and the first category, signs. A sign thus becomes "an abbreviated expression for a known thing. But a symbol is always the best possible expression for a relatively unknown fact."[5] From this perspective, then, "Talmud," "cross" and "traffic light" are all signs insofar as we can exhaust their meaning by simply citing a dictionary definition. If, however, any of these terms carry deeper unconscious significance, they are to be considered true symbols.

We need not pause here to ask what it is that makes things symbols: whether, for example, there exists a collective unconscious, as Jung would have it. We need simply note that though everything we communicate is couched in some form of symbolic language, there exist some items of experience which we seem to relate to on a level that eludes our conscious awareness. Moreover, since this symbolic meaning is not immediately evident to us, it is obviously not something we think about or discuss. We do, of course, recognize the symbol, immediately and automatically, as representing something, and as being very important. What that "something" is, though, is not a matter for rational debate, since we ourselves cannot identify it with certainty. We know only that it has tremendous meaning for us and that people who deny its existence evoke our consternation, even our wrath. We are emotionally bound to these symbols that awaken within us automatic responses which we feel but cannot clearly explain.[6]

So, a true symbol has three qualities:

1) Verbal description of a symbol's significance can never exhaust a symbol's depth of meaning.[7] In fact, to the extent that the symbol is still a living item in the life of the community, such verbalizations are generally superfluous. When we say, for example, "Light is the symbol of the Divine," or "Light is the symbol of Israel's mission,"[8] we use the word "symbol" loosely. If light really symbolized either entity, we would not have to say so. We would recognize it automatically, and explain it only when called on to do so by people who are not members of our "group" and are not familiar with the symbolic code which we have been trained to recognize instantly.

2) Liturgically, where we deal with a group experience (at least in the Jewish tradition), the symbol's significance must be shared by the members of the group.[9] In fact a prime indication that various individuals really do constitute a group is their ability to respond similarly to a common symbol. Light may indeed symbolize the divine for an individual worshipper who is truly struck by the reality of God's presence

whenever Sabbath candles are lit. But if this response is not shared by other worshippers, that symbol remains part of the individual's own private language and is irrelevant to group worship.

3) Since the attribute of symbolism is apprehended most immediately on an emotional level, and since words simply fail to encompass fully and clearly exactly what it is that the symbol awakens within us, we find challenges to our symbolic system frustrating to deal with. Our symbols are self evident to us and we cannot fathom the inability of others to comprehend their importance.

Thus, in sum, a liturgical symbol is an item in the service which directs the community of worshippers, immediately and with absolutely no commentary or explanation, to an awareness of an experience or value which they hold in common; one to which they are either attached or repelled strongly; but whose exact significance they cannot verbalize.[10]

The best example of a symbol for our time is, unfortunately, a negative one. But its symbolic impact, negative though it may be, testifies to the crucial event of our age: the holocaust, with the swastika its symbol. No one feels compelled to explain it; we cannot verbalize what it conjures up in the Jewish mind and heart, precisely because what it denotes is truly symbolic. Verbal description would be superfluous. But it fulfills our three criteria: its response is beyond verbal explanation; it is shared by the whole community; and we react emotionally just by looking at it. Scholars may tell us that the swastika was used by ancient cultures for purposes entirely remote from the Nazi context. But such logic is irrelevant to a Jewish community for which the swastika has become symbolic of that evil which mere words cannot begin to describe.

Now prayerbooks are full of symbolic items whose symbolism is by definition never fully explained, since as soon as the prayerbook presumes to inform us exactly what a particular symbol means, we can be sure it is not a symbol at all but a sign. The only means of identifying whether a term has true symbolic meaning is to scrutinize how the community reacts to it, and the prayerbook, by its very nature, rarely offers such third-person objective reports. You will, therefore, have to analyze your own reaction to prayers, words, phrases, acts, and objects that make up a service, to decide whether they have symbolic meaning. The *Kaddish* for example will probably prove to be symbolic, because for most of us it evokes an automatic response; yet aside from some general explanation that it relates to death, or mourning, it is difficult to explain our depth of emotional investment in reciting it. Indeed, few Jews even know the English translation. Though it was composed, and originally recited, in the vernacular (Aramaic, then), the depth of its symbolic message for us results in its being the sole prayer which we would never recite in our vernacular, English. And who would dare omit it from a service when those who would normally say it are present? It is a community symbol which touches the heart of even those Jews who relate positively to little else in the prayerbook—even though we cannot agree precisely on the reason why.

In like fashion people may find themselves inexplicably attached to the Torah, the Shofar, the prayer "Grant us peace," *Kol Nidrei,* or any number of different things. For some, the *Union Prayer Book* is itself a symbol, and the very idea of replacing it with *Gates of Prayer* will be resisted for that reason alone. But without exploration in depth, we are usually aware only of the strong feelings we have about the matter in question. So debates over symbols usually revert to irrational arguments with neither party to the debate appreciating the other's profound emotional investment.

In the past, when the makeup of the Jewish community was fairly stable, most people shared the same sort of Jewish experience, and, hence, the liturgical symbolism which referred to it. A basic problem today is that the Jewish community is no longer so monolithic.[11] Despite a broad base of upper-middle-class, college-educated laity, the truly free society in which we live allows everyone to develop along remarkably individual lines, so that what we call the Jewish community is in many ways no community at all. Though banded together in temples for certain common ends—our children's education, for example—the membership really spans broad differences in background and Jewish aspirations. It is virtually impossible to find a Jewish symbolism common to all, the result being that any given service will fail to elicit complete support from all worshippers. As we shall see later, when we discuss prayerbook structure, this very division of the community into various parts is reflected by the structural component of *Gates of Prayer,* which, in effect, officially recognizes the existence of Jewish sub-groups by providing a large variety of services.[12] For the time being, however, we can summarize the symbolic factor by noting that we are just as dependent on symbols as humanity has always been; that prayerbooks achieve our impassioned support or rejection partly because they do or do not display the symbols we hold dearly; that the precise symbolic complex of the *Union Prayer Book,* as with any other prayerbook, has yet to be studied in depth; and, most importantly, that we would err grievously to mistake the absence of a common understanding on the subject of symbolism for the absence of symbolic messages themselves. Indeed the symbolism of a prayerbook as the epitome of what the community holds dearest or dreads the most, may well be the most significant factor in determining whether a new book is written, and if written, whether and by whom it is accepted.

III

If the symbolic content is the hardest element to isolate, the manifest content is the easiest. The statements about faith, the nature of the universe and humanity that constitute the plain meaning of the liturgy are there for all to see. One simply compares the content of one prayerbook with that of another, and comes up with different statements of community identity. Of course the picture is not complete without our taking into account the other elements, but the study of manifest content has in its favor the fact that it is amenable to empirical verification. From the examination of a text—not merely some presumed symbol—one can determine whether a community did or did not accept anthropomorphic descriptions of God, optimistic statements about humanity, passionate references to Zion, and so on.

Now, as long as we remember that whatever we find in the manifest content is amenable to changes forced upon us by the other elements of the whole, this is a perfectly justifiable method for arriving at what the community accepts as binding from its inherited worldview, and what it wishes to alter. It is certainly a valid index for Reform liturgy, since the decision to translate it made its literal meaning suddenly, and often uncomfortably, obvious to all, while at the same time eliminating any positive symbolic overtones which might have made the Hebrew text palatable. Moreover, the German founders of Reform hailed from a society where intellectuals studied philosophy and theology. They were, therefore, conditioned to search out the theological implications of the plain text and to take them seriously.

It is worth remembering, however, that not all ages have been so concerned with theological niceties. Past generations have intoned many prayers which defied literal acceptance. People took them as poetry or allegory, and identified with the symbolism inherent in the prayers themselves or the method of their recitation. Even today, for example, we would be painfully mistaken to assume that the nominal Orthodox Jew—that is, the Jew who says he is Orthodox because he attends an Orthodox synagogue, even though he may not subscribe to the totality of Orthodox Jewish law—really subscribes to the literal meaning of the entire *Siddur*. As often as not it is the symbolic significance of the chant, the davening, the tallit, and the other Orthodox rituals which prompt his attendance at services. He believes in angels, bodily resurrection, and the like, no more than does the average Reform Jew. But the Reform Jew, lacking the positive symbolic association with the Hebrew, has translated the prayers and then is forced to worry about their meaning.

So Reform Judaism's concern for theology in the prayerbook is as much a consequence of its losing its symbolic connection with the traditional service, as anything else. And it was buttressed by the natural theological proclivity of Reform intellectuals who received their "enlightened" education in the philosophically oriented German universities of the eighteenth and nineteenth centuries. But to this must be added yet another factor: the practical concerns of the Reform laity at the time. For Reform Judaism did not begin as an academic movement.

Reform Judaism was lay-inspired. However cultured and philosophically oriented they may have been, these pioneering spirits had other motives for articulating the need for reform. Israel Jacobson is generally accorded the honor of ushering in the Reform movement when, in 1809, he introduced liturgical changes in his school in Westphalia (Germany). What gave him the opportunity to do so was the advent of Napoleon, who swept through Europe and reorganized it, wiping out irrational geographic and national distinctions typical of the medieval world, and reordering it on the foundations of reason and enlightenment, which the French revolution proclaimed as common to all people.[13] Jacobson believed himself entrusted with the task of bringing the Jews in his region into the modern world, and he, therefore, designed a school with divine services which would inculcate the young with the liberal spirit of the new age and eschew the narrow medievalism of the old. Since the Napoleonic reforms were grounded on the absolutism of the modern nation state, it was senseless for European Jews to define themselves as another (and therefore potentially disloyal) nationality; so Jacobson joined other Jewish leaders of the time in formulating the doctrine that Jews were a religious body, not a nation, who had been denied the opportunity to develop freely as other religions had, but whose commitment to reason and modernity would shine forth ever so brightly if but given the chance.

So Jacobson's practical orientation led him to emphasize not theology but another element of the liturgical message with which we have yet to deal; service choreography: a German sermon and German prayers; a choir and unified congregational participation; in short, "the victory of modern occidental decorum over oriental emotions."[14] But this modernization of worship procedure carried with it the dominance of vernacular prayer, and thus it was that Reform prayerbook editors from then on have struggled with the difficulty of harmonizing the manifest content of the English translation with their modern consciousness.[15] The result has been an overemphasis on theological emendation, as if the purging of theologically reprehensible dogma from the prayerbook would automatically produce prayerful Jews. Yet, despite all such efforts, decade after decade of *CCAR Yearbooks* repeatedly present eulogies for past generations that knew how to worship with fervor.[16] It has taken 150 years to discover that the manifest content of the prayerbook is only part of the complex interaction of factors which constitute the prayerbook message.

Yet as long as prayers are in the vernacular, content is an important factor. It is the most obvious part of the liturgical message, offering a variety of statements of faith with which the worshippers are asked to identify. As we read them, we receive a picture of what the prayerbook authors think we do or do not believe in, and to the extent that the authors have correctly recorded our identity, the book will be accepted as a valid communal self portrait.

Based as it is on nineteenth-century western European models, the *Union Prayer Book* provides us with a clear example of this process. The theological message of the classic *Siddur* was entirely medieval in substance.[17] Its world view preceded the age of reason, the birth of the modern nation states, and the growth of capitalism. It reflects an era when names like Darwin, Kant, and Hegel; and concepts like evolution, progress, science,—even religion—were unknown, at least in their modern connotations. The Reform community of Germany, on the other hand, was composed of that very vanguard of Jewish society most at home in the world of modernity. The manifest content of the *Siddur* was simply at odds with this community's self-perception. Judaism for them was a religion; their nationality was that of their Christian neighbors. Envisaging the gradual progress of all humanity—a process whose existence was guaranteed by science, substantiated by the Enlightenment, and illustrated by the French Revolution—they painted the future in the most optimistic terms imaginable. They did not expect God to interrupt the natural course of history, and awaited no messiah to appear miraculously and do His bidding; they looked instead to the ethical achievements of enlightened humanity, linked arm in arm in the march of human progress that was inherent to the evolutionary spiral and that led inevitably to the perfect age of universal peace and harmony. Much of the medieval legacy of Jewish law seemed inapplicable now, but in its place there was the undeniably Jewish moral basis for all that was good in the Judeo-Christian heritage: the monotheistic principle in which morals were grounded, and the prophetic legacy which both promised a better day, and demanded an 'ethic' which would realize it.

So the community's self image was a positive one. Despite any temporary setbacks in their drive for equal civil rights, they did not doubt the happy future which Napoleon's destruction of the ghetto walls had presaged. A Jew could be proud to have initiated the monotheistic ideal and could look ahead with certainty to the fruition of the prophetic dream.

This view was only underscored in America. True, in the wake of the French Revolution, Europe had retreated into reactionary politics reminiscent of the Middle Ages, but the American Revolution was alive and well, and its sons and grandsons welcomed Jews to these shores, offering unparalleled freedom of opportunity to all creeds. So the self-image of German Reform Jews required no substantial change in America. As Americans, now, they saw themselves as championing the prophetic message and hastening the messianic age through cooperative ethical endeavor with their neighbors.

It was precisely this vision which the *Union Prayer Book* presents. The best example of this novel explication of Jewish identity is its version of the *Tefillah,* the petitionary prayer par excellence, which, traditionally, emphasized the rabbinic doctrine of messianism. Worshippers recited a prayer for the ingathering of the diaspora, those presumed to be in *galut,* exile; this was followed by a request for the restoration of Jewish leadership in a reconstituted Jewish state; these leaders would cut off the wicked and reward the righteous. Jerusalem would be rebuilt as of old under the messianic rule of a descendent of King David. The Temple would be reconstituted and the cult restored.

Almost none of this traditional vision of the future was palatable to the new communal self-image. These Jews considered themselves no nation, and desired no return to Palestine. They were not in exile and had no yearning whatsoever for a restoration of past national glories. Visions of an avenging God visiting His wrath on Israel's enemies, understandable perhaps in the depths of the Middle Ages, could hardly be held at the glorious dawn of the twentieth century. And the idea of a divinely sent personal messiah seemed painfully simplistic when contrasted with the modern scientific concept of the evolution of humanity, moving inevitably toward the golden age of the future. Finally, the very notion that a cult of animal sacrifice might be reinstituted was beyond consideration.

So the *Union Prayer Book* eliminated these prayers. (Considerations of decorum suggested abbreviating the service anyway.) Moreover, the other petitions that were included—for health, wisdom, etc.—now were accorded secondary status, as the *Union Prayer Book* changed the traditional practice of requiring the worshippers to stand during their recitation. It was not the *Tefillah,* even in truncated form, but the *Shema,* the declaration of monotheism, which became the center of the Reform service; worshippers were instructed to rise for it, instead.

Space prohibits a complete listing of the dozens of similar emendations which, together, constitute the manifest content of the *Union Prayer Book* message, but there is no doubt that American Reform Jews recognized its portrait of Jewish existence as an accurate reflection of their lives.[18] In essence, it was merely an importation of the European books which had preceded it; but then, the American identity was not very different from the European one. From time to time minor alterations in the community's self perception were integrated into the *Union Prayer Book* picture by equally mild revisions. But the picture in its essence was never repainted. It remained virtually intact until the present.

IV

The structure of the *Union Prayer Book,* no less than its content, contributed to a prayerbook message reflective of the reality of Reform Jewry. Before we consider this, however, we must define the role of prayerbook structure, generally, in providing a liturgical message. As the medium which carries the prayers, it has considerable impact on the worshipper.

One must first recognize that prayerbook structure is only to a limited extent fixed. Even traditionalists who hesitate to deviate from the statutory order of prayers must decide how those prayers are to be presented in written form. Rav Amram Gaon's ninth-century prayerbook mentioned above, for example, offered them as part of an extended legal commentary, each prayer being introduced by citations of the talmudic law which governs its recitation. Thus worshippers were subtly informed that they were part of a religious community which derived authenticity from talmudic law. Eight centuries later, the same prayers could be found in mystical prayerbooks, interspersed with meditations and diagrams composed of different combinations of the letters of the Divine Name.[19] The average worshipper may have lacked a full appreciation of the complexity of the mystical system thereby represented, but the barest glance at these diagrams sufficed to indicate that the goal of worship was the apprehension of the underlying mystical meaning of the prayers, in which the Hebrew alphabet generally, and the letters of the Tetragrammaton specifically were major parts. In each case, worshippers received a structural message reflective of their own particular time and place.

These are just two examples of how structural decisions give subliminal messages to Jewish worshippers. Other equally decisive considerations can be multiplied. Is there a translation, and if so, how is it arranged relative to the Hebrew? Is the title in Hebrew or the vernacular? What prayers are printed in large letters, and what prayers are relegated to almost unnoticeable type? Are there pictures, diagrams, philosophical treatises, rabbinic commentaries or other extraneous material, which signify the intended role of prayer or Jewish life generally? What services are placed at the front of the book, and which ones are relegated to the end? How detailed are the instructions to the worshippers, and what titles are employed for the officiants? These and all other aspects of layout and design provide the structural input to the overall liturgical message regarding Jewish identity.

Any worshipper considering the *Union Prayer Book* from this perspective will realize that various structural characteristics which we usually take for granted go a long way toward presenting a picture of Jewish identity consistent with the content message discussed above. Unlike the traditional *Siddur,* the *Union Prayer Book* opens from left to right and carries an English title.[20] English predominates even in the latest edition (1940) which has much more Hebrew than the original. This is obviously a book for Jews who are at home in the American milieu, and accept its cultural and aesthetic values unhesitatingly.

Moreover, compared to the *Siddur,* the *Union Prayer Book* is relatively small. Unlike the *Siddur* which opens with services for weekdays, the *Union Prayer Book* begins with five Friday evening services; the weekday services are relegated to the back of the book. So this is a book for people who have a very circumscribed opinion of how much a Jew should pray. Thrice daily worship is no longer seriously intended; Friday night represents the main celebration of Jewish identity; the services are abbreviated; the Friday evening options to some extent express a Reform commitment to freedom, but there are few real theological choices. So the alternatives are provided primarily to avoid boredom,[21] a boredom which is explainable only in a community for whom prayer has lost a good deal of its vitality.

Most important are the stage directions for the service. The traditional *Siddur* gave relatively few directions, summarizing at most what was mandated by the standard law codes, and depending beyond that on the force of local custom. Since prayer was a living part of Jewish life, any attempts to alter popular preferences which were not actually

144

illegal were bound to fail anyway. The *Union Prayer Book,* however, presupposes that worshippers are ignorant of synagogue etiquette, and assumes the necessity of instructing them on their every action. Each paragraph is labeled as "Responsive Reading," "Choir," "Reader," or "Congregation." The congregation is told to rise or to be seated, and the reader is informed when to open the ark, remove the Torah, and so on.[22] These detailed instructions reflect both an attempt to standardize local customs, and to provide a mood of total decorum (a consideration we shall return to when we discuss service choreography).

The background for all of this is the Reform community's denial of the binding quality of Jewish law. With the absence of authoritative legal precedents, nearly everything becomes possible and, predictably, early Reform prayerbooks preceding the *Union Prayer Book* portray just such an enormous variety of liturgical practices. So the *Union Prayer Book* reflects a community whose centrifugal forces have effectively robbed it of the right to claim a sense of Jewish community at all, and who now must regroup around another system of law, not one bit less authoritarian than that which it has just denied. It is the law of social convention promising respect from one's non-Jewish peers;[23] and, theologically, the opportunity to fulfil the Jewish mission of spreading the prophetic ethic in America while working to realize the messianic age. So this community no less than the Orthodox was constrained by forces antithetical to true freedom. But the ideational underpinnings of its constraint were compatible with the times. Its prayerbook's content voiced the feelings of those times—its promise, its biblical basis, and its ethical demands. And its structure, every bit as constraining as the *Shulchan Aruch,* laid down specific liturgical roles which would reeducate a rootless dissipating community to new and acceptable standards of common liturgical propriety.

Naturally these instructions used technical terms in line with the general message of the book. Early editions entitled the officiant "Minister," provided for "anthems" and "hymns" by a choir, prescribed the "sermon," and labeled prayers by novel English names like "Sanctification" and "Adoration."

So the structure itself told the worshippers that they were praying as part of American Israel, a community at home in and acculturated to American values. There is no sense of living in exile here. And the choreography, as we shall see, was effectively fixed to exclude whatever might be perceived as unbecoming tumult or aspiritual confusion. Yet, as the word "Union" in the title indicates, there are stage directions which attempt to fix an American rite, limiting local custom as much as possible, and instructing people who no longer predicate Jewish custom on traditional Jewish law how best to constitute a modern Jewish community.

V

We have, so far, pointed to the existence of a three-part message in the prayerbook: content (both manifest and symbolic), structure and choreography. In each of the first two cases we have analyzed briefly the way the message is shaped to encompass what its authors believe to be a true representation of the Jewish people. If the people consider it accurate, they identify with it and adopt it as their prayerbook; if not, they do not. We have shown how the content and structure of the *Union Prayer Book* reflected nineteenth-century European roots and their outgrowth, the early American Reform community. Before extending our discussion to the *Union Prayer Book*'s choreography, it is necessary to add one more theoretical consideration.

We must realize that the prayerbook message we have been discussing does more than merely reflect an already existent community image. Without in any way denying what has been said above, we must extend our understanding of the message to allow for its capacity to change the community's identity. Suppose a particular prayerbook reflects a heightened sense of mysticism. Suppose also that the people accept the prayerbook because they are inclined toward its mystical perspective, even though they may not be as deeply committed to it as are the prayerbook's authors, who, after all, are in a position to write the book in the first place because they already are leaders and, therefore, opinion molders in the community. Once the people do begin using the book, however, the book's message acts as a socializing agent to heighten the ideal image it represents. What we have is partially an example of a self-fulfilling prophecy. A prayerbook editor discerns a readiness to accept mysticism. That trend is congenial to him. The prayerbook he edits serves to accelerate the trend so that a mere inclination now becomes a popular commitment to a particular view of Judaism. Thus a positive reception of the book does not necessarily indicate that the people accept its image of themselves as completely accurate; only that they prefer it to any other image available. But once accepted, barring historical events that might change the community's direction, the prayerbook message now becomes an active ingredient in forming group identity.

146

As we have seen, the structure of the *Union Prayer Book* functioned in this active sense. In the 1890's there were many competing prayerbooks in America. This liturgical variation mirrored the community which was anything but united on Jewish belief and practice. But the movement toward the end of the century was plainly toward some form of general unity. From the 1850's onward, a series of conferences was held in an attempt to achieve some form of consensus.[24] National institutions were founded, and a *Union Prayer Book* adopted.

Perhaps the most significant catalyst to successful standardization was the flood of eastern European immigrants that began arriving here in the 1880's. Imagine the dismay of those American Jews who had already reached the high degree of acculturation mentioned above, but who now felt their security threatened by the importation of an eastern European Jewish culture which was the very antithesis of enlightenment.[25] Now, more than ever, it became important to mark themselves off as the enlightened Jewish community they believed themselves to be. So when it came to choosing a prayerbook to represent their self-image, the decision was made to choose one that stood relatively far to the left of center.[26] Most Jews had, in any event, already passed beyond the point where a prayerbook with but a few conservative changes from the tradition could satisfy them. Few understood the Hebrew prayers. Old symbols lacked vitality now, anyway. But above all it was the spectre of seeing the Jewish community's essential nature "regress" overnight into the eastern European mold that made the legislation of a unifying prayerbook mandatory.

Thus, as we have seen, the *Union Prayer Book* adopted detailed stage directions which limited variation in custom and mandated a certain choreography. Just as the nature of a musical score is realized in practice, so the structure of the prayerbook acted to guide services into a certain mold.[27] We may now look at the choreography of the prayerbook message, understanding that it is in many ways but an activation of the structural score.[28]

Jews have in fact prayed in a great many ways, ranging from "davening" to silent meditation, from highly elaborate synchronized dramatics to informal spontaneous worship. Reform choreography of this century stands out merely as one more instance in which the structural score and content-message combine to make a certain type of worship that is consistent with a Jewish community's self-image at a particular time and place.

No doubt the choreography of *Union Prayer Book* worship services did vary from place to place. Nevertheless the spirit of the time exercised its influence over this aspect of the liturgical message no less than over the content and structural coordinates. Thus the self-image of the Jewish community as a religion fully in step with the progress of western society was, not unexpectedly, mirrored by a manner of worship similar to that which prevailed in upper-middle-class American churches. We have seen how the *Union Prayer Book* structure ruled out the possibility of free expression and we noted earlier in this book how the CCAR from its inception tried to foster choral singing and unified congregational participation in hymns.[29] The architectural discovery of the cathedral-like temple, the movement of the reader's desk from the center of the room to the front, and the introduction of organ and choir hastened this transformation.[30]

The description of such services should not, however, be confused with an evaluation of them. Opponents of Reform labeled them cold, boring, and churchlike; advocates saw them as majestic, uplifting and spiritual. Once we realize that such terms are evaluative rather than designative,[31] we can see that both parties to the debate were equally right, their evaluation corresponding not to the service itself but to the extent to which the choreographic message accorded with their own sense of Jewish identity. Those imbued with the western European heritage pictured Judaism as another western religion. Like the Episcopalian or Roman Catholic Mass it would feature highly dramatic ritual, but stripped of any vestige of medieval superstition. Like the Protestant church it would feature magnificent congregational hymns. The Jewish heritage would provide moral preachments befitting the religion which had fostered the monotheistic principle in the first place. The whole would be presented with a sense of staid decorum fully in keeping with an upwardly mobile middle class who had been taught by French *philosophes* and German idealists alike to view detached philosophical speculation as the highest form of human activity. Such decorum was compatible also with the Puritan-American tradition which frowned on excessive display of emotion; and it seemed particularly important now, as immigrants threatened to inundate America with their *shtetl* form of worship which was so heavily laden with Hasidic abandon, medieval symbolism, and, in general, a choreography completely alien to the self-image which German Jews had been developing for an entire century.

Consider, however, the following eyewitness account of a worship service.

> [There is] a large pulpit of wood, on which they have spread beautiful coverings of blue, purple, and scarlet silk. . . . Below the pulpit there enters [a choir] of young and old people

[alike], trained in voice and in the melodies. Their voices are sweet and they are expert in prayer and all related matters . . . . The Chazzan of the synagogue begins [the prayers] and the choir responds, word for word . . . . When he says, "A Psalm, a song for the Sabbath day" (Ps. 92), they reply, "It is good to give thanks unto the Lord." All the people [then] read the psalm verses in unison until their conclusion, at which time the Chazzan begins with, "The soul of every living being," and the choir responds "shall bless Thy name." [Thus] he recites a line and the choir answers him until they reach the *Kedushah*. The congregation recites this in a low voice and the choir sings it aloud. Then the choir falls silent, and the Chazzan alone completes [the prayer] . . . . The entire congregation rises for the *Tefillah* . . . and when they resume their seats, [the dignitary involved] steps forward. When all the people see him, they rise, until he is seated on the dais . . . . He begins his sermon for the day . . . He speaks fervently, . . . and while he speaks, no one in the congregation opens his mouth, moves around, or says a word. (The account now continues with the Torah reading, and the conclusion of the service.)

This description could well have been taken from the annals of many a Reform temple of our time. But, in fact, it is an account of a tenth-century service in Babylonia, the very center, then, of Jewish "orthodoxy."[32] Though it is not typical of all services of the time,[33] it does reflect an attempt by a certain segment of the Jewish population to adapt its worship to a particular self-image current among the philosophically enlightened upper class. The dominant Moslem culture then valued philosophy, decorum, and order quite as much as did the environment which was later to breed Reform Judaism. Indeed, no less a personage than Moses Maimonides preferred such services. He was, after all, the Jewish upper-class philosopher par excellence, and he looked askance at worship patterns unbecoming to the intellectual grandeur which he saw as the hallmark of Judaism. It was no nineteenth-century Reform Jew, but Moses Maimonides himself who first argued against the customary silent recitation of the *Tefillah* prayer, on the grounds that decorum would best be served if people would just remain quiet, listening intently to the Chazzan's chant, and answering 'amen' in pious unison.[34] So the attempt to heighten congregational decorum by doing away with individual displays of emotion is neither good nor bad, and not even Reform in its essence. It is simply a natural result of a community's decision to see itself in a certain way. For Reform Jews it correlated with the content and structure of the *Union*

Prayer Book to present a harmonious reflection of a Jewish identity conditioned by western European enlightenment, and underscored by middle-class America. If Jews hailing from eastern Europe failed to be moved by the majesty of such services, it was simply because their self-image had been shaped by forces of an entirely different nature. To them, such services really were cold and churchlike; to Reform Jews they were the very essence of religious respectability and spirituality. So the *Union Prayer Book* whose content encapsulated the message, and whose structure determined the choreography, was the epitome of emergent Reform Jewish identity in America.

VI

But life in America was too volatile for that identity to remain unchanged for long. Even as the first edition of the *Union Prayer Book* rolled off the presses, the sociological makeup of the Jewish community was undergoing a transformation. German Jews, up to now the majority, were fast becoming a minority, as Jews from Russia and Poland continued to arrive in ever increasing numbers.[35] As the latter became socialized into American life, some found a home in the emerging Conservative movement which combined a commitment to American mores in the world at large with a maintenance of Jewish ethnicity within the synagogue.[36] Others, however, had been "marginal men" in Europe, who had participated in both the western and eastern European models of religious identity. They joined Reform temples but brought a self-image that included room for ethnic expression. Membership was later swelled by second and third generation eastern European Jews whose social class or geographic location made Reform appealing. The very homogeneity of the *Union Prayer Book* message was becoming an anachronism, and within a very few years the need for a revision was voiced.

A detailed account of these revisions would serve little purpose here. But they too could be revealed as alterations in the prayerbook message intended to speak meaningfully to this new Reform constituency. When one considers the magnitude of the social change wrought in this century, one is surprised not at how much but at how little Reform liturgy was altered. The eastern European migration did not end until the 1920's. It was followed on a global scale by the Great Depression, the Holocaust, and the birth of the State of Israel. Here in America, meanwhile, anti-Semitism had surfaced in the thirties and a new life style was developing by an unprecedented move to suburbia in the fifties. The gulf between German and Russian Jews disappeared as intermarriages between children of the two Jewish communities became commonplace, and all Jews found themselves brought together to oppose Hitler and to support Israel. The post-war baby boom is just now bringing to maturity the largest native born Jewish adult population this country has known.[37] To them, the concerns of their immigrant grandparents are ancient history. They are wholly and fully Americans, for whom freedom is a given. Neither German nor Russian, they take their cues for Jewish identity from a milieu which presupposes a viable State of Israel, a communications system which unites all Jews everywhere, and a newly found freedom to experiment in a novel synthesis of American and Jewish culture.

Gates of Prayer is neither the end nor the beginning of that synthesis. It was preceded by a movement which bore the name Creative Liturgy. How really "creative" it was is a matter of aesthetics on which I have no desire to pass judgment. Seen in its historical context, however, the thousands of mimeographed services which constitute the Creative Liturgy movement represent a significant attempt to present a novel Jewish consciousness. Like prayerbooks at other times and places, these services provide their own message in which content (manifest and symbolic), structure, and choreography all combine to give a consistent picture of American Judaism as defined by the services' authors. Like it or not, this became the staple liturgical diet for many Jews, a fact which alone testifies to its valid comprehension of how some Jews, at least, viewed themselves.[38]

But for all its assets—and I am among the minority who think the movement had assets—the Creative Liturgy craze was full of problems. How many people, after all, have the requisite combination of scholarship, artistry, and time to write new liturgy on a regular basis? Moreover, even those who can, or think they can, find that the very regularity of novelty soon results in novelty itself becoming conventional and boring.

It is, I think, not novelty per se that Jews crave, but a new perspective on themselves, one which is truly American in origin. Neither western European (classical Reform) nor eastern European (classical Conservative) will do any longer. It is a new American Judaism which we now must fashion, and a new liturgy to express it.

So people experimented with such expressions, in a variety of weekly Creative Services. And out of it all, we groped our way toward a definition of what we are. It is this definition which finds its expression in Gates of Prayer, whose message we must now consider.

VII

If we turn first to content, we find ourselves overwhelmed immediately by the number of traditional concerns which have been reintroduced, though not equally in all services, and frequently with significant alterations from their original. Where the *Union Prayer Book* found concepts objectionable, the prayers which expressed them were usually omitted, as we saw above regarding the blessings of the *Tefillah. Gates of Prayer,* on the other hand, displays a hesitancy to divest ourselves so completely of the classic expression of our past; but our past now includes two hundred years of Reform Judaism no less than the medieval world which preceded it. So prayers which are still wholly alien to the conceptual framework of Reform Jews may indeed be found reinstated, but only with significant emendations.

Consider the *Tefillah* which we looked at above. The traditional tenth blessing for the ingathering of the exiles, omitted in the *Union Prayer Book,* is here reinserted, but now reinterpreted as a prayer for freedom. Blessing 11, originally a plea, "Restore our judges as of old," has also been readmitted but asks, "Pour Your spirit on the rulers of the land." Blessing 12, the malediction against heretics, is still judged to be morally unacceptable and is, therefore, absent, but the next blessing, for the reward of the just, has been reintroduced. Even the blessings for Jerusalem and the advent of the Davidic monarchy are restored, but the former now asks for the peace of Jerusalem, and the Davidic messianic thrust has been reinterpreted to be deliverance for all the world.[39]

Significantly, these benedictions present not one serious deviation from the ethical perspective of the *Union Prayer Book.* Neither Wise nor Einhorn nor any of the pioneers of Reform would have found them morally unconscionable. Reform worshippers, now as then, are optimistic and universal in their concerns.

The most major revision in content is our openly zealous commitment to Zionism. But, then, it was not Reform Judaism per se that denied the Zionist enterprise. A prayerbook commentary by Samson Raphael Hirsch, the founder of the Neo-Orthodox movement in nineteenth-century Germany, indicates that he too opposed any implication that Jews should uproot themselves from German soil.[40] There was a difference of course. Hirsch still accepted the traditional hope of an *ultimate messianic* return to Zion. But this was not Zionism! The questions separating Orthodoxy from Reform, therefore, were theological—was the ultimate hope a national personal messiah, or a universal messianic age? and legal—do Jews have the right, or not, to alter time-honored prayers? The difference is clear in the ways the two movements handled the seventeenth benediction of the *Tefillah* which traditionally concludes with praise for God who "will return His divine presence to Zion." Hirsch, who felt bound to include the prayer without change, added a German commentary emphasizing the faith in an ultimate return, but avoiding any mention of leaving Germany prematurely. Many Reform prayerbooks, including the *Union Prayer Book,* replaced the troublesome conclusion with an alternative formula, drawn from the Holiday Liturgy and going back to the ancient Palestinian ritual: "Blessed art Thou whom alone we serve in reverence."[41] *Gates of Prayer* has, however, readmitted the concept of a return of God's presence to Zion, but rephrased the English to read: Blessed is the Lord "whose presence gives life to Zion and all Israel."[42]

It is no surprise to find, also, a special service for the Sabbath before Israel Independence Day and another service for Independence Day itself.[43] Interestingly enough, some of the prayer versions found there hail from ancient fragments of Palestinian prayers which history had consigned to desuetude.[44] Lost for centuries, they were rediscovered at the turn of this century.[45] As world Jewry has reclaimed the physical heritage of our land, so Reform Judaism now reclaims our spiritual legacy. When Israel Independence Day fell in 1976, Reform Jews prayed from reconstituted prayer texts which had not been part of official public worship for centuries! This very undertaking of reclaiming our roots and planting ourselves firmly amidst an eternal people of cosmic significance is part of our new Jewish vision of ourselves.

To what do we owe the rediscovery of ourselves as a people, not just as a religion? Israel's birth certainly, but also the Holocaust preceding it, which tragically underscored the Zionist argument. This too is part of our heritage now. Just as similar disasters of the past gave rise to prayers expressive of their role in the changing configuration of Jewish identity, so, now, does Holocaust literature find a place in our prayerbook. The haunting words of Hannah Senesh *(Eli Eli)* who died behind enemy lines trying to rescue her fellow Jews has long been sung by youth groups and incorporated in creative services. It is now in *Gates of Prayer.*[46] Similarly, our introduction to the *Kaddish* speaks of our martyrs who fell at Dachau and at Buchenwald;[47] and special readings speak plaintively, yet comfortingly, of Jewish suffering.[48] The chant of *Ani ma-amin* (I believe with perfect faith in the Messiah's coming, and even if he be delayed, I will await him) does not correspond to the highly rationalistic theology of early Reform Judaism. But our time is

153

one of heightened romanticism and a rediscovery of symbolic language. The fact that this song evokes memories of victims marching to the gas chambers entitles it a place in our prayerbook.[49]

Our calendar itself has been altered to include liturgical recognition of the Holocaust. Tish'a be-Av, the commemoration of the Temple's destruction, was a favorite fast day in medieval times, when the fact of living in exile was real, not just theological. It became, literally, a day of mourning, as whole communities donned sackcloth and ashes, sat on the floor, recited elegies, and remembered Zion. But it epitomized the medieval mind-set Reform Judaism denied, and it quickly earned the wrath of leading Reformers who argued that the dispersal of Jews among the nations was part of Israel's mission to spread light there. But Tisha Be-Av is now back with us, connected inseparably with Yom Hashoah, the day of the Holocaust. A special service for the occasion includes the vow of Abraham Shlonsky, "I have taken an oath: to remember it all/ to remember, not once to forget!/ Forget not one thing to the last generation/ When degradation shall cease/ To the last, to its ending . . ."[50]

It will be recalled that in the wake of Napoleon's rationalization of Europe, Reform Jews in Germany defined themselves as religion, not nation. But with the Holocaust, the ongoing drama of the struggling State of Israel, and the tragic situation of Jews behind the Iron Curtain and in Arab lands, it is no wonder that Jews in America have come to emphasize their peoplehood. Moreover, twentieth-century America, unlike nineteenth-century Europe, has come to appreciate the unique contribution of ethnic groups with emotional and cultural ties to different mother countries. If one can talk of Hispano-Americans, Black-Americans, Italian-Americans, and so on, one can surely talk of Jewish Americans, where the definition of "Jewish" is not limited to religion. So without in any way denying an essential religious component of Judaism, American Reform Jews have expanded their sense of self to include also a group ethnicity, a family tie that makes all Jews responsible for each other.

These experiences have breathed new life into old prayers which once sounded outmoded or unthinkable. So we find, for example, a return to the original text of the *Aleinu* or Adoration.[51] Its particularism, so jarring to Reform Jews of the past, and therefore omitted from the *Union Prayer Book,* now strikes a familiar chord: "We must praise the Lord of all, the maker of heaven and earth, who has set us apart from the other families of the earth, giving us a destiny unique among nations." There will, of course, be some who prefer to emphasize the universalistic element of the same prayer, its vision of God "Who spread out the heavens and established the earth," as the *Union Prayer Book* put it, and for them, an alternative Adoration, this familiar one, can be substituted; there are also a third and a fourth version, equally universalistic, the latter being reworded in the Hebrew so as to fit the rhythm of the traditional melody. But the particularistic version of the original is an option for those who wish it.

The message of content then, emphasizes expansion, not contraction; affirmation, rather than denial; inclusion instead of exclusion. As we have grown in numbers, so we have grown in the variation of theological views represented among us, and the vision of Reform Judaism as a confirmation of the individual's right to choose intelligently from within Jewish tradition finally becomes reality. So alternative services offer real choices within, of course, certain broad parameters representative of the Reform community's conception of itself: services reminiscent of the *Siddur;* others derived from the *Union Prayer Book;* yet another which leans toward religious naturalism; and, everywhere, individual prayer options written by philosophers and mystics, saints and sages of all generations.

This 800 page volume, in fact, bespeaks an attempt to include even more than the traditional *Siddur* did, to make available the full potential of Jewish tradition from which individual theological self-images may be sustained and nurtured. Some prayerbook staples like prayers for *tallit* and *tefillin*—for those who use them—have been restored to Reform liturgy. Other prayers found in only a few rituals have been added too—*Yedid Nefesh,* for example, a mystical hymn dating from the sixteenth century.[52] An anthology of new readings representative of today's concerns make up the latest stratum of this multi-dimensional volume.

VIII

But above all, it is the structural impact of *Gates of Prayer* which impresses the worshipper. We have already seen how the *Union Prayer Book,* though liberal in theory, was very constricting in structure. It contained only a meager sampling of the traditional *Siddur's* contents, and it arranged what little it did include so as to eliminate local congregational deviations from the norm, as well as idiosyncracies of personal worship. Also, it was clearly the English which predominated, in a book which opened from left to right, virtually did away with Hebrew (at least in the first editions), called the officiant "Minister" and had no noticeable Hebrew title at all.

The structural message of *Gates of Prayer,* on the other hand, can be summed up as the opposite of both these qualities. As for its liberalism, it allows more choice than any prayerbook in the history of Jewish worship. And its Hebrew sources drawn from the totality of our tradition are arranged so as to give the impression that they have as much claim to our attention as do the English translations and paraphrases.

The latter point, easily demonstrable, can be dealt with first. The book itself bears two titles, one in Hebrew *(Shaarei Tefillah)* and one in English *(Gates of Prayer)*, each being an exact translation of the other. In perfect, bilateral symmetry, the Hebrew title is on the front cover and front page, as Hebrew books go—the right side, that is—while the English title is displayed in the same way on the left side of the book. The major clue as to the priority of the two aspects is the numbering of the pages: i.e., how the book is bound, from left to right or vice versa. Here, the commitment to liberalism comes in. One can order the book bound either way.

This dual commitment to both Jewish and American identity factors is generally carried through the book's titles and subtitles. They are listed in both Hebrew and English. Even the numbers of the services are in both Roman and Hebrew numerals.

Most significant of all, however, is the first point, the commitment to genuine liberalism. This is a prayerbook which not only allows, but actually demands a choice of what and how to pray. Ironically, this very liberal structure may mistakenly suggest the amorphous bulk of prayers which constitutes the Orthodox *Siddur.* Since this is decidedly not what the *Gates of Prayer* is, we would do well to investigate the factors behind this confusion, an investigation which will prove useful in comprehending why *Gates of Prayer* is really a liberal prayerbook.

We must first elaborate on what we said previously about the early Reformers' concern with decorum, and their subsequent decision to organize worship in staid non-individualistic ways. The traditional *Siddur* which they inherited and to which they reacted was in many ways an open-ended document. Depending on who printed it, it could, and usually did, appear without too many instructions for the worshipper. Of course considerable depth underlay what instructions there were; the mystical diagrams, for example, presupposed an elaborate Kabbalistical system of thought. But the average worshipper was not aware of the fine points of this mystical system. He saw an introductory mystical meditation as just another prayer, to which certain local customs regarding its usage had been attached, and even these usages, as often as not, were alluded to in but a few words or even omitted from the text completely.

The result was that despite much similarity in services, there were substantial variations from place to place. Without structural impediments to alternative interpretations of how the service was to be conducted, local custom reigned supreme, and even within the same locality, individual worshippers often appropriated the right to exercise their own intuitive notion of how they should worship. Thus was born the typical eastern European *shtetl* service, in which people arrived at different times, and seemingly "did their own thing," with only a modicum of leadership from the prayer leader who generally contented himself with reciting aloud the last part of each paragraph, so that people would not get too far ahead of each other. But within long prayers some people did finish well ahead of others. Thus, while some, either by choice or by necessity, read the prayer more slowly, others who had finished were busy looking around the room, talking to each other, and so on. In sum, the *Siddur* was basically structureless in the eyes of the worshipper, putting relatively few restraints on the individual's manner of saying the prayers, doing little to make sure people did the same thing at the same time in the same way.

It was this 'defect' which liberal prayerbooks set out to eliminate, by imposing strict structural demands on each and every prayer. They were eminently successful, as the congregation became in effect passive receptacles for instructions given to them by a service leader who simply followed the prayerbook instructions to the letter.

Now *Gates of Prayer,* structurally, has returned, to a great extent, to the freedom offered by the *Siddur.* Given our congregational histories, it is not to be expected that spontaneous individualism will emerge. But congregations do now have the structural liberty to develop their own brand of worship which is most reflective of their image of themselves as Jews.

To begin with, there is an abundance of services, ten for Sabbath evening, six for Sabbath morning, and so on. There are also five different Torah rituals, and four different sets of concluding prayers. It is not expected that everyone will use all the services. People may select their own prayer combinations. This optionality is deliberately designed to mirror the diversity of the liberal movement for whom the book is intended.

Even within each service there are optional choreographic possibilities. Some instructions are still given, particularly regarding standing or sitting for major prayers. But the striking feature of the book is the choice still available for the congregation. Passages are not labeled as congregational or choir or leader selections. People are not told whether to say the Hebrew or the English. Instead, two structural devices have been drawn on to provide some guidance for those who wish it, without in any way denying individual experimentation along novel lines.

First, one finds three different kinds of print, each one being intended as a suggested type of worship technique. On the other hand, no instructions make this division mandatory. Each congregation can offer any prayer it likes in any way it likes.

Secondly, the English and Hebrew begin at their respective left or right margins but do not run to the margin at the opposite side of the page. Thus one can pray in English and bypass the intermediary Hebrew, since his English orientation results in his seeing the Hebrew as indented, and optional. The same is true of the Hebrew reader, who will view the page from a right to left orientation and consider the English indented and optional. At first a page looks like a patternless jumble to someone familiar with the highly formalized structure of the *Union Prayer Book*. But selective perception can be counted on to make worshippers see each page according to a gestalt which they themselves invent as their congregational norm. One can, theoretically, read an entire service in either Hebrew or English; or alternate languages as one sees fit. A service can be sung (either all or in part) by everyone, musical specialists alone (choir and/or cantor), or by no one. *Gates of Prayer* is, in truth, nothing less than an official declaration that diverse worship patterns are perfectly acceptable, even desirable, from a religious perspective which emphasizes liberalism within Jewish parameters.

Finally, it should be noted that the structure assumes an educated Jewry. Unlike most traditional *Siddurim,* which were printed poorly, with no indication of the traditional structural mandates of the liturgy, this book is provided with logical divisions between separate structural entities and it gives both Hebrew and English titles for each one. The traditional Hebrew titles appear whenever relevant, but English equivalents vary from service to service. The services most dependent on the traditional liturgy bear relatively exact English equivalents, while other services carry creative titles chosen to parallel the content of the English rendition. In either case it is hoped that the titles will not interrupt the experience of worship, but enhance it, by providing the opportunity for reflection on the themes and structure of prayers which have come down to us through the centuries. They form the backbone of *Gates of*

Prayer, no less than they did for any Jewish prayerbook since the first one was written in the ninth century.

Our assumption of the existence of a searching, educated Jewish laity deserves reemphasis. The inclusion of so many traditional sources is predicated on the belief that the Reform constituency wants to know what the tradition in all its fullness is; and a prayerbook whose structure demands choices assumes that the worshippers really want to choose. Presumably, Reform Jews in America, overwhelmingly college graduates and used to exercising mature judgment based on informed inquiry in all other aspects of life, are just the type of Jews who will find such an approach appealing.

IX

The final aspect of the liturgical message, it will be recalled, is choreography, the "how" of prayer. Certainly this is the hardest aspect to predict, and all one can do is provide some perspective, survey some trends, and note the possibilities inherent in the structural "score."

The first and third tasks have already been done. We have seen that unlike the *Union Prayer Book, Gates of Prayer* is virtually structureless in terms of its allowing or prohibiting certain choreographies. One can imagine services predominantly in Hebrew or in English. The choir may be a major or a minor factor with this book. Similarly, the roles of the reader and cantor may be drastically altered as congregations decide how to use a book with a host of options. Certain guidelines exist, of course, in terms of the typeface and the selection of songs at the back of the book. But there is no reason to believe that either of these will be the determining influences in the worship modes of the future.

We have already seen how various choreographies reflected different community self-perceptions. Three specific illustrations of this process seem to be particularly relevant today: the use of space, dress and music.

As the microcosm of the Jewish society at large, the community at worship tends in many ways to reflect considerations of class and status. The Levitical choir and the role of priests in the worship of the Second Temple, for example, no less than the decision in Eastern Europe in the last century to seat those with wealth and status by the Eastern wall, gave ample recognition to the class structure of the society as a whole. Similarly, the reader will recall that dignitaries sat separately in the tenth-century Babylonian service cited above and that the congregation rose when they entered. In our own day, similar considerations have led at times to the practice of selling family pews, seating temple board members on the dais, and adopting clerical garb for rabbi and cantor.[53]

On the other hand, the earliest synagogue, perhaps in reaction to the class division of the Temple cult, emphasized a more democratic community perception. A knowledgeable lay person led the prayers and he did so, for the *Shema* and its blessings at least, without leaving his seat in the congregation. Similarly, despite the separate seating arrangements mentioned above, the Eastern European service, with its small *minyans* and plethora of little crowded *shuls,* was a faithful reproduction of the intimacy and population density of society itself. This was especially true of Hasidism which emphasized the worth of the common man; yet provided for the recognition of the *Rebbe* by giving him a special seat, reserving certain prayers for him to lead, and so on.

The trend today seems to be aimed at recapturing a mood of intimacy and the consequent blurring of social distinctions. An innovative use of space is used, for example, to break down the social distance between congregation and officiants. Changing roles of the clergy generally in our society are involved here, as are current psychological models emphasizing persons, relationship and community. Once again, therefore, liturgical choreography functions to carry a message regarding the Jew's view of self and society. But since the social changes involved are still so much in flux, it is impossible to predict the ultimate choreography that will result.

As for music, our search for a suitable musical idiom has been sketched earlier.[54] Consonant with their general liturgical goals, Isaac Mayer Wise and his contemporaries saw music's role as facilitating congregational singing. This would provide a spiritually uplifting experience; it would end the individualistic clamor of the Orthodox *shul;* and standardize worship throughout the country. They were eminently successful, except that the decorum and standardization derived not from singing but from listening together. Few congregants dared to compete with the battery of trained voices by singing with the choir. Moreover, the music itself relied on organ accompaniment, since experience with the organ in Europe showed that instrument to be uniquely suited to provide a broad range of musical expression while imparting a sense of dignity.

Lately we have seen several new developments in synagogue music, all of which can be related to the American Reform community's search for identity. Most striking has been the adoption of American folk or folk rock music, and the increasing utilization of Israeli melodies.[55] In both cases we see an American Jewish community turning its back on music hailing from Europe, and opting instead for music which they consider more immediate to contemporary culture. The American idiom is often accompanied by the "folk" guitar, that most American of instruments. The Israeli songs convey a message, both manifestly and symbolically, of our overall concern for Jewry in Israel. Musically speaking, however, we tend to select those melodies which could as easily have been composed in New York as in Tel Aviv, and again the guitar frequently predominates. This musical mode has characterized, particularly, what I have called the Creative Liturgy movement. Overwhelmingly democratic and participatory, it appealed to the search for "community," a dominant value in America generally since the sixties, and a growing desideratum in the minds of Reform Jews, to judge by a survey of the Reform laity, published in 1972.[56]

This musical preference was but the most obvious example of a liturgical style representing a general reaction to the formal choreography which accompanied the *Union Prayer Book*. And it parallels similar experimentation in contemporary Christian worship.[57]

In sum, the Reform movement has been reconsidering its classical worship choreography, a trend which began with its teenagers—who were most Americanized from birth—but which has spread rapidly as that youth grew to maturity and began joining temples as they were presently constituted. They replaced the highly dramatic orchestration of the organ–choir–reader–cantor complex, and adopted informal, congregationally active modes of worship, emphasizing simple songs of American and Israeli youth, and various Jewish traditions amenable to the assertion of individuality, such as brightly colored *kippot* and home-made *talleitim*. If we assume such people are typical of Americans born in the baby boom of the 40's and 50's, and now just reaching child-bearing age; if further, we assume people generally exercise influence over liturgical modes only after their children reach educable age and force their parents to take a stand on Jewish identity; then we can expect this model of worship choreography to expand rapidly in the next decade.

But this is only the beginning of a new choreography, the "excess of the revolution," as it were. Based on the past, one would hypothesize that more sophisticated music dependent on the American milieu would also be composed; and in fact it has. Thus, some congregations have developed compositions based on motifs of American jazz or the Modernist modes of composers like Berg and Schoenberg. Elsewhere, one hears echoes of Bernstein and the American theater or a neo-

Hasidic *nigun* set to modern percussion accompaniment. One would expect the vastly more difficult process of nurturing a Jewish-American musical heritage to take time to mature, its development depending largely on the amount of money American Jews want to invest in the process.[58]

In any case the musical heritage typical of Reform temples for decades is undergoing serious challenge. The old choreography in which passive congregations listen quietly to performing choirs and music dependent on the organ is felt increasingly to be inadequate. True, it represented the Jewish self-image of early Reform whose ideological roots and active leadership hailed from Germany. But it no longer suits many in the new generations who make up our congregational rolls. That they will express their own uniqueness in the end is certain; but the musical idioms they will ultimately prefer cannot be predicted.

X

In the end then, *Gates of Prayer,* like all prayerbooks which preceded it, provides a picture of the Jews who use it. The factors of the liturgical image have been explored above, and we might conclude simply by drawing a concise picture of the type of Jewish community which *Gates of Prayer* assumes.

It is a community born and bred in America, but committed to membership in the Jewish people. Our Jews are intelligent and informed, though they are still struggling with the Jewish aspect of their education. They are exploring the fullness of the Jewish tradition, giving no necessary priority to any specific aspect of it. In fact they are still in the first stage of discovering many traditional themes of whose existence they have often been completely unaware.

Their Reform heritage is evident by the openness they show to all aspects of the tradition, their refusal to compromise intellectual honesty and ethical imperative, and their candid admission that religion is a commitment to search and to wonder, to affirm and to doubt. The events of the Holocaust and the birth of modern Israel stand foremost in their mind, but the increasing necessity for developing a synthesis of Americanism and Judaism is high on their agenda. As Reform Jews they want to be free to draw nourishment from the totality of the Jewish tradition, be it Hasidic joy, Talmudic wisdom, philosophic wonder, Kabbalistic mystery, prophetic idealism or liberal openness to experimentation and change. And they want to blend this with the best of modern culture: colloquial English, modern poetry, new music, American democracy, and the commitment (both Jewish and American) to an educated constituency.

To the extent that this portrait is correctly drawn and that *Gates of Prayer* reflects it, the Reform movement will have found a liturgy responsive to its constituents' self-image. It will be Reform liturgy come of age—a creative synthesis of Jewish liberalism and American freedom—that will truly be a liturgical rite for American Jews. Our founder, Isaac Mayer Wise, called his prayerbook *Minhag America,* envisioning a ritual appropriate for America; one hundred years later, his vision may be becoming a reality.

NOTES

1 See Peter Berger's discussion of what he calls the "plausibility structure." Peter L. Berger, *The Sacred Canopy* (1967. Paperback ed. New York: Doubleday Anchor, 1969), pp. 45–51.

2 See discussion by Cronbach, above, p. 42.

3 See discussion by Clifford Geertz, *The Interpretation of Cultures: Selected Essays* (New York: Basic Books, 1973), p. 91.

4 Jung made this differentiation frequently, returning to it again and again in his writings. The most popular treatment is his introductory essay in *Man and His Symbols* (1964. Reprint. ed. New York: Dell Publishing Co., 1968), p. 41. Cf. Jolande Jacobi, *Complex Archetype and Symbol in the Psychology of C. G. Jung* (New York: Pantheon Books, 1959), pp. 74–124.

5 Jung (1949), p. 601. Cf. Victor Turner, *A Forest of Symbols* (Ithaca and London: Cornell Paperbacks, 1970), p. 26, who cites this passage, and adopts its perspective to anthropology; and Erwin R. Goodenough (*Jewish Symbols in the Greco-Roman Period,* New York: Pantheon Books, 1953–65, 12:69) who notes that the data for him—as for us—are, unlike Jung's, not individual dream symbolism, "but public ones. . . . As does a scientist, I had to construct what they call a 'model,' a working hypothesis . . . So I have come quite pragmatically to define a symbol as a form which means more than we actually see." On the other hand, Goodenough does not accept the full Jungian perspective (*Jewish Symbols,* 4:49). Nor need we.

6 As Rollo May puts it, "The psychological essence of the symbol is that it has the power to grasp the person as a totality." It is totally beyond "all the objective, intellectualized talk in the world with words which have become signs and have lost their symbolic power." (Rollo May, ed., *Symbolism in Religion and Literature,* New York: 1960, p. 22). Cf. Goodenough, *Jewish Symbols* 12:69/70. "To be a symbol, a form must be felt to have inherent potency. It not only recalls, but acts to move us, to inspire. . . . What then is meaning or value in a symbol? Simply emotional impact."

7 Cf. Goodenough's discussion, *Jewish Symbols* 12:69. "In symbols . . . an attempt to approximate even verbal precision is entirely out of place;" and citation by May, above, n. 6.

8 *Union Prayer Book*, p. 7. For the symbolic aspect of light, generally, in the religious milieu of the first century C.E., see Erwin R. Goodenough, *By Light, Light* (New Haven: Yale University Press, 1935); Peter Berger (*The Sacred Canopy*, p. 40) calls light and darkness "the fundamental confrontation" symbolizing "nomic security and anomic abandonment."

9 "To be a symbol . . . the form must seem symbolic to the group at least," Goodenough, *Jewish Symbols*, 12:68, and his references there.

10 See above n. 6 and 7; People do, of course, try to verbalize symbolic meaning, and what they say has to be taken seriously. Reality is, as Robert Bellah observes ("Christianity and Symbolic Realism," *Journal for the Scientific Study of Religion* 9 [1970]: 94) amenable to "multiple schemas of interpretation . . . (and) various levels of consciousness." But such verbalized expressions would, in our sense, generally be signs, not symbols. Cf. Turner, *A Forest of Symbols*, p. 26.

11 See the comments by Alvin Reines, above, pp. 90–91, and Bettan, above, pp. 112–14.

12 See the essay by Stern, "Guide to the Services and their Themes," below, pp. 171–6, for a short description of the different points of view represented by the different services for *Shabbat*. Their theoretical bases are elaborated upon in Part Two, "What We Believe."

13 For a general treatment of the role of Napoleon in spurring enlightenment among Jews, see "Napoleon" in index of: Raphael Mahler, *A History of Modern Jewry 1780–1815* (New York: Schocken, 1971), and Ellis Rivkin, *The Shaping of Jewish History* (New York: Charles Scribner's Sons, 1971). For an extended discussion, see Franz Kobler, *Napoleon and the Jews* (New York: Schocken, 1976).

14 Jacob Rader Marcus, *Israel Jacobson* (Cincinnati: HUC Press, 1972), pp. 86/7.

15 For a discussion of prayer in the vernacular, see the chapter, "Hebrew and Vernacular Prayer" in Jakob J. Petuchowski, *Understanding Jewish Prayer* (New York: Ktav, 1972), pp. 43–56; for data regarding the Reform movement in Europe, see "Vernacular" in the index of: David Philipson, *The Reform Movement in Germany* (1907. Reprint. ed. New York: Ktav, 1967); Jakob J. Petuchowski, *Prayerbook Reform in Europe* (New York: World Union for Progressive Judaism, 1968); and W. Gunther Plaut, *The Rise of Reform Judaism* (New York: World Union for Progressive Judaism, 1963).

16 See, for example, Albert Goldman's remarks (*CCAR Yearbook* 66 (1956): 185). In discussing what he calls "the lethargic indifference to worship," he suggests, "One need but turn back to the *Yearbooks* of the late twenties and early thirties to read of the struggles of this Conference with the problems of prayer. In 1947 another discussion of prayer was held and we are no closer to affording further solutions."

17 The themes of this message are summarized in Petuchowski's essay, pp. 13–22. See also Max Margolis, "The Theology of the Old Prayerbook," *CCAR Yearbook* 7 (1897/8): pp. 1–10; and Leonard Kravitz, "The *Siddur*," *CCAR Journal* 14:1 (January, 1967): pp. 6–11.

18 See the illuminating tribute by Nathan A. Perilman, "The Union Prayer Book," *CCAR Journal* 14:1 (January, 1967): pp. 24–27. And for the period in which the *Union Prayer Book* was conceived, see Gershon Greenberg, "The Significance of America in David Einhorn's Conception of History," *AJHQ* 63:2 (December, 1973): pp. 160–184.

19 For an example, reproduced in a readily available English book, see Abraham Millgram, *Jewish Worship* (Philadelphia: Jewish Publication Society, 1971), p. 377.

20 The front page does carry a Hebrew title, *Seder Tefillot Yisrael,* but it is not printed on the cover, and its very existence is virtually unknown by Jews who worship from it.

21 Jonah B. Wise put the problem succinctly in 1930. "It [the *Union Prayer Book*] is intended for use in congregations where the preacher is the reader, which normally meets regularly and repeats the service or hears it repeated weekly.... Briefly the reading preacher faces the serious implications of a shortened manual of translated prayers read weekly to the same group." ("The Devotional Value of the Union Prayer Book," *CCAR Yearbook* 40 [1930]: p. 295.)

22 The best of many illustrations, perhaps, are the instructions to the rabbi at the beginning of the Yom Kippur eve service, of the Newly Revised *Union Prayer Book,* Vol. 2, pp. 126 and 129. This is lacking in earlier editions which do not carry the prayers to which they relate. But these earlier editions do not hesitate to be equally explicit. Cf. *Union Prayer Book* (1894), Vol. 2, p. 191; and the High Holy Day prayerbook of Isaac S. Moses (1916), p. 268 which echoes it. This labeling of prayers to provide westernized decorum, though most evident in Reform prayerbooks, can also be seen in the official Conservative prayerbook (1946) as well as modern Orthodox *Siddurs* such as the Birnbaum *Siddur,* where the English word "Reader" indicates where the cantor's repetition of each paragraph should begin.

23 An example of what John Murray Cuddihy (*The Ordeal of Civility* [1974. Reprint. ed., Delta Paperback, 1976], p. 148) calls the "Gentile halakah of civility."

24 See Gunther Plaut, *The Growth of Reform Judaism* (New York: World Union for Progressive Judaism, 1965), Chapters 2 and 3; Joseph Buchler, "The Struggle for Unity: Attempts at Union in American Jewish Life, 1654–1868," *AJA* 2:1 (June, 1949): pp. 26–38; and Jacob Rader Marcus, "The Theme in American Jewish History" *Publication of the American Jewish Historical Society* 48:3 (March, 1959): pp. 141–146.

25 "The Americanized Jews observed this downtown world (of new immigrants) and were appalled at the jangle of provincial loyalties, religious 'medievalism,' and strident radicalism." Arthur A. Goren, *The New York Jews and the Quest for Community: The Kehillah Experiment, 1908–1922.* (New York: Columbia University Press, 1970), p. 21. See also references provided by Goren, p. 258, n. 17. Esther L. Panitz ("The Polarity of American Jewish Attitudes Towards Immigration, [1870–1891]" *AJHQ* 53 [1963]) explains attempts by German Jews to restrict immigration by economic considerations. Certainly that was the explanation offered. Yet, "studies of the Jewish community's economic standing would, at first blush, tend to disprove such reasoning" (Panitz, p. 108). So the economic burden, considerable though it may have been, was aggravated by the perceived threat to an enlightened Jewish identity, which, unlike the new immigrants, was both westernized and highly patriotic. Cf. Zosa Szajkowski, "The Attitude of American Jews to East European Jewish Immigration (1881–1893)," *Publications of the American Jewish Historical Society* 40 (1950/51), esp. pp. 230–235, where letters citing various prejudicial images of Russian Jews are marshaled, and Irving Aaron Mandel, "Attitude of the American Jewish Community Toward East-European Immigration," *AJA* 3:1 (June, 1950), pp. 30–32, which notes that Russian Jews were feared as strikers, nihilists, socialists and anarchists.

26 For a detailed history of the *Union Prayer Book,* see Lou H. Silberman, "The Union Prayer Book: A Study in Liturgical Development" in *Retrospect and Prospect,* Bertram W. Korn, ed., (New York: Central Conference of American Rabbis, 1965), pp. 46–80.

27 Herbert Bronstein notes the choreographic effect of structural rigidity. ("In Defense of Kevà" *CCAR Journal* 14:1 [January, 1967]: pp. 79/80).

28 One should perhaps cite Einhorn, himself, who, for example, prints the words of the priestly benediction in two parallel columns, each word standing alone on a line, and being repeated in the parallel position of the line opposite (1858 ed., p. 113). The first column is labeled "Prayer Leader" and the other, "Choir and Congregation." Not only does such an arrangement guarantee word for word repetition, but it also singles out this particular prayer as especially significant. Such was Einhorn's aim, no doubt, in his book which he named for and patterned after the Temple Cult. Cf. Eric L. Friedland, "Olath Tamid by David Einhorn," *HUCA* 45 (1974): pp. 311–313 for a discussion of the cultic model.

29 See above, pp. 27–34.

30 The history and significance of the placement of the *bimah,* or reader's desk deserves more study. S. D. Goitein (*Mediterranean Society,* Vol. 2 [Berkeley and Los Angeles: University of California Press, 1971], pp. l46/7) notes the existence of a central *bimah* in 11th–12th century Egypt and vicinity, and suggests the Jewish community took over its usage from the church some time between 400 and 600. The Torah was read from it, but not the prayers. Maimonides refers to it as a place, also, from which sermons were given (*Tefillah* 11:3). This central *bimah* came to characterize Ashkenazic synagogues as early as the twelfth century. It is, however, unclear exactly when or why prayers as well as the Torah reading were recited from there. For a contemporary perspective see William Sharlin, "Music of the Synagogue: When the Chazzan 'Turned Around,'" *CCAR Journal* 9:4 (1962): pp. 43/4.

31 Again using Cronbach's terminology; see above, pp. 42–43.

32 The report of Nathan Hababli, carried in *Seder Olam Zuta.*

33 Contrast, for example, the summaries carried by S. D. Goitein, *A Mediterranean Society* 2:167/8.

34 A thorough description of Moslem worship patterns, the cultural values they exhibited, and the influence they had on men like Maimonides is carried in Naphtali Wieder, "Islamic Influences on the Hebrew Cultus" (Hebrew) *Melilah* 2 (1946): 37–121.

35 "Thanks to these arrivals, the approximately 280,000 Jews of 1880 increased to about 1,000,000 in 1900, 3,500,000 in 1915, and were 4,500,000 when mass immigration was shut off in 1925." Lloyd P. Gartner, "Jewish Education in the United States" in Marshall Sklare, ed., *The Jewish Community in America* (New York: Behrman House, 1974), p. 232. For precise figures see Robert Gutman, "Demographic Trends and the Decline of Anti-Semitism" in Charles Herbert Stember et al., *Jews in the Mind of America* (New York: Basic Books, 1966), p. 354.

36 See Marshall Sklare, *Conservative Judaism* (Glencoe: Free Press, 1955), pp. 66, 246/7. Sklare also explores the worship pattern of Conservative Judaism in terms of its form (= choreography) and content, pp. 83–128; and reprinted with some adaptations in Marshall Sklare's *The Jews: Social Patterns of an American Group* (Glencoe: Free Press, 1958), pp. 357–77.

37 See Martin Mayer, "Growing Up Crowded," *Commentary* 60:3 (September, 1975), pp. 41–46. The post-war "baby boom" did not peak until the mid 1950's. "More than half the girls born in our baby boom have not yet reached the age of reproduction." (p. 46).

38 A summary of the liturgical message of Jewish identity contained in these services is contained in Lawrence A. Hoffman, "Creative Liturgy," *Jewish Spectator* (Winter, 1975): 42–50. See also Abraham G. Duker ("Emerging Culture Patterns in American Jewish

Life," *Publications of the American Jewish Historical Society* 39:4 [June, 1950]: 351–89) for a vivid account of how Jewish acculturation in America has altered "traditional" customs and rituals.

39 *Gates of Prayer*, pp. 41/42.

40 See Hirsch's commentary in his *Siddur Tefillot Yisrael* (English Translation), (New York: Feldheim Publishers, 1969), p. 138. "Redemption will begin only once all [Jews] will be gathered together out of this dispersion in order to be reunited. But such a reunion cannot be brought about by human action or even through the intermediary of human effort; we must wait for God Himself to sound the Shofar." Cf. Hirsch's *Nineteen Letters* (English Translation), Jacob Breuer, ed. (New York: Philipp Feldheim, Inc., 1960), p. 108. "For this future . . . we hope and pray, but actively to accelerate its coming is prohibited to us."

41 See Petuchowski, *Prayerbook Reform*, pp. 231–238 for a full discussion of this benediction.

42 *Gates of Prayer*, p. 66.

43 *Gates of Prayer*, pp. 412–414; 590–601.

44 *Gates of Prayer*, p. 599, for example.

45 For a fine synopsis of the geniza discovery, see S. D. Goitein's introduction to *A Mediterranean Society*, Vol. 1 (Berkeley and Los Angeles: University of California Press, 1967), pp. 1–29.

46 *Gates of Prayer*, p. 267.

47 *Gates of Prayer*, p. 628.

48 *Gates of Prayer*, pp. 407–11. Compare also the reading for *Shabbat Zachor*, p. 400. This is the Sabbath immediately before Purim, and is one of four such special Sabbaths of the Jewish calendar. Though the Torah readings for all four have been included in the Torah lectionary (below, p. 271), *Shabbat Zachor* alone, with its reminder of Amalek the archevil would-be destroyer of the Jewish people (Ex. 17:8–16), is singled out for its own liturgy.

49 *Gates of Prayer*, pp. 411, 575.

50 *Gates of Prayer*, p. 575.

51 *Gates of Prayer*, pp. 615–20.

52 *Gates of Prayer*, p. 159.

53 Other customs include special mention of benefactors, a practice going back to G⌐onic times; mentioning the complete pedigree of a man called up to the Torah; the once-common practice of auctioning off Torah honors to the highest bidder; and the traditional seating division of men and women. Evidence from the geniza is summarized by S. D. Goitein, *A Mediterranean Society*, Vol. 2, pp. 161–5. cf. Samuel C. Heilman, *Synagogue Life* (Chicago: University of Chicago Press, 1976). Index, s. v. *kibbud*.

54 See above, pp. 27–34.

55 See the analysis by Sharlin, above, pp. 122–127.

56 Leonard Fein, et. al., *Reform is a Verb* (New York: Union of American Hebrew Congregations, 1972), p. 140. "Through all of our work, no single conclusion registers so strongly as our sense that there is . . . a powerful, perhaps even desperate, longing for community . . ." Fein's concluding chapter, "Impressions and Judgments," should be read at length. It is reproduced with some changes in Marshall Sklare's *The Jewish Community in America* (New York: Behrman House, 1974), pp. 204–218. Cf. Sklare's observations regarding community, pp. 197/8.

57 See, for example, Robert Bellah's observations on his participation in such a service, *Beyond Belief* (New York: Harper & Row paperback, 1976), pp. 211–216.

58 See remarks by Gutmann, above, pp. 117–120.

Part Five

On Shaarei Tefillah

Guide to the Services and Their Themes

Chaim Stern

Introductory Meditations (pp. 3–28)

Our prayerbook begins with readings for individual meditation before the public service begins; they may also be inserted within the actual service itself. Approximately half the passages discuss worship and prayer. Others discuss the nature of God, the Jewish people, and religion in general. The latter half of the readings come from *Pirkei Avot*, that collection of rabbinic aphorisms traditionally studied on Saturday afternoon (particularly between Pesach and Shavuot); but included for meditation generally in Reform prayerbooks for over a century.

Shabbat Evening Services

Service One (pp. 117–141): The Classical *Siddur*

Service One adheres closely to both the structure and the content of the classical *Siddur*. Thus, for example, the candles may be kindled before dark, and, therefore, before the service begins; the candle lighting ritual, if read at all, would then be considered as retrospective. Its contents, in any case, set the tone, since the prayer introducing the actual blessing *(Av Harachamim)* is traditional, coming from the *Techinah* literature.

The English of this service consists entirely of translations of traditional Hebrew prayers. The *Kabbalat Shabbat* contains all the traditional psalms (95–99, 29, 92/93), though some are abridged, and a complete version of *Lecha Dodi.* The *Tefillah* contains several innovations as compared with the old *Union Prayerbook*: inserts for Shabbat Shuvah, Rosh Chodesh, Chol Hamo-eid, and Chanukah; a new *chatimah* for the *Gevurot;* some novel Hebrew and some old Hebrew restored for the *Avodah.*

The service is clearly divided according to traditional rubrics. Each prayer bears a brief descriptive heading in both Hebrew and English. The former are generally drawn directly from rabbinic literature, and the latter are corresponding translations, assuming at times, however, the viewpoint of covenant Theology.* The *Chatsi* (hereafter referred to as the "Reader's") *Kaddish* introduces *Barechu.*

Service Two (pp. 142–157): Religious Naturalism**

Service Two follows the thematic development of the traditional service, but its English, apart from standard passages like *Barechu* and *Shema,* is, in the main, new. Its general tone, moreover, is humanistic, emphasizing our obligation to grow in godliness. Like other services, however, it contains passages which belie any simplistic label. As a totality, it is richer and more polyphonic than any label can denote. Thus, though humanism remains the dominant theme, the service also celebrates God, the universe and their impact on us. Perhaps a more adequate statement of the theme would be our human responsibility in relation to our partnership with God.

Service Three (pp. 158–175): Mystical Search

This is a lyrical song of praise to God, with strong mystical overtones. The recurring image of light serves as a unifying motif. Much of the *Kabbalat Shabbat* derives from the Jewish mystical tradition, newly compiled, creatively translated, and arranged in a novel way.

The English surrounding the *Shema* consists of selected biblical citations regarding the traditional themes of creation, revelation, and redemption. But revelation is viewed from the human perspective, being seen as a continuing possibility for *us.* And redemption, too, is seen from our side of the divine-human relationship. This service also provides four passages for silent meditation, one of them (p. 168) from the *Zohar;* and a new continuation of the *Hashkiveinu* (p. 168) which extends the metaphor of light.

As for the *Tefillah,* its English (as in most other services) is almost

---

*Ed. note: See Eugene B. Borowitz, "The Individual and the Community in Jewish Prayer," above, pp. 53–70. **Ed. note: See Roland B. Gittelsohn, "No Retreat From Reason," above, pp. 80–88.

entirely new; but here, even the Hebrew is somewhat unique. For example, the Hebrew of the *Hoda-ah* is a slightly adapted version of the *Modim Derabbanan.*

Although the prevailing mood is primarily an exuberant celebration of faith, a challenging note is injected regarding the shadows that darken our lives and shake that faith. See, for example, the meditations on pages 173 and 174. So faith, here, is not predicated on a blissful ignorance of reality; rather, it is affirmed in the face of full recognition of all that challenges our trust.

Service Four (pp. 176–188): Social Justice

Social justice and personal uprightness are the themes of Service Four. In the *Kabbalat Shabbat,* the Sabbath is itself designated as a day with moral dimensions (pp. 177/8); so, too, the synagogue (p. 179), in a passage adapted from the *Union Prayer Book.*

The blessings before the *Shema* are adapted from the *Union Prayer Book,* Service Three. The *Ge-ullah,* however, is new. It utilizes biblical passages and interpretative responses to spell out our responsibilities as a covenanted people. The Hebrew of *Hashkiveinu* comes from the Sefardic rite. A meditation on our human nature leads us to the *Tefillah,* which contains all the traditional themes, but in an abbreviated Hebrew, some of it untraditional in this context (e.g., *Kedushat Hashem,* p. 186). The result is a novel *Tefillah* emphasizing personal righteousness as our response to the Divine imperative.

Service Five (pp. 189–203): Our Reform Heritage

This service will be recognized as coming essentially from the *Union Prayer Book,* enriched, however, by Bialik's *Hachama* (p. 190), and the Reader's *Kaddish* (p. 192). The English passages represent several *Union Prayer Book* services, but the English is somewhat revised. In a number of blessings, the Hebrew, too, resembles the *Union Prayer Book* (e.g., *Avodah,* p. 200; *Hoda-ah,* p. 201). The service includes all the traditional themes.

Service Six (pp. 204–218): Equivocal Service*

Service Six is quite unusual in that its English (almost entirely new) is equivocal; that is, theological language is either omitted completely from the English, or is phrased so as to allow for the possibility of a multiplicity of subjective interpretations by individual worshippers.

---

*Ed. note: See Alvin J. Reines, "Polydoxy and the Equivocal Service," above, pp. 89–101.

Thus, for example, no passages intended for English reading contain the word "God." The word appears only in translations of Hebrew that are meant to be sung in the original. Otherwise, all references to Deity use wording that may be understood in a variety of ways.

The service follows the traditional thematic pattern, but its treatment of these themes is unconventional. The *Kabbalat Shabbat,* for example, emphasizes the related concepts of creation and freedom.

To maintain the concept of equivocation, thus avoiding theologically biased English, this service leaves basic recurring Hebrew passages (*Barechu, Shema,* etc.) untranslated. The English is rich in thought and feeling. It can be experienced equally profoundly by people of diverse religious viewpoints.

Service Seven (pp. 219–234 or 219–229 and 235–243): Covenant and Commandment*

The unifying complex of this service is the constellation of life, choice, and covenant, bound together. The theme appears first in the *Kabbalat Shabbat* where there is also a meditation on the Holocaust, as a counterpoint. This service views us as God's partners, called to labor for a better world, a more abundant existence for all.

The *Shema* and its blessings, particularly, are of interest here. The Hebrew is traditional, but the English is arranged to connect the themes of creation, revelation and redemption (e.g., p. 226). The English of *Ve-ahavta* contains responses which are a commentary on the *Ve-ahavta.* Though the general tenor of the service is humanistic/active, the English that follows the *Hashkiveinu* (p. 228) is quiet and philosophical. Yet the responsive reading before *Veshameru* (p. 228) returns to the basic theme of life/choice/covenant, and to the active mood that stance entails. The *Tefillah* continues this theme, but leaves room for others as well: heritage, peoplehood, prayer, etc.

An alternative *Tefillah* (pp. 236–238) is unusually free in its text and themes. It is preceded by an optional meditation and litany of praise and thanksgiving (p. 235). It is in turn philosophical, meditative, and affirmative. Its major themes are the nature of humanity, our relation to God, our peoplehood and responsibilities.

Service Eight (pp. 244–259): Confrontation with Estrangement

This is the last "adult" service (Services Nine and Ten are intended as

---

*Ed. note: See Eugene B. Borowitz, "The Individual and the Community in Jewish Prayer," above, pp. 53–70.

Family Services). This service assumes in the worshipper a degree of alienation from Shabbat and Jewish tradition, and provides a way back through a confrontation with this estrangement. So the theme of this service, sounded immediately and most particularly, in the *Kabbalat Shabbat,* is *Shabbat* itself; and those affirmations inherent in our worship and faith, as well as the difficulties people may have in understanding or accepting them. A number of the traditional Hebrew passages are omitted from this service, but the English content is both stimulating and eloquent.

Services Nine and Ten (pp. 260–268; 269–279): Family Services

Service Nine is brief and its language simple. Some traditional Hebrew is omitted, but much retained. There are several new passages, some adapted from the *Union Songster.* In general the classic themes are touched upon, to familiarize young children with the adult service.

Service Ten is also brief and linguistically simple. But it is somewhat longer than Service Nine, a trifle less conventional in its arrangement, and very slightly more humanistic in its tone.

Shabbat Morning Services

Service One (pp. 282–317): The Classical *Siddur*

Service One for the morning, like its numerical counterpart for the evening, is the most classical or traditional one. It includes a ritual for those who wear the *tallit* (this ritual is not repeated, but its placement allows it to be used in conjunction with any of the services). The service proper begins with an extensive selection from the *Birchot Hashachar,* numbered to facilitate reference; and a representative, though relatively smaller, series of readings from the *Pesukei Dezimrah.* Two versions of *Yotser* are provided, with insertions for special calendrical events, as in Evening Service One.

Service Two (pp. 318–331): Doubt and Affirmation; the Struggle to Believe

This service offers an opportunity for a contemporary affirmation of faith. It contains many humanistic prayers, and freely acknowledges both our doubts and our struggle to believe.

Its introduction (pp. 318–319) consists of Psalm 100 and three English passages from the *Union Prayer Book* (though the first two and part of the third are much older in origin). A number of the other passages first appeared in *Service of the Heart,* and have been revised for inclusion here. Others derive from the Evening Services, especially Service Two.

Service Three (pp. 332–347): Our Reform Heritage

With few exceptions (most notably, the meditation on p. 333, and the Reader's *Kaddish*), this service comes from the *Union Prayer Book*. It is the equivalent of Evening Service Five, from which the *Tefillah* is largely derived. There are, however, some passages that appear nowhere else in this prayerbook (pp. 333, 342/343 and 345/346).

Service Four (pp. 348–363): The Search for Truth

This is a philosophical service. Its introductory prayers sound the theme of searching for "the way," a theme developed further in the *Shema* and its blessings. But there a complimentary theme appears: the Divine Presence which we believe to stand fast, despite our uncertainties, guaranteeing moral truths, and promising hope in the future and direction in the present.

Service Five (pp. 364–377): Bar/Bat Mitzvah

This service is designed expressly for a Bar or Bat Mitzvah service; that is, its English has been written with the view toward making it possible for one or two young people becoming Bar or Bat Mitzvah to lead the service. The selections are lyrical, celebratory and affirmative.

Service Six (pp. 378–382): Family Service

This is, obviously, the morning equivalent of Services Nine and Ten in the evening. It contains most of the traditional themes, but in a very simplified format and language.

Conclusion

Gates of Prayer is an intensely Jewish prayerbook with endless possibilities of worship inherent in it. Every rabbi and cantor has his or her own path of prayer and sense of responsibility, just as each congregation has its own inherited customs and traditions. All, we hope, are open to novelty and an earnest search for truth; and all will find opportunity here to deepen discoveries, to heighten one's sense of commitment, and to rejoice and sing of the creation and its Creator.

NOTES

TO SHAAREI TEFILLAH

Introduction

THE PURPOSE of the notes is to identify the sources of the prayers and meditations contained in *Shaarei Tefillah, Gates of Prayer;* to draw attention to, and explain, any textual changes that have been made as well as features of the translations which require special comment; and to explain something of the history and structure of the services and their relation to the traditional Jewish liturgy.

To make the notes more intelligible, a few explanatory remarks may be helpful.

For our knowledge of the early history of the Jewish liturgy, we are largely dependent on Rabbinic literature. This is the work of *a*) the Palestinian Rabbis down to about 200 C.E., known as *Tannaim,* and *b*) the Palestinian and Babylonian Rabbis of the next three centuries, known as *Amoraim.* The chief Tannaitic source is the *Mishnah,* a compendium of laws arranged in tractates. The most important of these for our purpose are: *Berachot,* on the daily liturgy, *Rosh Hashanah,* on the New Year Festival, and *Yoma,* on the Day of Atonement. Also Tannaitic are the *Tosefta,* another compendium of laws, similarly arranged, and a small number of *Midrashim* (collections of Scripture interpretations), such as the *Sifrei* to Numbers and Deuteronomy. The chief Amoraic source is the *Talmud,* a vast amplification of the Mishnah and divided into the same tractates. There is a Palestinian version of this, known as the *Jerusalem* (or *Palestinian*) *Talmud,* and a Babylonian version, known as the *Babylonian Talmud.* Also Amoraic (and post-Amoraic) are a large number of Midrashim, such as *Midrash Rabbah* to the Pentateuch and the Five *Megillot.*

The centuries after the compilation of the Talmud, down to about 1000 C.E., are known as the Gaonic Age from the title, *Gaon,* of the heads of the Babylonian academies of that period. From that period, perhaps the 8th century, we have a tractate called *Soferim,* which is a compendium of laws relevant to the liturgy, as well as the first Jewish prayerbook (for until then the Jewish liturgy was handed down orally): *Seder Rav Amram,* compiled by Rav Amram, Gaon of Sura, around 860 C.E.

During both the Gaonic Age and the Middle Ages, the Jewish liturgy was enlarged and enriched by the inclusion of new compositions, especially liturgical poems called *piyyutim*, written in Palestine, Germany, Spain, and other countries. Of these, different communities made different selections. This, among other causes, led to the emergence of a diversity of liturgical traditions called *Minhagim* (Rites), the broadest distinction being between the *Ashkenazi* Rite, that of German Jewry, and the *Sefardi* Rite, that of Spanish Jewry. Among early prayerbooks, the one which exerted the greatest influence on the former was *Machzor Vitry*, by Simchah ben Samuel of Vitry (France), around 1100 C.E.

Further amplifications of the liturgy are due to the Kabbalists of 16th century Safed in Palestine.

The terms *Seder* or *Siddur* (both meaning 'Order') and *Machzor* ('Cycle') were at first used without distinction. Later it became customary to use the former for a daily and Sabbath prayerbook, the latter for a Festival prayerbook, usually with an elaborate structure of *piyyutim*.

The Middle Ages also saw the appearance of a large number of codifications of Jewish Law, sections of which are relevant to the liturgy. The most important are: the *Mishneh Torah* by Moses ben Maimon, known as Maimonides (1135–1204, Egypt) and the *Shulchan Aruch* by Joseph Karo (1488–1575, Turkey and Palestine).

The Reform Movement in Judaism, which began in Germany early in the 19th century, has repeatedly revised the traditional liturgy. Its aims have been, first, to shorten the services, which had grown inordinately long, by dispensing with repetitions and eliminating a large proportion of the *piyyutim*, especially the more obscure ones; secondly, to bring the doctrinal content of the liturgy into accord with modern thought, by omitting or recasting passages expressive of beliefs which were deemed to be antiquated, e. g., referring to a personal Messiah as distinct from a messianic age, the restoration of the sacrificial cult, the resurrection of the dead and the existence of angels; thirdly, to enrich the liturgy with modern material; and fourthly, to provide a variety of services in order to avoid monotony.

The earliest Reform prayerbook was that of the Hamburg Temple, 1819. In America, David Einhorn's *Olat Tamid*, 1858, and Isaac Mayer Wise's *Minhag America*, 1866, were the forerunners of the *Union Prayerbook*, adopted by the Central Conference of American Rabbis in 1894, last revised in 1940. The present volume, *Gates of Prayer: the New Union Prayerbook* was adopted by the Central Conference of American Rabbis in 1973.

Among the more innovatory prayerbooks of the English-speaking Jew, besides the *Union Prayerbook*, have been: the *Sabbath Prayer Book* of the Jewish Reconstructionist Foundation (1946); the *Liberal Jewish Prayer Book* (Vol. I), edited by the late Rabbi Israel I. Mattuck of the Liberal Jewish Synagogue,

London, in 1926 and revised in 1937; and *Service of the Heart*, edited by Rabbis John D. Rayner and Chaim Stern for the Union of Liberal and Progressive Synagogues, London, 1967.

The primary source of the present volume is, of course, the traditional Jewish liturgy. But it also draws extensively on Jewish literature generally as well as previous Reform prayerbooks, especially those which have been named. In addition, many items have been written specially for this volume by the Editor and his colleagues.

As regards the literary character of the contents, the following broad distinction may be useful. The Jewish liturgy evolved out of the use of Biblical passages, especially Psalms, and prayers in the *berachah* form. A *berachah* ('benediction'), for this purpose, is either a single sentence beginning *Baruch ata Adonai Eloheinu melech ha-olam*, literally, "Blessed (or, Praised) are You, O Lord our God, Ruler of the universe . . ." or a longer prayer on a single theme which is then 'sealed' or summarized in a short 'concluding eulogy' (*chatimah*) beginning *Baruch ata Adonai*, literally, "Blessed (or, Praised) are You, O Lord. . . ." The Gaonic and medieval compositions are in large part poetic, obeying their own metrical rules. Modern compositions tend to be prayers or meditations of no fixed form.

In spite of this stylistic diversity and the vast span of time from which it stems, the Jewish liturgy has a pervading unity, partly because of the abundant use which has been made in every period of the Bible and its language, and even more because of the *basically* unchanged and unchanging universe of ideas and aspirations which it expresses.

The Notes that follow owe much to Rabbi John D. Rayner, who compiled the Notes to *Service of the Heart*. Rabbi A. Stanley Dreyfus and Rabbi Lawrence A. Hoffman are responsible for many corrections and improvements in the text.

Rabbi Chaim Stern

Abbreviations

BOOKS OF THE BIBLE

N.B. The references are to the Hebrew (Masoretic) division into chapters and verses, as maintained in Jewish translations of the Bible; Christian translations differ slightly in this respect.

CHRON.	Chronicles	JER.	Jeremiah
DEUT.	Deuteronomy	LAM.	Lamentations
DAN.	Daniel	LEV.	Leviticus

ECCLES.	Ecclesiastes	MIC.	Micah
EXOD.	Exodus	NEH.	Nehemiah
EZEK.	Ezekiel	NUM.	Numbers
GEN.	Genesis	PROV.	Proverbs
HOS.	Hosea	PS., PSS.	Psalm, Psalms
ISA.	Isaiah	SAM.	Samuel
	ZECH.	Zechariah	

OTHER ABBREVIATIONS

Abrahams   Dr. Israel Abrahams (1858–1925), *A Companion to the Authorised Daily Prayer Book*, Hermon Press, N. Y., 1966 (first published 1922).

ASD   Rabbi A. Stanley Dreyfus

B.   Babylonian Talmud

b.   ben (son of)

B.C.E.   Before the Common Era

Baer   Seligman Baer: *Seder Avodat Yisrael*, Roedelheim, 1868, and often reprinted.

Ber.   Berachot (tractate of Mishnah, Tosefta, or Talmud)

C.   Century (Common Era, unless otherwise stated)

c.   *circa*

Cant.   Canticles (Song of Songs); used only in connection with **Canticles** Rabbah

CCAR   Central Conference of American Rabbis

C.E.   Common Era

cf.   Compare

ch.   chapter

CS   Rabbi Chaim Stern

DP   Rabbi David Polish

E   English

ed.   edited, edition, editor

e.g.   for example

f., ff.   following (one or two pages)

H   Hebrew

HC   Rabbi Henry Cohen

HF   Rabbi Harvey J. Fields

Ibid.   In the same place

Idelsohn	Dr. Abraham Z. Idelsohn (1882–1938), *Jewish Liturgy and its Development*, Schocken Books, N. Y., 1967 (first published 1932).
IIM	Rabbi Israel I. Mattuck (1883–1954), ed. of LJPB
J.	'Jerusalem' Talmud
JE	*The Jewish Encyclopedia*, Funk and Wagnalls Company, N. Y. and London, 1901
JPS	Jewish Publication Society, Philadelphia
JR	Rabbi John D. Rayner
JRU	Jewish Religious Union (London), *Orders of Service*, 1903
Levi	Eliezer Levi: *Yesodot Hatefillah* (1961 ed.)
lit.	literal, literally
LJPB	*Liberal Jewish Prayer Book* (vols. I and III, 1937 and 1926 eds.), ed. IIM
LJS	Liberal Jewish Synagogue (London)
Loc. cit.	In the passage cited
LXX	The Septuagint (early Greek translation of the Bible)
M.	Mishnah
Meg.	Megillah (tractate of Mishnah, Tosefta, or Talmud)
MV	Machzor Vitry
NH	Rabbi Norman Hirsh
p., pp.	page, pages
PB	Prayerbook
q.	quoting
R.	Rabbi, Rav
RBG	Rabbi Roland B. Gittelsohn
RIK	Rabbi Robert I. Kahn
R.H.	Rosh Hashanah (tractate of Mishnah, Tosefta, or Talmud)
RL	Rabbi Richard N. Levy
SB	Rabbi Sidney Brichto
SH	*Shaarei Habayit* (*Gates of the House*)
Soferim	'Minor Tractate' Soferim
SOH	*Service of the Heart* (1967), ed. CS and JR
SPJH	*Services and Prayers for Jewish Homes* (ULPS, 1955 ed.)
SRA	*Seder Rav Amram Gaon*, ed. Daniel Goldschmidt, Hotza'at ha-Rav Kook, Jerusalem, 1971
ST	*Shaarei Tefillah* (*Gates of Prayer*)

sw	Rabbi Stephen E. Weisberg
trad.	tradition, traditional, traditionally
trsl.	translated by, translation, translator
ULPS	Union of Liberal and Progressive Synagogues (London)
UPB	*The Union Prayerbook for Jewish Worship*, Newly Revised, Part I, 1940
v., vv.	verse, verses
vol.	volume

Notes

Meditations and Readings for Worship

No. Page

1   3   *The pious ones* ... M. Ber. 5.1.

2   3   *The Rebbe of Tsanz* ... From *The Hasidic Anthology*, ed. Louis I. Newman, p. 332. The Tsanzer Rebbe, i. e., the (Chasidic) Rebbe (Rabbi) of Tsanz, was Chayim Halberstam (1793–1876).

3   3   *If I knew* ... *Ibid.*, p. 327. A saying of the Kobriner, i. e., R. Moses of Kobrin (d. 1858).

4   3   *Once the Baal Shem* ... The substance of this story is found in Martin Buber, *Tales of the Hasidim*, vol. 1, p. 73. The Baal Shem Tov ('Good Master of the Name') was Israel b. Eliezer (1700–1760), founder of Chasidism.

5   3   *I have always found* ... From *A Private House of Prayer*, by Leslie D. Weatherhead.

6   4   *Make every effort* ... From Louis I. Newman, *op. cit.*, p. 340. A saying of the Bratzlaver, R. Nachman of Bratzlav (1770–1811), great-grandson of the Baal Shem Tov.

7   4   *The Lord will scatter you* ... Deut. 4.27a, 29.

8   4   *Know the God of your ancestors* ... 1 Chron. 28.9.

9   4   *The Lord is near* ... Ps. 145.18.

10   4   *Consider how high* ... J. Ber. 9.1.

11   4   *I do not pretend* ... From Claude G. Montefiore (1858–1938), *Outlines of Liberal Judaism* (1923 ed.), pp. 97f. The present version is condensed.

12   5   *True prayer* ... Based on a meditation by IIM. For the original, see SOH, p. 7.

No. Page

13 5 *Prayer gives us* ... A meditation by IIM, published in the *Liberal Jewish Monthly*, London, High Holydays, 1961. Slightly adapted.

14 5 *Out of the depths* ... From *The Zohar: the Book of Splendor*, selected and ed. by Gershom G. Scholem, p. 8. Taken from the Zohar, II.63b. The quotation is Ps. 130.1. The Zohar, the central work of Jewish mysticism (Kabbalah), is generally considered to date from the latter part of the 13th C.

15 5 *Chief among the duties* ... From *The Duties of the Heart*, by Bachya ibn Pakuda, 11th C. Jewish moralist. Taken from SOH, p. 8, which took it from LJPB, p. 251.

16 6 *Prayer is speech* ... A revised version, by CS, of a meditation written by him that appears in SOH, pp. 8f.

17 6 *I regard the old* ... From "Prayer," by Henry Slonimsky, in *Essays*, Hebrew Union College Press, Cincinnati, Quadrangle Books, Chicago, 1967, p. 120.

18 6 *If anyone comes* ... From IIM's Introduction to LJPB, p. xii.

19 7 *Normally, we are compelled* ... A meditation by Rabbi Dr. Leslie I. Edgar, from LJPB, pp. xxvii f.

20 7 *Public worship* ... By IIM, from *LJS Newsletter*, 28th January 1943.

21 8 *Why fixed prayers? To learn* ... New, by CS.

22 8 *It is not you alone* ... Micah Joseph Berdichevski (1865–1921), one of the founders of modern Hebrew literature. From *Tefillah Shebalev*, in essays entitled *Baderech*, vol. 1, pp. 47f. The English is a paraphrase by Rabbi Dr. Aaron Opher in the CCAR *Tikkun* for Confirmation.

23 8 *Unless we believe* ... Slightly adapted from *Ten Rungs: Hasidic Teachings*, by Martin Buber, pp. 51f.

24 8 *Who rise from prayer* ... By George Meredith (slightly adapted), quoted by Louis Jacobs, *Jewish Prayer*, p. 15.

25 8 *Where is God? Wherever* ... A saying of the Kotzker, R. Mendel of Kotzk (d. 1859).

26 9 *There is no room* ... From Martin Buber, *Ten Rungs*, p. 102. Attributed to the Baal Shem Tov (See No. 4).

27 9 *Wherever you find* ... Mechilta to Exod. 17.6.

28 9 *To love God truly* ... From Martin Buber, *Ten Rungs*, p. 82.

29 9 *A father complained* ... From Louis I. Newman (See No. 2), p. 116.

30 9 *If God is not* ... From *Belief Unbound*, by William Pepperell Montague, quoted in *A Treasury of the Art of Living*, ed. by Sidney Greenberg, p. 332.

From Chapters of the Fathers

The *Pirkei Avot*, "Chapters of the Fathers," are a collection of ethical maxims by the early Rabbis and their forerunners, c. 200 B.C.E.–200 C.E., which were included in the Mishnah. The custom of studying this tractate on Sabbath afternoons is already attested in SRA, p. 80. Among Ashkenazim it became customary to study it after Pesach until Shavuot or Rosh Hashanah — the practice varies. *Pirkei Avot* has for centuries held a special place in the hearts of the Jewish people as a source of ethical inspiration and instruction. The present trsl. is in part derived from that of SOH, pp. 13–22. It has benefited from the suggestions of JR, who studied it in manuscript. Our selection is more inclusive than the one in SOH. Both follow the numbering in R. Travers Herford's edition, which has also been consulted on questions of trsl. In 3.22 we have omitted the proof-texts, Jer. 17.6, 8. In 4.1 we have omitted the proof-texts, Ps. 119.99, Prov. 16.32, Ps. 128.2, 1 Sam. 2.30. Similarly omitted from 6.9 are Prov. 6.22 and Haggai 2.8. A number of the passages have been abridged. In 1.15, it may be that "Say little" is intended in the sense "Promise little." For this suggestion we are indebted to the late Dr. A. S. Dorfler. In 2.15, "Repent one day before your death" means "Repent every day, since you do not know when you will die." In 2.18 the quotation is from Joel 2.13. In 4.23 we are called upon to be sensitive to the feelings of one who is, or may be, shaken at a time of crisis. It enjoins us to give such a person a little time to gain control over his or her emotions. In 6.4 the quotation is Ps. 128.2. In 6.9 the quotation is Ps. 119.72.

Weekday Services

EVENING SERVICE

51 31 *The synagogue is the sanctuary* . . . Adapted by CS from a prayer by Louis Witt in UPB, p. 327.

52 31 *Praise the Lord* . . . Based on Neh. 9.5 and cited in M. Ber. 7.3, this invocation trad. introduces the 'Recitation of the *Shema*' (See No. 55). The *Barechu*, as this invocation is called from its opening word, is followed by a congregational response that is first attested in the Sifrei to Deut. 32.3.

53 32 *Praised be the Lord* . . . *whose word makes evening fall.* The first major section of the service is the 'Recitation of the *Shema*,' introduced by the *Barechu* and comprising, apart from the *Shema* itself, a series of benedictions which, in the evening service, number four: two before the *Shema* and two after it. So the Mishnah ordains, M. Ber. 1.4. The present benediction, whose theme is Creation, is the first of the series, and is known as *Ma-ariv Aravim* ('makes evening fall'). It is partly cited in B. Ber. 11b.

No. Page

54 32 *Unending is Your love* ... The second of the two benedictions preceding the *Shema* in the evening service, known from its opening words as *Ahavat Olam* (Cf. Jer. 31.2), and having as its theme Revelation. Cited in B. Ber. 11b.

55 33 *Hear, O Israel* ... Trad., the *Shema* consists of three Scriptural passages: Deut. 6.4–9 (to which the term primarily refers), Deut. 11.13–21, and Num. 15.37–41. The antiquity of its liturgical use, at any rate of the first paragraph, is attested by the Nash Papyrus, 2d-1st C. B.C.E., and as regards all three paragraphs, by Josephus, 37–100 C.E., Antiquities IV, 8.13. M. Tamid 5.1 asserts that it was recited already in the days of the Second Temple, and in the Temple itself. According to M. Ber. 2.2, the third paragraph was originally recited in the morning only. The *Shema* was intended as a daily Scripture lesson, to be recited evening and morning in accordance with the phrase 'when you lie down and when you rise up.' It is a solemn affirmation of the unity and uniqueness of God, and of the Jew's duty to study His Torah and to obey His commandments. The *Shema* remains what it has always been: the central statement of Jewish faith. In Reform PBs, the second paragraph is often omitted because of the doctrine of retribution, and the third because of the commandment concerning fringes; they are regarded as questionable or unessential within the present liturgical context. We include Num. 15.40f., extending this somewhat further than UPB, p. 15 (See SOH, p. 33). The congregational response, 'Blessed is His glorious kingdom ... ,' is not Scriptural, though reminiscent of Ps. 72.19 and Ps. 89.53. It apparently goes back to the days of the Second Temple (Cf. M. Yoma 3.8), and may be related to the response in the *Kaddish* (See No. 58), 'Let His great name be blessed for ever and ever.'

56 34 *All this we hold* ... An abridged version of the first of the two benedictions that follow the *Shema* in the evening service. It reaffirms the unity of God, proclaimed in the *Shema*, and alludes to the Exodus from Egypt. For the latter reason it is known as *Ge-u-lah*, Redemption. There are allusions to it in the Talmud (B. Ber. 9b, 12a). The Scriptural quotations at the conclusion are Exod. 15.11, 18, and Jer. 31.10. We trsl. the concluding eulogy (lit., 'who has redeemed Israel') as 'Redeemer of Israel,' to emphasize the redemptive role of God in all ages, past, present, and future. Cf. the ancient Palestinian *Chatimah* to this benediction: *Tsur Yis-ra-eil ve-go-a-lo*, 'Rock of Israel and its Redeemer.'

No. Page

57 35 *Grant, O Eternal God* ... The second of the two benedictions that follow the *Shema* in the evening service, known from its opening word as *Hashkiveinu*, 'Cause us to lie down.' There are allusions to it in the Talmud (e. g., B. Ber. 4b). Its theme is Divine Providence, although it is referred to in the Talmud, *ibid.*, as an extension of the *Ge-u-lah*. Most Reform PBs abridge or emend this benediction, but we retain the classical text here, rendering *satan*, 'adversary', as 'our inclination to evil.'

58 36 *Let the glory of God* ... The name *Kaddish*, Aramaic for 'holy,' is first found in Soferim 10.7, but the doxology itself is believed to date from early Rabbinic times, probably from before the destruction of the Second Temple. There are allusions to it in the Talmud (e. g., B. Ber. 3a and J. Ta-anit 1.3; in the latter instance some of its phrases occur in a prayer of thanksgiving for rain). Its central response is reminiscent of Dan. 2.20 and Ps. 113.2. There may be a connection between this response, 'Let His great name be blessed ...' and the response to the *Shema*, 'Blessed is His glorious kingdom ...' (See No. 55). It is generally thought that the *Kaddish* originated in the *Beit Hamidrash* (House of Study) rather than the Synagogue, as a way of concluding a public discourse on a messianic note. Then it entered the Synagogue liturgy as a concluding prayer marking the end of a service, or of a section of a service. Later still it became also a mourner's prayer (Soferim 19.12), on the principle that one should praise God in sorrow as well as in joy (Job 1.21). Ultimately several versions of the *Kaddish* developed for different occasions and purposes. The version used in this PB at the end of services is the *Kaddish Yatom*, 'Orphan's *Kaddish*,' and is intended to serve both as a mourner's prayer for those recently bereaved or observing the anniversary (Yahrzeit) of a near relative's death, and as a concluding prayer for all. Apart from the last paragraph (based on Job 25.2b), the *Kaddish* was written in Aramaic 'so that all might understand it, for this was their vernacular (*Tosafot* to B. Ber. 3a).' Here, however, we offer not the *Kaddish Yatom*, but a shorter version known as *Chatsi Kaddish*, 'Reader's (lit., 'half') *Kaddish*,' which is trad. recited at the end of a section of the service. Since it is not intended to be recited by mourners, it may be sung rather than spoken. Our use of the *Chatsi Kaddish* marks a return to the older Reform practice which follows the trad. liturgy. More recent Reform liturgy, through its exclusive use of the *Kaddish* as a memorial prayer, has obscured the Messianic

NOTES TO SHAAREI TEFILLAH

significance of this prayer. By introducing the *Chatsi Kaddish*, therefore, we emphasize its message of the coming of the divine kingdom, the essential point of all the forms of *Kaddish*. It is worth noting that the *Kaddish* has no reference to death, for it looks forward to the Messianic time when 'death will be swallowed up for ever (Isa. 25.8).' It may be pointed out that the opening sentences of the 'Lord's Prayer' (Matthew 6.9, cf. Luke 11.2), are very likely based on an ancient version of the *Kaddish*.

59   37   *Eternal God, open my lips* ... Ps. 51.17 trad. introduces the next major section of the service, the *Tefillah* ('Prayer,' i. e., par excellence) or *Amidah* ('Standing'), a custom going back to the 3rd C. *Amora*, R. Yochanan b. Nappacha, B. Ber. 9b. The *Tefillah* originated in the days of the Second Temple but continued to develop thereafter. According to B. Meg. 17b, its text was fixed under the authority of Rabban Gamaliel II, around 100 C.E. For weekdays it consisted for some time of eighteen benedictions (hence its other name, *Shemoneh Esrei*, 'Eighteen') to which, perhaps in the 2nd or 3rd C., a 19th was added. On Sabbaths and Festivals only the first three and the last three are recited, and the intermediate ones are replaced by a single benediction peculiar to the day. Along with the *Shema* and its accompanying benedictions, the *Tefillah* is the chief constituent of the daily liturgy. However, the *Shema* and its benedictions are recited only twice daily, in the morning and evening, while the *Tefillah* is recited three times daily—morning, afternoon, and evening. The practice of praying three times a day is already alluded to in Dan. 6.11 and Ps. 55.18. Some of the blessings of the *Tefillah* are paralleled by a psalm included in the Hebrew text of chapter 51 of Sirach (Ecclesiasticus, c. 200 B.C.E.). But the Hebrew may belong to a later time.

60   37   *We praise You* ... *Shield of Abraham.* The first benediction of the *Tefillah*, known as *Avot*, 'Fathers' or 'Ancestors' (M. R.H. 4.5). Like all the benedictions of the *Tefillah*, it borrows much of its language from Scriptural phrases. It praises the God of all generations for His loving and redemptive acts. We trsl. the Hebrew אבותינו, 'our fathers,' somewhat freely, here and elsewhere, to avoid exclusive use of the masculine. Many Reform PBs in Europe and America have emended the Hebrew text to read 'redemption' instead of 'a redeemer;' among them are Isaac Mayer Wise's *Minhag America* (1866), and David Einhorn's *Olat Tamid* (1856–8), in its later editions. Like UPB and SOH, we follow these precedents. The para-

No. Page

graph beginning 'Remember us unto life' is an insertion peculiar to the Ten Days of Repentance, first found in SRA, p. 135. See Soferim 19.7.

61   38   *Eternal is Your might* . . . The second benediction of the *Tefillah*, known as *Gevurot*, 'Powers [of God]' (M. R.H. 4.5). Following Einhorn's *Olat Tamid*, UPB and SOH emend the text to affirm that God is the Source of all life and that He has.'implanted within us eternal life' (in the concluding eulogy, derived from the benediction after the reading of the Torah). Originally, the trad. text emphasized God's power in the physical and moral realms, but its main theme came to be the Resurrection of the Dead, a doctrine not accepted by Liberal Judaism; hence the emendation. Other Reform PBs (e. g., LJPB) retained the trad. text but interpreted it in terms of spiritual immortality. In the body of the text, we have followed UPB and SOH, emending it to read *Mechayei Hakol*, '[You] give life to all,' and, unlike UPB and SOH, have followed the form of the trad. liturgy by using these words also for the concluding eulogy, trsl. it there as 'the Source of life.' The sentence beginning 'Who is like You, Source of mercy' is another insertion peculiar to the Ten Days of Repentance, first found in SRA, p. 135.

62   38   *You are holy* . . . The third benediction of the *Tefillah*, known as *Kedushat Hashem*, 'The Holiness of God' (M. R.H. 4.5). The Hebrew that we have rendered by 'those who strive to be holy' might be more lit. rendered as 'holy beings' (i. e.. the angels). SOH emends the text to say, 'and every day we will praise Your holiness.' UPB retains the trad. text (as we do), and renders it by 'Thy worshippers.' The alternative concluding eulogy is prescribed so for the Ten Days of Repentance by Rav (3rd C.), B. Ber. 12b.

63   39   *You favor us with knowledge* . . . The first of the thirteen (originally twelve) intermediate benedictions of the *Tefillah*, which are recited on weekdays only. Most of them are mentioned in B. Meg. 17b. The present one, known as *Binah*, 'Understanding,' is mentioned also in M. Ber. 5.2 and B. Ber. 34a. Most Reform PBs omit some or all of these intermediate benedictions, or they summarize them (Cf. UPB, pp. 323 and 349). In the present service, we give twelve, recasting those which seemed to us in need of modification on doctrinal grounds. Cf. SOH, pp. 48–52.

64   39   *Help us to return* . . . The second of the intermediate benedictions, known as *Teshuvah*, 'Repentance.'

65   39   *Forgive us, our Creator* . . . The third of the intermediate benedic-

No. Page

tions, known as *Selichah*, 'Forgiveness.'

66   40   *Look upon our affliction* ... The fourth of the intermediate benedictions, known as *Ge-u-lah*, 'Redemption.' It is interesting to compare the usage of the first benediction following the *Shema*, also
known as *Ge-u-lah*, where the concluding eulogy is, in the Hebrew,
Ga-al Yisraeil, 'who has redeemed Israel.' Here the usage is parti-
cipial, *Go-eil Yisraeil*, 'the Redeemer of [or, who is redeeming]
Israel.' *Ga-al* refers to the deliverance from Egypt, while *go-eil*
more generally refers to the God who constantly redeems us from
bondage and suffering (Cf. No. 56).

67   40   *Heal us, O Lord* ... The fifth of the intermediate benedictions,
known as *Refuah*, 'Healing.' It is based on Jer. 17.14, the singular
being changed to the plural (so already SRA, p. 25). Our form of
the concluding eulogy, 'Healer of the sick,' may well be older than
the trad. 'who heals the sick of His people Israel.' The latter seems
to be based on a formula used when visiting the sick on the Sabbath (B. Shabbat 12b). The former, which we prefer as being more
comprehensive, is found in J. Ber. 2.4 and *Sifrei* to Deut. 33.2. Cf.
Idelsohn, p. 100.

68   40   *Bless this year* ... The sixth of the intermediate benedictions,
known as *Birkat Hashanim*, lit., 'The Blessing of the Years' (We
render it 'For Abundance'). It is mentioned in M. Ber. 5.2. We
have omitted one phrase ('Bless our year like other good years')
and trsl. the concluding eulogy somewhat freely (lit., 'who blesses
the years').

69   41   *Sound the great horn* ... A new version of the seventh intermediate
benediction. It is known as *Kibbuts Galuyot*, 'The Ingathering of the
Exiles.' Our version begins in the same way as the trad. text, but
in place of the petition for the ingathering of the exiles goes on to
emphasize the hope for universal freedom. We therefore entitle it
Cheirut, 'Freedom.' The phrase 'Let the song of liberty be heard
... ,' is based on Lev. 25.10, and was first utilized in this context by
R. Manuel Joel in his *Israelitisches Gebetbuch*, Breslau, 1872, an example followed in several subsequent German Reform PBs. (See
Petuchowski, *Prayerbook Reform in Europe*, pp. 218ff.) Our concluding eulogy was suggested by the phrase, 'Redeem me from man's
oppression,' in Ps. 119.134.

70   41   *Pour Your spirit upon the rulers* ... A new version of the eighth
intermediate benediction, known as *Birkat Mishpat*, 'The Blessing
of Justice.' The second half is virtually identical with the trad.
text. The first half trad. voices the hope for the restoration of Is-

No. Page

rael's judges, for which we have substituted the hope for universal justice. Our version of the first half is based on phrases occurring in such Scriptural verses as Isa. 40.23; Ps. 148.11; Joel 3.1; Zech. 12.10; Ezek. 39.29; Pss. 25.9; 119.7, 25, 106.

71 41 *Have mercy* . . . An abridged version of what is trad. the tenth intermediate benediction, known as *Birkat Hatsadikim,* 'The Blessing concerning the Righteous.' We entitle it, somewhat freely, 'For Righteousness.' We omit the ninth intermediate benediction, a malediction against slanderers or informers (originally heretics), composed, according to B. Ber. 28b, c. 100 C.E.

72 42 *And turn in compassion* . . . A new version of what is trad. the eleventh intermediate benediction, known as *Bonei Yerushalayim,* 'The Builder of Jerusalem,' and by us entitled *Shelom Yerushalayim,* lit., 'The Peace (or, Welfare) of Jerusalem.' In its trad. form this benediction beseeches God to rebuild Jerusalem and to reestablish the Davidic monarchy. Partly for doctrinal reasons, and partly because the trad. theme of the present benediction is repeated by the next one, our version has been altered so that it is a prayer for the present and continuing welfare of the land and people of Israel, as symbolized by Jerusalem. Thus it reflects the events of our time. It contains, as well, an allusion to the connection between Zion and the messianic hope, expressed by the reference to Zion and Jerusalem as a source of enlightenment to all humanity. Our text is based on phrases occurring in such Scriptural verses as Pss. 69.17; 122.7; Isa. 2.3; Lev. 26.6; Haggai 2.9.

73 42 *Cause the plant of justice* . . . A new version of what is trad. the twelfth intermediate benediction, known as *Birkat David,* 'The Blessing concerning [King] David,' but by us entitled *Yeshuah,* 'Deliverance.' We have broadened the hope expressed here for the restoration of the Davidic commonwealth into the concept of the Messianic Age, i. e., universal righteousness leading to universal deliverance. The phrase 'plant of righteousness' is taken from Jer. 33.15, and was first used in this context by Joel in 1872 (See Petuchowski, *Prayerbook Reform,* pp. 229f.). The concluding eulogy is trad., but we trsl. it freely so as to bring out the enlarged meaning we wish to convey.

74 42 *Hear our voice* . . . The last of the intermediate benedictions (our twelfth, trad. the thirteenth), known as *Shomei-a Tefillah,* 'Who Hearkens to Prayer.' Our version is abridged.

75 43 *Be gracious* . . . The first of the three last benedictions of the *Te-*

No. Page

fillah, known as *Avodah*, 'Worship' (M. Tamid 5.1, M. R.H. 4.5). Following UPB and SOH, and many other Reform PBs, we have omitted the trad. references to sacrificial worship, substituting a thought (based on Pss. 145.18; 25.16) on the theme of God's nearness to all who seek Him with sincerity. The Hebrew for 'Let our eyes behold Your presence in our midst' is also new in the present benediction and is based on phrases occurring in such Scriptural verses as Ezek. 39.29 and Joel 3.2. Unlike UPB and SOH, we retain the trad. concluding eulogy, which we trsl. rather broadly to carry out the more universal theme we wish to convey, i. e., God's presence in Zion and wherever our people worships Him in truth.

76 43 *Our God ... be mindful* ... On Sabbaths, Festivals, and High Holy Days, the *Kedushat Hayom* ('The Holiness of the Day'), replaces the weekday intermediate benedictions. On Festivals and High Holy Days, the present passage is part of that benediction. It is trad. inserted before the concluding eulogy of *Avodah* on the first day of the new month and on the intermediate days of Pesach and Sukkot. It is alluded to in B. Ber. 29b, Tosefta Ber. 3.10, Soferim 19.7. Our version is abridged, and we have placed it after the *Avodah*. We trsl. the Heb. אבותינו, 'our fathers,' somewhat freely, to avoid exclusive use of the masculine.

77 44 *We gratefully acknowledge* ... The penultimate benediction of the *Tefillah*, known as *Hoda-ah*, 'Thanksgiving' (M. Ber. 5.2, 3; M. R.H. 4.5). Unlike UPB and SOH, we give here the complete text, but we trsl. the Heb. אבותינו, 'our fathers,' somewhat freely, to avoid exclusive use of the masculine. 'Let life abundant ...' is a somewhat free trsl. of an insertion peculiar to the Ten Days of Repentance, first found in SRA, p. 137.

78 45 *We give thanks ... In the days of the Hasmoneans* ... Trad. inserted in the *Hoda-ah* (No. 77), after the first paragraph, to be recited on Chanukah. First attested, in a shorter version, in Soferim 20.8. The present version, which we have very slightly abridged, is found in SRA, pp. 97f., with minor variations.

79 46 *We give thanks ... In the days of Mordecai* ... Trad. inserted in the *Hoda-ah* (No. 77), following No. 78, to be recited on Purim. Cf. Soferim 20.8. The present version, which we have slightly abridged, is found in SRA, p. 100, with minor variations. We have placed both the present passage and the preceding one after the *Hoda-ah*. For that reason, we have added one English sentence to the present passage to serve as a fitting conclusion.

No. Page

80 46 *O Sovereign Lord of peace* ... The evening version of the last benediction of the *Tefillah*, known as *Birkat Kohanim*, 'The Priestly Benediction' (and called by us *Birkat Shalom*, 'The Benediction concerning Peace'), in reference to Num. 6.24ff., on which this benediction
(especially the longer morning version) is based, and which is
trad. recited here in the morning service (M. Tamid 5.1, M. R.H.
4.5). This shorter evening version has been traced back only to the
eleventh C., though it is probably older. Here we retain the trad.
text, unlike those Reform liturgies which universalize this benediction either by abridgement and paraphrase (UPB, pp. 22f.) or
emendation (SOH, p. 78). Other versions are noted as they appear
in the present PB. The alternative conclusion is trad. for the Ten
Days of Repentance, first found in SRA, p. 137, with some variation. Its concluding eulogy, trad. during these days, is found in
some Reform liturgies (including the present one in some services)
throughout the year. Here the alternative conclusion is somewhat
abridged, with a rather free trsl.

81 47 *O God, keep my tongue* ... A meditation which trad. follows the
Tefillah, composed by the Babylonian Rabbi, Mar bar Rabina (c.
400 C.E.), cited in B. Ber. 14b, 17a. Our trsl. is somewhat compressed, with the effect of slightly abridging the Hebrew.

82 47 *May the words* ... Ps. 19.15, from the trad. meditation following
the *Tefillah* attributed to Mar bar Rabina (See No. 81).

83 47 *May He who causes peace* ... This verse, first found as the conclusion of the *Kaddish* (See No. 58) in SRA, p. 39, trad. forms the conclusion of the meditation that follows the *Tefillah*. It is based on
Job 25.2b. We have added the English words 'and all the world.'

MORNING SERVICE

84 48 *Praise the Lord* ... *like a curtain.* Ps. 104.1f. The wearing of a *Tallit*
at a morning service (and by the leader at every service) is attested
often in the Talmud and Midrash (e. g., B. Shabbat 147a, B. Menachot 41a, b). It is derived from the Scriptural injunction to attach
fringes to the corners of one's outer garment as a reminder of the
Mitzvot. See Num. 15.38ff., Deut. 22.12.

85 48 *Blessed is the Lord* ... *in the fringed Tallit.* B. Menachot 43a. We trsl.
vetsivanu, (lit. 'commands') as 'teaches.'

86 48 *In the Torah it is written* ... A meditation derived from the *Siddur*
of R. Isaiah Horowitz (c. 1555–1633, Prague-Safed) and widely re-

printed. The custom of wearing *Tefillin* ('Phylacteries') during the morning service (and, in Talmudic times, throughout the day by the pious) is of great antiquity, traced back at least to the 4th C. B.C.E. In one form or another, it is in all probability older still. The Scriptural foundation for this practice is Deut. 6.8, 11.8; Exod. 13.9, 16. Worn on the head and arm, the leather boxes of the phylacteries contain these Scriptural passages: Exod. 13.1–10, 11–16; Deut. 6.4–9; 11.13–21. On the subject in general, see JE, vol. 10, pp. 21–28. There is little in the sources on the attitude of Reform Judaism's earlier generations toward *Tefillin*, but it is clear that they felt doubts as to the value of the use of *Tefillin*. Petuchowski, in *Prayerbook Reform*, pp. 122f., shows that *Tefillin*, though not abolished, were viewed ambivalently, in some quarters at least. It should also be kept in mind that the weekday morning service, when *Tefillin* are worn, became a rarity in Reform congregations. We restore the ritual to our liturgy, for use by those who wish to wear *Tefillin*. *Tefillin*, a sign of the covenant between God and Israel, are worn at weekday morning services only, since the Sabbath and the Festivals are themselves 'signs,' thus rendering *Tefillin* superfluous on those days (B. Eruvin 96a).

87 48 *Blessed is the Lord . . . to wear Tefillin.* Recited upon putting *Tefillin* on the hand. B. Menachot 60b. We trsl. *vetsivanu*, (lit. 'commands') as 'teaches.'

88 49 *Blessed is the Lord . . . the Mitzvah of Tefillin.* For the head. B. Menachot 60b. We trsl. *vetsivanu*, (lit. 'commands') as 'teaches.'

89 49 *Blessed is His glorious kingdom . . .* See No. 55.

90 49 *I will betroth you . . .* Hos. 2.21ff.

91 51 *How lovely are your tents . . .* This, the *Mah Tovu*, is a mosaic of Scripture verses (Num. 24.5; Pss. 5.8; 26.8; 95.6 [with change from plural to singular]; 69.14), trad. recited on entering the synagogue. Early PBs vary with regard to their selection of verses.

92 51 *Blessed . . . who has made our bodies . . .* An appreciation of the wondrous complexity of the human body. Cited in B. Ber. 60b, SRA, p. 2, this benediction dates from the beginning of the 4th C.

93 52 *Blessed is the Eternal . . . the study of Torah.* Cited in B. Ber. 11b, in the name of Samuel (3rd C.).

94 52 *Eternal our God, make the words . . .* Cited in B. Ber. 11b, in the name of R. Yochanan bar Nappacha (3rd C.), as a benediction to be recited before the reading of the Torah, but trad. found in the liturgy

No. Page

in the first section of the morning service, known as *Birchot Hashachar*, 'Morning Blessings.'

95 52 *These are the obligations* ... B. Shabbat 127a, an elaboration upon M. Pei-ah 1.1. (See also B. Kiddushin 39b.) Trad. found in *Birchot Hashachar*.

96 53 *The soul that You have given me* ... From *Birchot Hashachar*. It goes back to B. Ber. 60b. Our version is slightly abridged, and we have changed the concluding eulogy (in H and E) from 'who restores souls to dead bodies' to 'in whose hands are the souls of all the living and the spirits of all flesh' (Job 12.10). Cf. UPB, p. 101; SOH, p. 141.

97 53 *Blessed is the One who spoke* ... This benediction, the *Baruch Sheamar*, trad. introduces the second section of the morning service, known as *Pesukei Dezimra* (lit., 'Verses of Song'), and consisting mainly of Psalms. It is first attested in SRA, p. 7. Our version is abridged.

98 54 *Let the glory of God* ... See No. 58.

99 55 *Praise the Lord* ... See No. 52.

100 55 *Praised be the Lord* ... *the Maker of light.* This, known from its key word as *Yotser*, 'Creator,' is the first of the two benedictions that precede the *Shema* in the morning service, corresponding to the *Maariv Aravim* in the evening service (See No. 53). The Talmud cites it partially (B. Chagigah 12b), and notes that in Isa. 45.7, which the benediction incorporates, 'Creator of evil' has been changed euphemistically to 'Creator of all things.' Also included is Ps. 104.24. This benediction, especially for Sabbaths and Festivals, contains mystical and angelological elements, which we omit here, but which we include (in part) in Sabbath Morning Service I.

101 56 *Deep is Your love* ... This, known from its opening words as *Ahavah Rabbah* (and also as *Birkat Torah*, 'The Benediction concerning the Torah'), is the second of the two benedictions that precede the *Shema* in the morning service, corresponding to the *Ahavat Olam* in the evening service (See No. 54). It is partly cited in B. Ber. 11b. Our version omits one sentence, a petition for the Ingathering of the Exiles.

102 57 *Hear, O Israel* ... See No. 55.

103 58 *True and enduring* ... *Redeemer of Israel.* An abridged version of the one benediction that follows the *Shema* in the morning service, known as the *Ge-u-lah*, 'Redemption'. (For the corresponding evening version, see No. 56.) According to M. Tamid 5.1, it was recited

already in the Second Temple. It includes Exod. 15.11, 18. It should be repeated that the three benedictions surrounding the *Shema* emphasize respectively these three basic themes of Jewish theology: Creation, Revelation, Redemption.

This is the *Keduŝhah*, 'Sanctification,' a doxology built around Isa. 6.3 which amplifies the *Kedushat Hashem* (See No. 62) of the evening service, being recited trad. during the Reader's repetition of the *Tefillah* in the morning and afternoon services on weekdays. It is also recited on Sabbaths, Festivals, High Holy Days, and Rosh Chodesh in the morning, additional (*Musaf*), and afternoon services, and in the concluding (*Ne-ilah*) service on Yom Kippur. It is mentioned already in the Talmud (B. Ber. 21b). The present text includes Isa. 6.3, Ezek. 3.12, and Ps. 146.10. The various liturgical rituals (e. g., the Ashḳenazic, Sefardic, Yemenite) have differing versions of the *Kedushah*. The weekday *Kedushah*, however, is the one most nearly standard in all the rituals, and it is the least elaborate. The alternative concluding eulogy is prescribed so for the Ten Days of Repentance by Rav (B. Ber. 12b).

The morning version of the last benediction of the *Tefillah*, known as *Birkat Kohanim*, 'The Priestly

No. Page

Benediction,' in reference to Num. 6.24ff., on which it is based, but which we call *Birkat Shalom*, 'The Benediction concerning Peace.' There are references to it in the Talmud, e. g., B. Meg. 18a. Here we retain the trad. text throughout, but we add, in English, to the first sentence, 'and all the world,' and to the penultimate sentence we add 'and all peoples.' For the corresponding, though shorter, evening version, and on the alternative conclusion, see No. 80.

126   71   *O God, keep my tongue* ... See No. 81.

127   71   *May the words* ... See No. 82.

128   71   *May He who causes peace* ... See No. 83.

EVENING OR MORNING SERVICE I

129   72   *And now, O Israel* ... Deut. 10.12; Exod. 19.5a, 6a; Isa. 42.7.

130   72   *Praise the Lord* ... See No. 52.

131   73   *Eternal God, Your majesty* ... Slightly adapted by CS from a prayer by Samuel S. Cohon, in UPB, p. 29, on the theme of *Aravim* and *Yotser*. On the Hebrew, see Nos. 53 and 100.

132   74   *You are our God, the Source* ... Adapted by CS from a prayer by Samuel S. Cohon, in UPB, p. 51, on the theme of *Ahavat Olam* and *Ahavah Rabbah*. On the Hebrew, see Nos. 54 and 101.

133   74   *Hear, O Israel* ... See No. 55.

134   75   *I, the Eternal, have called you* ... An arrangement of Scripture verses by HF and CS on the theme of *Ge-ulah* (See No. 56), with new congregational responses. The quotations are Isa. 42.6; Jer. 31.33 (with one omission and a change in person from third to second); Isa. 45.20c (with one small change and the addition of three connective words), 21b; Amos 5.15a, 24; Lev. 19.13a, 16b; Isa. 60.18a; 54.13; 43.10a. The concluding portions are from the trad. evening and morning *Ge-ulah*, Nos. 56 and 103.

135   78   *Eternal God, open my lips* ... See No. 59.

136   78   *Blessed is the Lord* ... *Shield of Abraham.* Slightly adapted from the UPB (p. 18) rendering of *Avot*. On the Hebrew, see No. 60.

137   78   *Eternal is Your might* ... Slightly adapted from the UPB (p. 18) rendering of *Gevurot*. On the Hebrew, see No. 61.

138   79   *You are holy* ... Slightly adapted from the UPB (p. 18) rendering of *Kedushat Hashem*. On the Hebrew, see No. 62.

139   79   *We sanctify Your name* ... See No. 107.

140   80   *Eternal Source of knowledge* ... A composite prayer, compiled by

No. Page

CS, and based on UPB, pp. 349, 350. It touches on a number of the themes of the intermediate and concluding benedictions of the *Tefillah.* See Nos. 63 *et seq.* The final four paragraphs, beginning 'Lord our God, Creator ...' are based on a prayer by Edward N. Calisch.

141 81 *May the words* ... See No. 82.

142 81 *May He who causes peace* ... See No. 83.

EVENING OR MORNING SERVICE II

143 82 *The greatness of the Eternal One* ... New, by CS, influenced by a prayer by Samuel S. Cohon, in UPB, pp. 353f.

144 82 *Praise the Lord* ... See No. 52.

145 83 *Heaven and earth* ... Based on a prayer by Samuel S. Cohon, in UPB, pp. 354f., on the theme of *Aravim* and *Yotser.* On the Hebrew, see Nos. 53 and 100.

146 84 *In the human heart, too* ... Adapted from a prayer by Samuel S. Cohon, in UPB, p. 355, by CS, on the theme of *Ahavat Olam* and *Ahavah Rabbah.* On the Hebrew, see Nos. 54 and 101.

147 84 *Hear, O Israel* ... See No. 55.

148 86 *Infinite God* ... New, by CS, on the theme of *Ge-ulah* (See Nos. 56 and 103), with these quotations: Pss. 43.3; 46.2f.; Isa. 25.9; Ps. 63.8. The concluding portions are from the trad. evening and morning *Ge-ulah,* Nos. 56 and 103.

149 87 *Let there be love* ... A free adaptation by CS of a prayer by R. Elazar (2nd C.), cited in B. Ber. 16b. The concluding eulogy is based on a bedtime prayer cited in B. Ber. 60b. Here it is offered as a form of *Hashkiveinu.* On the Hebrew text, see No. 57.

150 88 *Eternal God, open my lips* ... See No. 59.

151 88 *God of ages past* ... New, by CS and SW, on the theme of *Avot.* On the Hebrew text, see No. 60.

152 89 *Your might, O God* ... New, by CS, on the theme of *Gevurot.* On the Hebrew text, see No. 61.

153 89 *You are holy* ... See No. 62.

154 89 *We sanctify Your name* ... See No. 107.

155 90 *A spark* ... New, by CS, utilizing a number of the themes of the intermediate benedictions of the *Tefillah.* See Nos. 63 *et seq.*

156 91 *May the words* ... See No. 82.

157 91 *May He who causes peace* ... See No. 83.

No. Page

EVENING OR MORNING SERVICE III

158 92 *Lord, You give meaning* . . . Freely adapted by CS from a prayer by Louis Witt, in UPB, p. 335.

159 92 *Praise the Lord* . . . See No. 52.

160 93 *Can we imagine* . . . New, by HC and CS, on the themes of the two benedictions that precede the *Shema*, i. e., Creation and Revelation (See Nos. 53 and 54, 100 and 101). The benedictions incorporated in the body of the prayer are from B. Ber. 59a, M. Ber. 9.2, and B. Ber. 58a. The first benediction is abridged. All may be found in SH; see SH Note No. 14.

161 94 *Hear, O Israel* . . . See No. 55.

162 95 *There lives a God* . . . New, by CS and SW, on the theme of *Ge-ulah*. On the Hebrew text, see Nos. 56 and 103.

163 96 *Cause us, our Creator* . . . This is the *Sefardi* version of *Hashkiveinu* for Sabbaths and Festivals, which we have adapted for weekdays by substituting for its concluding eulogy the one that is used on weekdays. For the trad. *Ashkenazi Hashkiveinu*, see No. 57.

164 97 *Eternal God, open my lips* . . . See No. 59.

165 97 *Our God and God of our fathers* . . . *length of our days.* New, by CS and HC, on the themes of *Avot* and *Gevurot*. On the Hebrew, see Nos. 60 and 61.

166 98 *You are holy* . . . See No. 62.

167 98 *We sanctify Your name* . . . See No. 107.

168 99 *O fill our minds with knowledge* . . . New, by CS, utilizing a number of the themes of the intermediate benedictions of the *Tefillah*. See Nos. 63 et seq.

169 100 *We pray for the peace* . . . New, by CS, on the theme of *Birkat Shalom* (on which see Nos. 80 and 125). The quotations are Isa. 32.16f.; Mic. 4.4. Cf. No. 366.

170 101 *May the words* . . . See No. 82.

171 101 *May He who causes peace* . . . See No. 83.

EVENING OR MORNING SERVICE IV

172 102 *Let us listen* . . . Ps. 85.9–14. We render the first word as 1st person plural rather than singular. Our trsl. accepts an emendation of the last clause of v. 9, attested by the Septuagint, reading וְאֶל יְשִׁיבוּ לִבָּם לֹה, though we retain the Masoretic text in the Hebrew. (The

No. Page

Masoretic text, וְאַל־יָשׁוּבוּ לְכִסְלָה, 'but let them not turn back to folly,' occurs nowhere else in the Bible in this sense and in this form.) The second clause of the last verse is obscure, and we render it as though the last word were 1st person plural rather than 3rd masculine singular.

173 102 *There are moments* . . . New, by CS.

174 103 *O give thanks* . . . Ps. 118.1.

175 103 *Praise the Lord* . . . See No. 52.

176 103 *O God, the keenest eye* . . . New, by CS; based in part on a prayer by Samuel S. Cohon, in UPB, pp. 353f. The theme is *Ma-ariv Aravim* and *Yotser*, on which see Nos. 53 and 100.

177 103 *Help me to know* . . . A compilation by CS of Scriptural verses on the theme of *Ahavat Olam* and *Ahavah Rabbah* (See Nos. 54 and 101). The quotations are Ps. 25.4, 5a; Hos. 6.6; Jer. 22.13, 15, 16b.

178 104 *Hear, O Israel* . . . See No. 55.

179 106 *True and enduring* . . . Slightly adapted from the UPB (p. 48) rendering of the *Ge-ulah*. On the Hebrew, see Nos. 56 and 103.

180 107 *Be praised, O Lord* . . . This short form of the *Avot* (See No. 60) is from the ancient Palestinian ritual, now preserved in the trad. liturgy only in *Mei-ein Sheva* (See No. 224). The somewhat free trsl. is by HF.

181 107 *For Your many blessings* . . . Adapted by CS from LJPB III (Festival vol.), p. 26, for use here as a *Gevurot*. On the Hebrew, see No. 61.

182 108 *You are holy* . . . See No. 62.

183 108 *We sanctify Your name* . . . See No. 107.

184 109 *Give us insight* . . . This, known as *Havineinu*, its first word, is a short form of the intermediate benedictions of the weekday *Tefillah*, recited by Samuel (3rd C.), and found in B. Ber. 29a. Such short forms are alluded to already in M. Ber. 4.3, 4. For doctrinal reasons, our version calls for 'the flowering of Your redemption' in place of the trad. 'establishment of Your temple, the flowering of David Your servant, and the clear-shining light of the son of Jesse, Your anointed.'

185 109 *Our God, the Guide* . . . A composite prayer by CS, adapting SOH, p. 292, and influenced by UPB, p. 349. In turn, the passage in SOH was slightly adapted from a prayer by IIM in LJPB, p. 274. See, as well, 'We humbly ask You . . .' in SOH, p. 292 (LJPB, p. 275).

186 110 *May the words* . . . See No. 82. *May He who causes peace* . . . See No. 83.

No. Page

AFTERNOON SERVICE

187 111 *Happy are those* ... This, known from its opening word as the *Ashrei*, consists of Ps. 145, prefaced by Pss. 84.5 and 144.15, and followed by Ps. 115.18. So 'framed,' Ps. 145 occurs three times in the daily liturgy, a practice recommended already in the Talmud (B. Ber. 4b). In trsl. Ps. 145.5, 6, we have changed the first person singular to third plural, following some ancient versions. Similarly, we have changed vv. 14 and 17 from 3rd to 1st singular. It should be noted that Ps. 145 is an alphabetical acrostic, with the letter *Nun* missing.

188 114 *Let the glory of God* ... See No. 58.

Sabbath Evening Services

SABBATH EVENING SERVICE I

189 117 *Source of mercy* ... A meditation before the kindling of the Sabbath lights taken from *The Authorised Daily PB* (London, 1891), and itself a version of an older *Techinah* ('Supplication'). Trsl. by CS. The concluding sentence is Ps. 36.10.

190 117 *Blessed is the Lord* ... *the lights of Shabbat.* The custom of kindling lights to usher in the Sabbath goes back to Pharisaic times. It is taken for granted in the Mishnah (e. g., M. Shabbat 2.6), but the benediction is not found before SRA. In some Reform congregations the lights are kindled as the service begins; in others, the lights are kindled earlier, and the service begins with the recitation of the benediction only. The kindling of Sabbath lights in the synagogue is a fairly recent innovation of Reform Judaism, and may be a revival of an ancient custom: 'The order of Sabbath is this: we enter the synagogues on Sabbath eve and recite the Afternoon Service *Tefillah* as usual. Then the one who kindles the Sabbath lights must recite the benediction' (SRA, p. 61). See also SH Notes No. 22.

191 117 *May God bless us* ... Slightly adapted from UPB, p. 7.

192 118 *Come, let us sing* ... Ps. 95.1–5, 7. As the benedictions surrounding the *Shema* express the themes of Creation, Revelation, and Redemp-

No. Page

tion, so too are these themes expressed, in that order, by the three Sabbath services in the trad. introductions to the *Kedushat Hayom* for each service. In the evening service, the theme is Creation; in the morning service, Revelation; in the afternoon, Redemption. This thematic scheme is not, however, limited to the *Kedushat Hayom*. It is also, and especially, evident in the evening service's introductory section known as *Kabbalat Shabbat*, 'Welcoming Shabbat;' in the provision, for the morning service, of the reading of Torah; and, in the afternoon service, the opening passage, 'A redeemer will come to Zion.' The custom of beginning the Sabbath evening service with a series of Psalms (95–99 and 29) and the *Lecha Dodi* (See No. 198) was introduced by Moses Cordovero, a leading Kabbalist of 16th C. Safed. The six Psalms represent the six days of creation leading to Shabbat; moreover, their themes are appropriate to Shabbat: they are nature-creation Psalms, and they call us to acknowledge the Creator by worship, and by acceptance of the divine Sovereignty. Finally, several of the Psalms are associated with Shabbat already in the Talmud (See, e. g., on Ps. 95.7, B. Shabbat 118b; on Ps. 29, B. Ber. 29a).

193 119 *Sing a new song* ... Ps. 96.1–8a, 9–13. As Ps. 95 begins with a call to worship, Ps. 96 may be regarded as a response to that call, a response carried forward by the remaining Psalms in this series.

194 120 *God reigns* ... Ps. 97.1f., 6, 8–10a, 11f. Our trsl. accepts several emendations: in v. 10, reading אֹהֵב יְיָ שֹׂנְאֵי רָע, 'The Lord loves those who hate evil' (instead of 'You who love the Lord, hate evil'); in v. 11, reading אוֹר זָרַח, 'Light dawns' (instead of 'Light is sown').

195 121 *Sing a new song to God* ... Ps. 98.1a, 2–4, 6–9. Here, as occasionally elsewhere, we render *Adonai* as 'God' rather than the more usual 'Lord' or 'Eternal.'

196 122 *Adonai reigns* ... Ps. 99.1–4, 9.

197 122 *A Song of David* ... Ps. 29. This Psalm, connected with the Sabbath already in the Talmud (B. Ber. 29a), describes a storm, and ends on the note of peace, thus making it an appropriate introduction to the Sabbath.

198 123 *Beloved, come* ... A poem composed, as the nominal acrostic of the text shows, by Solomon Halevi (Alkabetz), another Safed Kabbalist, brother-in-law of Cordovero (See No. 192). It is largely a mosaic of Scriptural verses, and yet is an original composition of great beauty and equally great popularity. We give here the entire

text, and elsewhere selected vv. from the text. The refrain is based on a Talmudic passage which relates that R. Chanina used to go out to the city limits, dressed in white, to welcome the advent of the Sabbath (B. Baba Kama 32a–b). Such was the custom, too, of the mystics of Safed. The concept of the Sabbath as Israel's bride is also Rabbinic (Gen. Rabbah 10.10), as is the legend that the two versions of the 4th Commandment (Exod. 20 and Deut. 5) were pronounced simultaneously (B. R.H. 27a, Shevuot 20b). The phrase 'the last of days, for which the first was made' is to be understood in the sense of goal or climax, in the light of the Rabbinic concept that the universe was created in accordance with a pre-existing 'architectural' plan — the Torah (Gen. Rabbah 1.2; B. Pesachim 54a; cf. Prov. 8.23). At the recitation of the last stanza, the worshippers trad. turn to the door of the synagogue to welcome the Sabbath Bride. Since in trad. Judaism, mourners remain in the synagogue foyer until the end of *Lecha Dodi* which, together with the preceding Pss., sets a joyous mood inappropriate for those recently bereaved, the custom of turning to the door also serves to welcome the mourners to the service. Trad. the daily services are read in the home during the week immediately following the burial of a close relative (*Shivah*) except on Shabbat, when mourners worship in the synagogue.

199 125 *A Song for the Sabbath Day* ... Ps. 92. Pss. 92 and 93, which trad. follow *Lecha Dodi*, do not appear in the early PBs, such as SRA and MV, but Maimonides mentions their recitation on Sabbath Eve as an ancient custom (Idelsohn, p. 130). The 2 Psalms are found as well in the ancient Palestinian liturgy as evidenced by *Genizah* fragments. According to the Mishnah (Tamid 7.4), Ps. 93 was recited in the Temple on Fridays, and Ps. 92 on the Sabbath. The Midrash (Eccles. Rabbah 1.2) says that Adam sang Ps. 92 on his first Sabbath.

200 127 *The Eternal is enthroned* ... Ps. 93.

201 128 *Let the glory of God* ... See No. 58.

202 129 *Praise the Lord* ... See No. 52.

203 129 *Praised be the Lord* ... *whose word makes evening fall.* See No. 53.

204 130 *Unending is Your love* ... See No. 54.

205 130 *Hear, O Israel* ... See No. 55.

206 131 *All this we hold* ... See No. 56.

207 133 *Grant, O Eternal God* ... See No. 57.

208 133 *The people of Israel* ... Exod. 31.16f. Trad. this passage follows the

No. Page

Hashkiveinu (No. 57) in the Sabbath evening service and occurs in the Kedushat Hayom (No. 511) in the Sabbath morning service. Its theme is the Sabbath, whose observance is a recognition by Israel of its covenant with God and of the divine creative activity. For this reason, we have, unlike UPB and SOH, retained the second half of v. 17 ('for in six days . . .'), holding this to be a poetical expression celebrating the creation, not a literal assertion that the world came into being in six days.

209 134 *Eternal God, open my lips* . . . See No. 59.

210 134 *We praise You* . . . Shield of Abraham. See No. 60.

211 135 *Eternal is Your might* . . . See No. 61.

212 135 *You are holy* . . . See No. 62.

213 136 *You set the seventh day apart* . . . This, part of the trad. introduction to the Kedushat Hayom (See below), is thought to be Talmudic in origin. It is based on Vayechulu, which follows it, and is first found in MV, p. 143 (Cf. SRA, p. 63, where it is noted as appearing in manuscript).

214 136 *Now the whole universe* . . . Gen. 2.1ff. This, known from its first word as Vayechulu, is first found in MV (and, in part, is noted in SRA, p. 63, as appearing in manuscript), but its liturgical use here as introducing the Kedushat Hayom is almost certainly Talmudic in origin. As with the second half of Veshameru (No. 208), we include it as poetry, not as an affirmation of the doctrine of creation in six days. Its use on the Sabbath, but not necessarily in the Tefillah, is discussed in B. Shabbat 119b.

215 136 *Our God and God of ages past* . . . This benediction, known as Kedushat Hayom, 'The Sanctification of the Day,' takes the place in the Sabbath Tefillah of the weekday intermediate benedictions. 'On the Sabbath . . . one says a Tefillah of seven benedictions, with the Sanctification of the Day in the middle' (Tosefta, Ber. 3.14). It is of course appropriate to refer to the Sabbath. Apart from that, however, is the thought that on the Sabbath it is inappropriate to turn the mind to one's needs, as the intermediate benedictions necessarily do. This would disturb the rest and serenity of the Sabbath, which, moreover, in itself is seen as an adequate fulfillment of our needs. The text itself is partly attested in B. Pesachim 117b. We trsl. the Hebrew אבותינו, 'our fathers,' somewhat freely, here and elsewhere, to avoid exclusive use of the masculine.

216 137 *Be gracious* . . . See No. 75.

217 137 *Our God . . . be mindful* . . . See No. 76.

224 141 *We praise You* . . . *abounding joy.* This, known as *Mei-ein Sheva,* 'Essence of the Seven [Benedictions],' and also as *Magein Avot,* 'Shield of the Ancestors,' is a summary of the Sabbath evening *Tefillah,* trad. understood as having been ordained for the benefit of late-comers to the service (Rashi on B. Shabbat 24b). The first paragraph begins like the trad. *Avot,* but its conclusion, quoting Gen. 14.19, is a variant harking back to the ancient Palestinian ritual. We utilize it elsewhere as well (See No. 180). The trad. text may be found, with slight differences, in SRA, p. 64. Our version replaces *Mechayei Meitim,* 'He revives the dead' with *Mechayei Hakol,* 'He is the Source of all life' (Cf. *Gevurot,* No. 61).

SABBATH EVENING SERVICE II

225 142 *As these Shabbat candles* . . . New, by CS.

226 142 *Blessed is the Lord* . . . *the lights of Shabbat.* See No. 190.

227 142 *Let there be joy* . . . New, by CS.

228 143 *In this quiet hour* . . . Based on a meditation by Mordecai M. Kaplan, adapted by Sheldon H. Blank.

229 143 *O Source of light* . . . New, by CS.

230 144 *How lovely* . . . Ps. 84.1–8, 11–13. Not in the trad. liturgy, except for the afternoon service in the *Sefardi* ritual. IIM put it into the Sabbath evening service, whose mood it fits (LJPB, pp. 3f., SOH, pp. 105f.). UPB (pp. 352f.) uses it as an introduction to a weekday morning service. In v. 7, the word usually trsl. as 'weeping' or left untrsl. as *Bacha* has been rendered by us as 'the driest [of valleys'] in light of the context. (Cf. A. Cohen's comment *ad loc.* in *The Soncino Books of the Bible.*) In the same v., the word usually trsl. 'blessings' should probably be vocalized בְּרֵכוֹת, 'pools.' We have trsl. it accordingly; but to bring out the dual possibility (which the word, however vocalized, would convey to the Hebrew mind) we have rendered יַעְטֶה (lit., 'covers it') 'blesses it.'

231 145 *We have come together* . . . Freely adapted by CS from LJPB, p. 62.

232 145 *How good it is* . . . . Ps. 133.1.

No. Page

233 146 *Many are the generations* ... New, by CS. Suggested in part by LJPB, p. 19, with an additional passage adapted from Frances Meyer.

234 146 *Let the glory of God* ... See No. 58.

235 147 *Praise the Lord* ... See No. 52.

236 147 *As day departs* ... New, by CS. Partially based on a prayer by CS and JR in SOH, pp. 77f. The Scriptural quotations are Ps. 8.2a, 5f. (with minor changes). On the theme (*Aravim*) and the Hebrew, see No. 53.

237 148 *O One and Only God* ... New, by CS, on the theme of *Ahavat Olam*. On the Hebrew, see No. 54.

238 148 *Hear, O Israel* ... See No. 55.

239 149 *In a world* ... A revision by CS of a prayer by JR and CS (SOH, pp. 80f.), on the theme of *Ge-ulah*. On the Hebrew (the concluding portion of which, beginning 'Who is like You ... ,' is trsl.), see No. 56.

240 151 *Let there be love* ... See No. 149.

241 151 *O God of Israel* ... New, by CS. An introduction to *Veshameru*, which follows.

242 151 *The people of Israel* ... See No. 208.

243 152 *Prayer invites God* ... Adapted from a passage by Abraham J. Heschel (1907–1973).

244 152 *Eternal God, open my lips* ... See No. 59.

245 152 *Source of all being* ... New, by CS, on the theme of *Avot*. On the Hebrew text, see No. 60. The concluding sentence derives from a prayer by JR and CS in SOH, pp. 81f.

246 153 *Your might, O God* ... See No. 152.

247 153 *A time can come* ... New, by CS, on the theme of *Kedushat Hashem*, quoting Isa. 6.3. On the Hebrew text, see No. 62.

248 154 *Those who keep the Sabbath* ... A passage alluding to Isa. 58.13; Gen. 2.3; Exod. 20.11; 31.17. It occurs in the *Kedushat Hayom* of the *Musaf* (Additional Service) both on the Sabbath and on a Festival when it falls on a Sabbath. Except for its opening words it also occurs in the *Kedushat Hayom* of the Sabbath morning service. Following SOH (p. 99), UPB (p. 32), and the *Sefardi* Ritual, we use it in the evening service as well. (UPB does not, however, use it as a prologue to the *Kedushat Hayom*, but as a replacement for *Veshameru*.) It is found, substantially as now, in SRA, p. 72. The English of the present version is based on a rendering by Samuel S. Cohon, in UPB. Its second half is not a translation, but a variation on the theme of the Hebrew.

No. *Page*

249 154 *God of Israel* . . . New, by RIK and CS, on the theme of *Kedushat Hayom.* On the Hebrew text, see No. 215.

250 155 *You are with us* . . . New, by CS, based on a prayer by JR and CS on the theme of the *Avodah,* in SOH, pp. 85f. The Hebrew text used here is the one found in UPB, p. 139, and SOH, p. 53. (Thus it differs from the text used previously; see No. 75.) The present text omits one passage from the trad. text, and substitutes for the trad. concluding eulogy a version 'whom alone we serve in reverence,' which is recorded in J. Sotah 7.6, and which is trad. recited in the Reader's repetition of the Festival *Musaf Tefillah.* This substitution goes back to the Hamburg Temple, 1841 (See Petuchowski, *Prayerbook Reform,* p. 231), and was followed thereafter by most Reform PBs.

251 155 *Eternal Source of good* . . . Adapted by CS from a new prayer by JR and CS, on the theme of *Hoda-ah* (See No. 77), in SOH, pp. 53ff. The Hebrew text is a shorter form of the *Hoda-ah,* trad. recited during the repetition of the *Tefillah.* It is known as *Modim Derabbanan,* 'Thanksgiving of the Rabbis' (B. Sotah 40a). The concluding eulogy is cited in J. Ber. 1.8. We have substituted, in the Hebrew, 'give us strength' for 'gather our exiles to Your holy courts' and made one slight omission. For an English version of this Hebrew, see No. 393.

252 156 *Let Israel Your people* . . . New, by CS, on the theme of *Birkat Shalom* (See No. 80). It begins, in Hebrew, with an amplified version of that benediction's opening words, and also alludes to the 7th intermediate benediction of the weekday *Tefillah* (See No. 69) and to the *Avodah* (See No. 75). It also utilizes, as a concluding eulogy, the one trad. recited only during the Ten Days of Repentance, but used also during the rest of the year by UPB and SOH, and first found in Lev. Rabbah 9.9.

253 156 *These quiet moments* . . . New, by Sidney H. Brooks, adapted by CS.

254 157 *May the words* . . . See No. 82.

255 157 *May He who causes peace* . . . See No. 83.

256 157 *Pray as if* . . . Source unknown.

257 157 *Who rises from prayer* . . . See No. 24.

SABBATH EVENING SERVICE III

258 158 *On this day* . . . New, by CS. The quotation is from the trad. *Yotser* (See No. 100), introduced there by the Gaonic period. It is omitted

No. Page

from SRA, but several manuscripts allude to it, and to the opposition of R. Saadya Gaon to its inclusion in *Yotser* (See SRA, p. 13).

259 158 *Blessed is the Lord . . . the lights of Shabbat.* See No. 190.

260 159 *Heart's delight . . .* A poem by Eliezer Azkari (Safed, 16th C.) a mystic who intended it as an introduction to worship. The initial letters of the Hebrew stanzas form an acrostic of the Divine Name, יהוה. Meditation upon the Name, and the Divine Mystery in general, would (he hoped) bring the worshipper nearer to God. Trsl. by CS.

261 160 *O God, this hour . . .* New, by CS, quoting Jer. 22.15b–16.

262 160 *Perfect truth . . .* Adapted by CS from LJPB, p. 94, with the following quotations added: Ps. 119.30; Isa. 54.14; Lev. 19.18; Eccles. 3.11a.

263 161 *Note: the mystics of Israel . . .* New, by CS.

264 161 *Beloved, come . . .* A selection of verses from *Lecha Dodi* (See No. 198).

265 162 *Sing a new song . . .* An arrangement by CS of verses from the *Kabbalat Shabbat* (See No. 192). Included are Pss. 96.1; 98.4a, 1a, 4b, 4a; 96.11f., 1b, 1a; 98.8; 96.1b; 98.4b.

266 162 *How can I sing . . .* By Joseph Zvi Rimmon (Poland-Israel, 1889–1958). Rimmon's Hebrew poetry shows strong mystical leanings.

267 163 *Let the glory of God . . .* See No. 58.

268 164 *Praise the Lord . . .* See No. 52.

269 164 *We praise You . . . revealed in creation.* A prayer by CS on the theme of *Ma-ariv Aravim* (See No. 53), first found, in a slightly longer version, in SOH, p. 108. It is an arrangement, with adaptations, of Pss. 104.19, 1; 113.4; 104.24. The concluding eulogy is based on a benediction found in M. Ber. 9.2, and trad. recited upon hearing thunder (See SH Notes No. 14).

270 165 *Give us understanding . . .* An arrangement by CS, mainly of Scriptural verses, on the theme of *Ahavat Olam* (See No. 54). The quotations (changed from singular to plural) are: Pss. 119.34; 86.11; 119.45a; 85.11; 86.12. The conclusion, suggested by ASD, is ancient, and does not appear in any contemporary ritual. See S. Schechter, 'Genizah Specimens,' reprinted in *Contributions to the Scientific Study of Jewish Liturgy*, ed. by Jakob J. Petuchowski.

271 165 *Hear, O Israel . . .* See No. 55.

272 165 *You shall love . . .* The insertions into the trsl. of *Ve-ahavta* ('For You are with us . . . ,' etc.) are adapted from a poem by Jesse Stampfer, suggested by HF.

273 167 *Happy is the one . . .* An arrangement by CS of Scriptural verses,

No. Page

      on the theme of *Ge-ulah* (See No. 56). The quotations are: Ps. 146.5, 6b, 7–9a; Isa. 61.1 (adapted). The conclusion is from the trad. *Ge-ulah*, with a small addition (in English) and some abridgement of the trsl.

274 168 *And God said* . . . Based on a passage from the Zohar, I.31b. The quotations are Gen. 1.3; Ps. 97.11. The theme of a supernal light hidden away for the righteous in time to come, and deriving from the light of creation, is Rabbinic in origin. See B. Chagigah 2a, Gen. Rabbah 3.6.

275 168 *The shadows fall* . . . New, by CS, on the theme of *Hashkiveinu* (See No. 57).

276 169 *The people of Israel* . . . See No. 208.

277 169 *Eternal God, open my lips* . . . See No. 59.

278 169 *Lord, You are the God* . . . New, by CS, on the theme of *Avot* (See No. 60). It alludes to Isa. 44.6; 41.8ff.; 42.6, and, in general, to Isa., chs. 41–49.

279 170 *Great is the power* . . . A revision by CS of a prayer by CS and SB in SOH, pp. 83f., on the theme of *Gevurot*. On the Hebrew text, see No. 61.

280 170 *Days pass* . . . New, by CS, on the theme of *Kedushat Hashem*, with allusions to Exod. 3.2; Gen. 28.16f. On the Hebrew text, see No. 62.

281 171 *Those who keep the Sabbath* . . . See No. 248.

282 171 *You are One* . . . From the prologue to the *Kedushat Hayom* in the trad. Sabbath afternoon service, first found in SRA, p. 79, and used here in place of the trad. evening *Kedushat Hayom* (See No. 215). The first sentence alludes to I Chron. 17.21. The reference to the observance of the Sabbath by the Patriarchs is Rabbinic in origin (e. g., B. Yoma 21b). James Michaels suggests it may have been intended as a polemic against those sectarians and early Christians who wanted to abrogate the ceremonial laws, including the Sabbath rituals.

283 172 *O God enthroned* . . . A new arrangement, by CS, of Scriptural verses on the theme of *Avodah* (See No. 75). The quotations are Pss. 22.4; 62.6; 42.9; 68.20.

284 172 *Eternal God, we give thanks* . . . New, by RIK, on the theme of *Hoda-ah*. On the Hebrew text, see No. 251.

285 173 *How can we give thanks* . . . New, by CS. It alludes to two songs of faith sung by Jews in the time of the Holocaust. The first, *Ani Ma-amin*, 'I believe,' is from a summary of Maimonides' 'Thirteen Principles of Faith' included in the trad. *Siddur*, and refers to the

No. Page

        Messianic Age. The second is from the 'Song of the Partisans,' Yiddish by Hirsh Glik.

286 173 *Let the day come* . . . A prayer based on a poem by R. Nachman of Bratzlav (See No. 6) entitled *Adon Hashalom,* 'Lord of Peace,' trsl. by CS, and adapted for use here for the theme of *Birkat Shalom.* On the Hebrew text, see No. 80.

287 174 *You are the world's beginning* . . . New, by CS. Suggested by a poem of Judah Halevi (foremost poet of the Spanish period, Spain-Palestine, 1086–1141). The Halevi poem is *Yah, Ana Emtsa-acha,* 'Lord, where shall I find You?'

288 175 *May the words* . . . See No. 82.

289 175 *May He who causes peace* . . . See No. 83.

SABBATH EVENING SERVICE IV

290 176 *These lights* . . . New, by HF and CS.

291 176 *Blessed is the Lord* . . . *the lights of Shabbat.* See No. 190.

292 177 *Lord, who may abide* . . . Ps. 15, adapted by changes from singular to plural. This Psalm does not appear in the trad. liturgy. It is found in SOH, but not in the *Kabbalat Shabbat.* 'Who give their word . . . retract' is an attempt to make sense of an unclear Hebrew text.

293 177 *There are days* . . . New, by HF and CS.

294 178 *Peace be to you* . . . This hymn, which seems to date from the 17th C., is trad. recited on returning home from the synagogue after the Sabbath evening service. Recently it has become popular also as a synagogue hymn, and we follow SOH in making it a part of the *Kabbalat Shabbat* in two services. It is based on the legend (B. Shabbat 119b) that two angels accompany the Jew on the way home from the synagogue on Sabbath Eve. If the home has been made festive in honor of the Sabbath, the good angel says: 'So may it be also next Sabbath;' and the evil angel says, reluctantly, 'Amen.' If not, it is vice versa.

295 179 *The synagogue* . . . A revision, by HF, of a prayer by Louis Witt in UPB, p. 327. For another version, see No. 51.

296 179 *Let the glory of God* . . . See No. 58.

297 180 *Praise the Lord* . . . See No. 52.

298 180 *O God, how can we know You* . . . Slightly adapted by CS from a prayer by Louis Witt in UPB, p. 39, on the theme of *Ma-ariv Ara-vim.* The Scriptural reference is to Exod. 33.19f. On the Hebrew text, see No. 53.

299 181 *When justice burns within us* . . . Adapted by CS from the second

No. Page

     half of the prayer in UPB, p. 39, noted above. On the theme of *Ahavat Olam.* On the Hebrew text, see No. 54.

300 181 *Hear, O Israel* ... See No. 55.

301 182 *I, the Eternal,* ... See No. 134. Here the concluding portion is of course from the evening *Ge-ulah* only.

302 184 *Cause us, our Creator* ... See No. 163. Here the concluding eulogy is the one used on the Sabbath.

303 185 *The people of Israel* ... See No. 208.

304 185 *Each of us* ... New, by HF, slightly adapted. At the conclusion, 'May our lips ...' is a variant on No. 59.

305 185 *Be praised, O Lord* ... See No. 180.

306 186 *God of eternal might* ... An abbreviation, with some variation in the English, of *Gevurot*, by CS. See No. 61.

307 186 *With acts of love* ... New, by HF, on the theme of *Kedushat Hashem* (See No. 62). The first line of the Hebrew is from the morning *Kedushah*. The second is Lev. 19.2b. The concluding eulogy is trad.

308 186 *God of all ages* ... A free trsl., by HF, of an abridgement of the *Kedushat Hayom* (See No. 215).

309 187 *O Lord ... in reverence.* A free trsl., by HF and CS, of Hebrew which combines (and abridges) several versions of the *Avodah.* For the body of the text, see No. 75. On the concluding eulogy, see No. 250.

310 187 *For the glory of life* ... A free trsl., by CS, of an abridgement of the *Hoda-ah* (See No. 77).

311 187 *Grant peace to our world* ... An arrangement by HF on the theme of *Birkat Shalom.* The first half is from the morning version of *Birkat Shalom* (See No. 125). The second half consists of lines from two poems by R. Nachman of Bratzlav (See, e. g., Glatzer, *The Language of Faith*, pp. 313, 315). One of those lines is in turn a quotation from the High Holy Day *Tefillah* ('Help us to establish ...'). The trsl. is somewhat free.

312 188 *Looking inward* ... New, by HF, somewhat adapted.

313 188 *May the words* ... See No. 82.

314 188 *May He who causes peace* ... See No. 83.

SABBATH EVENING SERVICE V

315 189 *Come, let us welcome* ... Slightly adapted by CS from UPB, p. 7. The quotations are Ps. 27.1a; Prov. 20.27; 6.23a; Isa. 42.6 (slightly adapted).

No. Page

316 189 *Blessed is the Lord . . . the lights of Shabbat.* See No. 190.

317 189 *May God bless us . . .* See No. 191.

318 190 *Lord of the universe . . .* Slightly adapted by CS from a prayer by Solomon B. Freehof, in UPB, p. 10.

319 190 *The sun on the treetops . . .* By Chaim Nachman Bialik (Russia-Palestine, 1873–1934), trsl. by I. M. Lask. This poem, whose second stanza we omit here, is a variation on the theme of *Shalom Aleichem* (See No. 294). We use it here as part of the *Kabbalat Shabbat*, to which it is appropriate. Bialik was the foremost Hebrew poet of modern times, and probably since Judah Halevi (See No. 287).

320 191 *We give thanks to You . . .* Adapted by CS from LJPB, pp. 44ff.

321 191 *This Shabbat sheds light . . .* New, by CS. Influenced by a prayer by Henry Berkowitz in UPB, p. 62.

322 191 *Blessed is the Sabbath . . .* Adapted by CS from a responsive reading by Samuel S. Cohon, in UPB, pp. 31f. The first response is from Ahad Haam ('One of the People,' pseudonym for Asher Ginsberg, Russia-Palestine, 1856–1927). Ahad Haam was a leading Hebrew essayist, editor, and propounder of 'Cultural Zionism.'

323 192 *Let the glory of God . . .* See No. 58.

324 193 *Praise the Lord . . .* See No. 52.

325 193 *Eternal God, Your majesty . . .* Slightly adapted by CS from a prayer by Samuel S. Cohon, in UPB, p. 29, on the theme of *Ma-ariv Aravim*. On the Hebrew, see No. 53.

326 194 *You are our God, the Source . . .* Based on UPB, p. 51, on the theme of *Ahavat Olam*. On the Hebrew, see No. 54.

327 194 *Hear, O Israel . . .* See No. 55.

328 195 *Eternal truth it is . . .* An arrangement of Scriptural verses together with some passages from the trad. *Ge-ulah*, adapted from UPB, pp. 41f. The quotations are Isa. 2.4 (adapted); Lev. 19.17a, 18b, 34. The passage beginning 'From the house of bondage' is new, by CS. The concluding English is a universalized paraphrase of the trad. Hebrew. On the Hebrew text, see No. 56.

329 197 *Cause us, O Lord . . .* This is the UPB (p. 56) trsl. of *Hashkiveinu*, slightly adapted, to which we have added the trad. concluding eulogy. On the Hebrew text, see No. 57.

330 198 *The people of Israel . . .* See No. 208.

331 198 *Eternal God, open my lips . . .* See No. 59.

332 198 *Blessed is the Lord . . . Shield of Abraham.* See No. 136.

333 199 *Eternal is Your might . . .* See No. 137.

334 199 *You are holy . . .* See No. 138.

No. Page

335 200 *Those who keep the Sabbath* ... See No. 248.

336 200 *Our God and God of all Israel* ... Slightly adapted from the UPB (p. 22) version of the *Kedushat Hayom*. On the Hebrew text, see No. 215. We trsl. the Hebrew אבותינו, 'our fathers,' somewhat freely, to avoid exclusive use of the masculine.

337 201 *Look with favor* ... The UPB (p. 138) version of the *Avodah*. On the Hebrew text, see No. 250.

338 201 *Lord, we give thanks* ... New, by CS, influenced by a prayer by Morris Lazaron, in UPB, pp. 68f.

339 201 *We gratefully acknowledge* ... Slightly adapted from the UPB (p. 138) version of the *Hoda-ah*. On the Hebrew text, see No. 77.

340 202 *Grant us peace* ... Based on the UPB (p. 22) prayer on the theme of *Birkat Shalom*. On the Hebrew text, see No. 80. Here, however, we add *Ve-al kol ha-amim*, etc., peace 'to all the nations,' and utilize the concluding eulogy referred to in No. 252 (Cf. SOH, p. 54).

341 202 *O God, guard my tongue* ... Adapted from SOH, p. 249. Cf. No. 81, and UPB, p. 24.

342 203 *May the words* ... See No. 82.

343 203 *May He who causes peace* ... See No. 83.

SABBATH EVENING SERVICE VI

344 204 *In every beginning* ... A free adaptation by CS of a reading found in *A Common Service*, by T. G. Falcon and H. B. Zyskind, revised and ed. by Alvin J. Reines. The (slightly adapted) quotations are Gen. 1.1, 3.

345 204 *Blessed is the eternal power* ... Based on *A Common Service*. On the Hebrew text, see No. 190.

346 205 *Now the whole universe* ... Gen. 2.1ff. Concerning the use of *Vayechulu* in the Sabbath service, see No. 214.

347 205 *These words* ... Adapted by CS from *A Common Service*.

348 206 *Shabbat is a day* ... New, by CS.

349 206 *Beloved, come* ... See No. 264.

350 207 *Now Shabbat is with us* ... Adapted by CS from *A Common Service*.

351 208 *Yitgadal Veyitkadash* ... See No. 58.

352 208 *Barechu* ... See No. 52.

353 208 *There was silence* ... New, by CS, on the theme of *Ma-ariv Aravim*. On the Hebrew text, see No. 53.

SABBATH EVENING SERVICE VII

No. Page

in Aramaic. Here it is used as part of the *Kabbalat Shabbat*, but trad. it is sung at the Sabbath evening meal.

374 221 *God of the beginning* ... New, by Henry Butler, slightly adapted by NH. We have added the Scriptural verses. They are Gen. 1.31; Pss. 33.5; 34.13f.; Amos 5.14; Ps. 36.10 (adapted).

375 221 *The universe whispers* ... New, by CS.

376 222 *Let the glory of God* ... See No. 58.

377 223 *Praise the Lord* ... See No. 52.

378 223 *There lives a God* ... *His creative will.* New, on the theme of *Ma-ariv Aravim*, by CS and SW. On the Hebrew text, see No. 53.

379 224 *There lives a God* ... *we call Him One.* New, on the theme of *Ahavat Olam*, by CS and SW. On the Hebrew text, see No. 54.

380 224 *Hear, O Israel* ... See No. 55.

381 225 *You shall love* ... The insertions into the trsl. of *Ve-ahavta* ('The path to the love of God ... ,' etc.) are new, by CS.

382 226 *There lives a God* ... See No. 162. The concluding English is a universalized paraphrase of the trad. Hebrew of the *Ge-ulah* (See No. 56).

383 228 *It is evening* ... New, by CS. On the Hebrew (*Hashkiveinu*), see No. 57.

384 228 *On the day* ... New, by DP and CS. It utilizes adapted quotations from Deut. 29.9; 30.15f., 18a, 19, and serves as an introduction to *Veshameru*, below.

385 229 *The people of Israel* ... See No. 208.

386 229 *Eternal God, open my lips* ... See No. 59.

387 229 *Our God and God of our fathers* ... See No. 165, and, on the concluding Hebrew (*Kedushat Hashem*), No. 62.

388 231 *Purify our hearts* ... From the *Kedushat Hayom* (No. 215).

389 231 *The world is sustained* ... M. Avot 1.2.

390 231 *Great is the gift* ... New, by CS and NH. On the Hebrew (*Kedushat Hayom*), see No. 215.

391 232 *Those who keep the Sabbath* ... See No. 248.

392 232 *Let me hear You* ... New, by CS, on the theme of *Avodah*. On the Hebrew, see No. 75.

393 232 *O God of Israel's past* ... A somewhat free trsl. of the *Modim De-rabbanan*, 'Thanksgiving of the Rabbis,' here used as the *Hoda-ah* (See No. 77). On the Hebrew text, see No. 251.

394 233 *God of all generations* ... Based in part on a prayer by Israel Bettan, in UPB, p. 58, and adapted by CS and HC.

395 233 *O Lord, may we never become complacent* ... Adapted from UPB,

No. Page

p. 350, on the theme of *Birkat Shalom*. On the Hebrew text, see No. 80.

396 234 *O God, keep my tongue* . . . A variation by CS on the meditation that trad. follows the *Tefillah* (See No. 81). Only the first verse (which is based on Ps. 34.14) and the last come from that meditation. The remainder comes from Pss. 143.8b; 51.12; 19.13; 25.5. First found in SOH, p. 102, with slight differences, and with an additional passage from Ps. 4.

397 234 *May the words* . . . See No. 82.

398 234 *May He who causes peace* . . . See No. 83.

399 235 *Rabbi Levi said* . . . Slightly adapted from Gen. Rabbah 14.9 which quotes Ps. 150.6. This begins an alternative set of prayers and meditations containing most of the themes of the *Tefillah,* in a looser setting than usual.

400 235 *Let us rejoice* . . . From *Hymns for the Celebration of Life* (The Beacon Press, Boston, 1964), No. 336.

401 236 *Eternal God, open my lips* . . . See No. 59.

402 236 *God of the past and future* . . . New, by Molly Cone and CS, on the theme of *Avot.* On the Hebrew text, see No. 60.

403 237 *When we call out* . . . New, by Molly Cone, slightly adapted, on the theme of *Gevurot.* On the Hebrew text, see No. 61.

404 237 *The dreams of prayer* . . . New, by CS and Molly Cone, on the themes of *Kedushat Hashem, Kedushat Hayom* and *Avodah.* On the Hebrew text (*Kedushat Hashem*), see No. 62.

405 238 *Those who keep the Sabbath* . . . See No. 248.

406 238 *As the seventh day* . . . New, by CS, followed by Ps. 8.4ff. (adapted).

407 238 *The stars of heaven* . . . New, by CS. The conclusion alludes to Ps. 8.6. Cf. Reconstructionist *PB for Rosh Hashanah*, pp. 122–5, by Eugene Kohn.

408 239 *Glory and honor* . . . New, by CS.

409 239 *Whither can I go* . . . Ps. 139.7ff.

410 240 *Through prayer we struggle* . . . New, by CS. The quotation is from Ralph Waldo Emerson (slightly adapted).

411 240 *Eternal God, like all* . . . Adapted by CS from a prayer by Morris Lazaron, in UPB, pp. 68f.

412 241 *It is written* . . . Zech. 8.16f.; Isa. 1.16c–17; Lev. 19.13f.; Deut. 15.7b–8a; Exod. 28.9; Lev. 19.34a; Deut. 16.20a; Lev. 19.18b; Joel 3.1 (to which an additional line has been added in the English).

413 242 *When we become aware* . . . Adapted by CS from a prayer by Louis Witt, in UPB, p. 45.

No. Page

414 243 *May the words* . . . See No. 82.

415 243 *May He who causes peace* . . . See No. 83.

SABBATH EVENING SERVICE VIII

416 244 *Out of the glaring darkness* . . . New, by RL, slightly revised and abridged.

417 244 *Blessed is the Lord* . . . *through light.* A variation on the theme of the blessing recited upon kindling the Sabbath lights, by RL. On the Hebrew text, see No. 190.

418 245 *Our noisy day* . . . New, by RL, somewhat revised.

419 245 *This is Israel's day of light* . . . From a poem, popular as one of the Zemirot (Table Songs), by Isaac Luria, leading Kabbalist of 16th C. Safed. Some versions preserve the acrostic of his name. For a fuller version, see Notes to Songs, No. 7.

420 246 *For our ancestors* . . . New, by CS.

421 246 *May the sense of God's presence* . . . New, by CS.

422 246 *Beloved, come* . . . See No. 264.

423 247 *If our prayer* . . . New, by RL, slightly adapted by CS.

424 248 *Let the glory of God* . . . See No. 58.

425 249 *Praise the Lord* . . . See No. 52.

426 249 *Aravim* . . . See No. 53.

427 249 *Once we learned* . . . New, by RL, on the theme of *Ahavat Olam.* For the Hebrew text, see No. 54.

428 250 *Hear, O Israel* . . . See No. 55.

429 251 *You shall love* . . . The responses to the trsl. of *Ve-ahavta* are by Abraham J. Heschel, *The Moral Outrage of Vietnam,* in *Vietnam: Crisis of Conscience,* © 1967 by Association Press. The last response (slightly adapted) is by Heschel, *The Insecurity of Freedom.*

430 252 *You shall be holy* . . . Lev. 19.2b.

431 252 *This is our truth* . . . New, on the theme of *Ge-ulah,* by CS and RL. It includes several passages adapted from M. Buber, *Ten Rungs.* For the Hebrew text (one passage of which has been placed before its trad. appearance), see No. 56. The concluding Hebrew paragraph is untrsl.

432 254 *The people of Israel* . . . See No. 208.

433 254 *Our Fathers prayed* . . . New, by RL and CS, on the theme of *Avot.* For the Hebrew text, see No. 60.

434 255 *We pray that we might know* . . . New, on the theme of *Gevurot,* by RL. On the Hebrew text, see No. 61. Here, however, the trad. text,

No. Page

without emendation, is utilized. Thus *Mechayei Hameitim*, 'Who revives the dead,' is retained here because of its interpretive use. The text also includes a passage trad. inserted into the *Gevurot* from Simchat Torah until Pesach, i. e., *Mashiv Haru-ach* ... , 'You cause the wind to blow ...' (this also used figuratively here), first attested in M. Ta-anit 1.1.

435 256 *Praised be the God* ... New, by RL, on the theme of *Kedushat Hashem*, slightly revised. On the Hebrew text, see No. 62. The concluding portion of the English, leading into *Yismechu*, is by CS.

436 256 *Those who keep the Sabbath* ... See No. 248.

437 257 *Our God, God of all generations* ... An interpretive version of *Kedushat Hayom*, by RL. On the Hebrew text, see No. 215.

438 257 *Words there are and prayers* ... New, by RL, somewhat revised, on the theme of *Birkat Shalom* (See No. 80). It quotes Isa. 2.4; Pss. 34.15b; 29.11; the concluding verse of the Kaddish (See No. 83); Num. 6.26. The latter three are freely trsl.

439 258 *I need strength* ... New, by RIK, slightly revised.

440 259 *May the words* ... See No. 82.

441 259 *May He who causes peace* ... See No. 83.

SABBATH EVENING SERVICE IX

442 260 *Come, let us welcome* ... New, by CS.

443 260 *Blessed is the Lord* ... *the lights of Shabbat.* See No. 190.

444 260 *May God bless us* ... See No. 191.

445 261 *When God made the world* ... New, by CS. Based on SOH, p. 206, Union Songster, p. 77.

446 261 *Let the heavens* ... Ps. 96.11.

447 262 *Praise the Lord* ... See No. 52.

448 262 *When woman and man* ... New, by CS.

449 262 *Hear, O Israel* ... See No. 55.

450 264 *True it is* ... New, by CS, on the theme of *Ge-ulah*. On the Hebrew text, see No. 56. Here the concluding Hebrew paragraph is omitted.

451 265 *Eternal God, open my lips* ... See No. 59.

452 265 *We praise you* ... *Creator of life.* Partly a trsl., partly new, on the themes of *Avot* and *Gevurot*, by CS. It includes the concluding eulogies of both benedictions. On the Hebrew (*Avot*) see No. 60. On *Gevurot*, see No. 61.

453 266 *We cannot see You* ... New, by CS, on the theme of *Kedushat Ha-*

No. Page

475 277 *Eternal God, open my lips* . . . See No. 59.

476 277 *Blessed is our God* . . . A simplified trsl., in part, of *Avot*, and in part a new prayer on its theme. On the Hebrew text, see No. 60. Cf. No. 452.

477 277 *Great is God's power* . . . New, on the theme of *Gevurot* and *Kedushat Hashem*, by CS. On the Hebrew texts (*Gevurot* and *Kedushat Hashem*), see Nos. 61 and 62. Cf. No. 452. On the concluding English text, '*You are holy* . . . ,' see No. 138.

478 278 *The people of Israel* . . . See No. 208.

479 279 *Our God and God of all ages* . . . See No. 454.

480 279 *May the words* . . . *the laws of life*. New, by CS, on the theme of *Avodah*. On the Hebrew text, see No. 75.

481 279 *May the words* . . . See No. 83.

Sabbath Morning Services

482 282 *Praise the Lord* . . . *like a curtain*. See No. 84.

483 282 *Blessed is the Lord* . . . *in the fringed Tallit*. See No. 85.

SABBATH MORNING SERVICE I

484 283 *How lovely are your tents* . . . See No. 91.

485 284 *Blessed* . . . *who has made our bodies* . . . See No. 92.

486 284 *Blessed is the Eternal* . . . *the study of Torah*. See No. 93.

487 284 *Eternal our God, make the words* . . . See No. 94.

488 285 *These are the obligations* . . . See No. 95.

489 285 *The soul that You have given me* . . . See No. 96.

490 286 *Blessed is the Eternal* . . . *who has implanted* . . . A series of benedictions found (except for the penultimate one, which is not attested earlier than MV) in B. Ber. 60b and incorporated in the *Birchot Hashachar*, 'Morning Blessings.' Of the 15 original benedictions, we include 12. Following some old manuscripts, we read *She-asani Yisraeil*, 'who has made me a Jew,' in place of *Shelo Asani Goi*, 'who has not made me a Gentile.' We also have *She-asani Ben Chorin*, 'who has made me to be free,' in place of *Shelo Asani Eved*, 'who has not made me a slave.' (Cf. *Sabbath and Festival PB*, Rabbinic Assembly [Conservative], p. 45).

491 287 *Lord our God* . . . *school us* . . . B. Ber. 60b, where it is a private prayer and therefore in the singular. Already changed to the

No. Page

plural in the trad. *Siddur*. There are some other variations as well. See also SRA, p. 3, where it appears still in its earlier form.

492 288 *At all times* ... Tana Debei Eliyahu Rabbah, ch. 21. The reference to 'inward' as well as 'outward reverence' may originally have been a reference to 'secret' as well as public reverence, thus reflecting a time of persecution when open adherence to Judaism was forbidden.

493 288 *Master of all worlds* ... A prayer cited in the Talmud, B. Yoma 87b, as intended for the Yom Kippur concluding service, where it still appears in part, but which also became part of the *Birchot Hashachar*. Our text is abridged, and we have inserted (in H and E) 'called to Your service.'

494 290 *Blessed is the One who spoke* ... See No. 97.

495 290 *The heavens declare* ... Ps. 19.2–5b.

496 291 *Let all who are righteous* ... Ps. 33.1–6, 9, 11, 15–17, 20–22.

497 292 *A Song for the Sabbath Day* ... Ps. 92. Cf. No. 199.

498 294 *Happy are those* ... See No. 187.

499 297 *Halleluyah* ... Ps. 150.

500 297 *Let every living soul* ... A somewhat abridged version of the *Nishmat Kol Chai*, which is trad. added to the *Pesukei Dezimra* on Sabbaths and Festivals. According to R. Yochanan in B. Pesachim 118a, the words 'the Benediction over song' in M. Pesachim 10.7 are a reference to this prayer. It is partly cited in B. Ber. 59b, Taanit 6b. It contains many Scriptural allusions and quotes Ps. 35.10. Starting with the words 'supreme and exalted,' it quotes Isa. 57.15 and Ps. 33.1. On the last paragraph, cf. M. Pesachim 10.5.

501 300 *Let the glory of God* ... See No. 58.

502 301 *Praise the Lord* ... See No. 52.

503 301 *Praised be the Lord* ... *the Maker of light*. See No. 100.

504 302 *Deep is Your love* ... See No. 101.

505 303 *Hear, O Israel* ... See No. 55.

506 304 *True and enduring* ... *Redeemer of Israel*. See No. 103.

507 306 *Eternal God* ... See No. 59.

508 306 *We praise You* ... *Shield of Abraham*. See No. 60.

509 307 *Eternal is Your might* ... See No. 61.

510 307 *We sanctify Your name* ... See No. 107. Here, for Shabbat, our *Kedushah* is somewhat more elaborate, adding, among other things, Ps. 8.10 (found in the Festival *Musaf*). Our version is composite, borrowing from both Morning and Additional (*Musaf*) Services, and omitting passages from each.

No. Page

511 309 *The people of Israel* ... See No. 208.

512 309 *Our God and God of ages past* ... See No. 215.

513 310 *Be gracious* ... See No. 75.

514 310 *Our God ... be mindful* ... See No. 76.

515 311 *We gratefully acknowledge* ... See No. 77.

516 312 *We give thanks ... In the days of the Hasmoneans* ... See No. 78.

517 313 *Peace, happiness, and blessing* ... See No. 125.

518 314 *O God, keep my tongue* ... See No. 81.

519 314 *May the words* ... See No. 82.

520 314 *May He who causes peace* ... See No. 83.

521 315 *Praised be the Lord ... the Maker of light.* This is a fuller, more elaborate version of *Yotser* (See No. 100). The passage *Hakol Yoducha*, 'All shall thank You,' is peculiar to the Sabbath, and is known by the Gaonic age. Our version is slightly abridged. The passage *El Adon*, 'God is Lord,' is from a hymn, with alphabetic acrostic, trad. interpolated in the Sabbath *Yotser*, by the Jewish mystics, possibly as late as the Gaonic age. Our version is slightly abridged, and we have made two small emendations (in H and E), as follows: in v. 4, reading 'He made them' instead of 'with understanding;' in v. 8, reading 'their King' instead of 'His kingdom.' Both passages are in SRA, p. 71, with slight variations. On *Or Chadash*, 'Let a new light ...,' see No. 258.

SABBATH MORNING SERVICE II

522 318 *Shout joyfully* ... Ps. 100. Trad. recited in the morning service on weekdays only. It appears in many ancient rites, but not in the oldest (e. g., SRA). It was associated, in Temple times, with thank-offerings (Lev. 7.2). It was the practice at times during the Middle Ages to recite this Ps. on Sabbaths and Festivals, and, following SOH, we offer it for the Sabbath.

523 318 *Praised be He* ... Adapted by CS from UPB, p. 115, from the UPB version of *Baruch She-amar* (See No. 97), trsl. by Samuel S. Cohon.

524 319 *You are One* ... Adapted by CS from the UPB version of *Ata Echad* (See No. 282). Found in UPB, p. 113.

525 319 *The heavens shall acknowledge* ... This consists of Scriptural passages and allusions. These are: Pss. 67.4; 81.10; Isa. 43.10; 42.6; Exod. 19.5b, 6a. Cf. UPB, pp. 344, 331f. The first three paragraphs are taken from the *Shirei Hayichud* ('Hymns of Unity'), one of which is sung at the end of the trad. morning service.

No. Page

SABBATH MORNING SERVICE III

No. Page

550 334 *Let the glory of God* . . . See No. 58.

551 334 *Praise the Lord* . . . See No. 52.

552 335 *Praised be the Lord* . . . *Creator of light.* Slightly adapted from the UPB version of *Yotser* (See No. 100), p. 118.

553 335 *Deep is Your love* . . . Slightly adapted from the UPB version of *Ahavah Rabbah* (See No. 101), pp. 118f.

554 336 *Hear, O Israel* . . . See No. 55.

555 338 *True and enduring* . . . An adaptation by CS of a UPB version (pp. 120f.) of the morning *Ge-ulah.* The three concluding English paragraphs are trsls. of the trad. *Ge-ulah.* On the Hebrew, which is not identical with the Hebrew that underlies the English, see No. 103.

556 339 *Eternal God, open my lips* . . . See No. 59.

557 339 *Blessed is the Lord* . . . *Shield of Abraham.* See No. 136.

558 340 *Eternal is Your might* . . . See No. 137.

559 340 *We sanctify Your name* . . . See No. 510.

560 341 *The people of Israel* . . . See No. 208.

561 342 *Our God and God of all Israel* . . . See No. 336.

562 342 *O God our Creator* . . . Adapted by CS from UPB, pp. 130f.

563 343 *Those who keep the Sabbath* . . . See No. 248.

564 343 *Look with favor* . . . See No. 337.

565 344 *Lord, we give thanks* . . . See No. 338.

566 344 *We gratefully acknowledge* . . . See No. 339.

567 345 *Grant us peace* . . . See No. 340.

568 345 *In this moment* . . . Adapted by CS from UPB, p. 46.

569 346 *Lord, who may abide* . . . See No. 292.

570 347 *May the words* . . . See No. 82.

571 347 *May He who causes peace* . . . See No. 83.

SABBATH MORNING SERVICE IV

572 348 *How lovely are your tents* . . . See No. 91.

573 348 *During the past week* . . . New, by CS and Molly Cone. The last paragraph alludes to Ps. 43.3

574 349 *Often our world is dark* . . . New, by CS. Suggested by UPB, p. 112. The quotation is an allusion to Ps. 16.11.

575 349 *Rabbi Chayim of Tsanz* . . . On the Tsanzer Rebbe, see No. 2. The tale has been slightly adapted.

576 350 *Happy are those* . . . Ps. 119.1f., 105, 130, 127, 165. This, the longest of the Psalms, is an eight-fold alphabetical acrostic on the theme of Torah.

No. Page

577 351 *Let the glory of God* . . . See No. 58.

578 351 *Praise the Lord* . . . See No. 52.

579 352 *Lord God of night and dawn* . . . New, by CS, on the theme of *Yotser* (See No. 100).

580 353 *You are manifest* . . . New, by CS, on the theme of *Ahavah Rabbah* (See No. 101). Suggested by a prayer by JR and CS in SOH, pp. 78f.

581 353 *Hear, O Israel* . . . See No. 55.

582 354 *Infinite God* . . . See No. 148. On the Hebrew text, see No. 103. Here, however, we omit the last Hebrew paragraph, and insert, as the penultimate English paragraph, an adaptation of Mic. 4.4.

583 356 *Eternal God, open my lips* . . . See No. 59.

584 356 *Lord, You are our God* . . . New, by RIK and CS, on the theme of *Avot* (See No. 60).

585 356 *Eternal God, the power* . . . New, by RIK and CS, on the theme of *Gevurot* (See No. 61).

586 357 *We sanctify Your name* . . . See No. 510.

587 358 *The dreams of prayer* . . . See No. 404.

588 359 *Those who keep the Sabbath* . . . See No. 248.

589 359 *The universe whispers* . . . See No. 375.

590 360 *You are One* . . . See No. 282. Here it takes the place of the trad. Sabbath morning *Kedushat Hayom* (See No. 215).

591 361 *Let us rejoice* . . . New, by Frances Meyer. On the Hebrew text (*Avodah*), see No. 75.

592 361 *Were the sun to rise* . . . New, by CS, on the theme of *Hoda-ah*. On the Hebrew text, see No. 251.

593 362 *We pray for the peace* . . . See No. 169.

594 362 *God of the beginning* . . . New, by Henry Butler and CS.

595 363 *May the words* . . . See No. 82.

596 363 *May He who causes peace* . . . See No. 83.

SABBATH MORNING SERVICE V

597 364 *God of the morning* . . . New, by SW, slightly adapted.

598 364 *Sweet hymns* . . . The first three vv. and the last v. of a poem known as *Shir Hakavod*, 'Hymn of Glory,' possibly by Judah b. Samuel of Regensburg (Yehudah Hechasid, d. 1217). The English is slightly adapted from a metrical version in UPB, p. 111.

599 364 *Let every living soul* . . . The first sentence of *Nishmat Kol Chai* (See No. 500).

No. Page

600 365 *Blessed is the Eternal ... who has implanted ...* See No. 490. Here slightly abridged.

601 366 *How greatly we are blessed ...* An extract from 'Master of all worlds' (See No. 493).

602 366 *Let the glory of God ...* See No. 58.

603 361 *Praise the Lord ...* See No. 52.

604 367 *Heaven and earth ...* See No. 145.

605 368 *O One and Only God ...* See No. 237.

606 368 *Hear, O Israel ...* See No. 55.

607 369 *I, the Eternal, have called you ...* See No. 134. Here the conclusion is from the morning *Ge-ulah* (See No. 103).

608 371 *Eternal God, open my lips ...* See No. 59.

609 372 *Lord, You are the God ...* See No. 278.

610 372 *Great is the power ...* See No. 279.

611 373 *Days pass ...* See No. 280. For the last paragraph, and for the Hebrew (*Kedushah*) see No. 510.

612 374 *The people of Israel ...* See No. 208.

613 374 *God of all ages ...* See No. 308.

614 375 *Those who keep the Sabbath ...* See No. 248.

615 375 *O Lord ... in reverence ...* See No. 309.

616 375 *God of all generations ...* See No. 394.

617 376 *Grant peace to our world ...* See No. 311.

618 376 *Pray as if ...* See No. 256.

619 376 *Master of the universe ...* By R. Nachman of Bratzlav (See No. 6), slightly abridged.

620 377 *May the words ...* See No. 82.

621 377 *May He who causes peace ...* See No. 83.

SABBATH MORNING SERVICE VI

622 378 *How lovely are your tents ...* Num. 24.5; Ps. 5.8. Cf. No. 91.

623 378 *For cities and towns ...* New, by CS. Based on SOH, p. 197.

624 379 *Praise Him, praise ...* Ps. 150.5, adapted. The English, by CS, is a paraphrase intended to be sung.

625 379 *Praise the Lord ...* See No. 52.

626 380 *We praise You ... Creator of light.* This is the SOH trsl. of *Yotser*. The text is abridged already in SOH, pp. 124f. On *Yotser*, see No. 100.

627 380 *Great is Your love ...* A simplified version of *Ahavah Rabbah* (See No. 101), based on SOH, pp. 198f. The Hebrew text is slightly abridged.

No. Page

628 381 *Hear, O Israel* ... See No. 55.

629 382 *Lord, You are One* ... A revision by CS of his prayer on the theme of *Ge-ulah* (See No. 103), in SOH, pp. 200f. Here we omit the last Hebrew paragraph. The concluding English paragraphs are trad.

630 383 *Eternal God, open my lips* ... See No. 59.

631 383 *We praise You* ... *Shield of Abraham* ... See No. 452. Here, however, we exclude the *Gevurot* theme.

632 383 *Great is Your power* ... A revision by CS of his prayer on the theme of *Gevurot* (See No. 61), in SOH, p. 202. It is partially included in No. 452.

633 384 *You are the holy God* ... New, by CS, on the theme of *Kedushah*, for which this is an introduction. The last English sentence is adapted from SOH, p. 202. On the Hebrew text, see No. 510.

634 385 *Our God and God of all ages* ... See No. 454.

635 385 *Those who keep the Sabbath* ... See No. 248.

636 386 *Lord our God, we pray* ... See No. 455.

637 386 *O God, we give thanks* ... New, by CS, on the theme of *Hoda-ah*. On the Hebrew text, see No. 251.

638 387 *May the God of peace* ... Author unknown. The last sentence quotes Isa. 9.5b. Here we use this passage as a *Birkat Shalom* (See No. 125).

639 387 *May the words* ... See No. 82.

640 387 *May He who causes peace* ... See No. 83.

Prayers and Reading for Special Occasions

THE SABBATH OF REPENTANCE

641 391 *Holy and awesome God* ... New, by CS. Based on a prayer in SOH, p. 275, which was adapted from LJPB, p. 291.

642 391 *Lord our God* ... *our own.* A prayer by R. Tanchuma b. Skolastikai, cited in J. Ber. 4.2. Our trsl. is slightly abridged.

643 392 *When heavy burdens oppress us* ... Freely adapted by CS from SOH, pp. 276f., where it was adapted from LJPB, pp. 186f. The responses are new, by CS.

644 392 *The Lord, the Lord God* ... Exod. 34.6f. Trad. found in the liturgy of the High Holy Days and in some other contexts. The passage is known as 'The Thirteen Attributes [of God].' This term, as well

No. Page

as the liturgical use of the passage, is attested in a saying of R. Yochanan (3rd C.) in B. R.H. 17b.

645 392 *Better one hour of repentance* ... M. Avot 4.22; B. Ber. 34b; M. Yoma 8.9.

646 393 *Avinu Malkeinu* ... The last verse of a famous penitential litany, recited during the Ten Days of Repentance. The words *Avinu Malkeinu*, which we transliterate, mean lit., 'Our Father, our King.' The first reference to this prayer, though not to this verse, is in B. Ta-anit 25b, where it is recited by R. Akiva, praying for rain during a drought. The prayer is generally attributed to Akiva on that account, although he may have been reciting an already-established formula. It is certain that many verses were added after his time (2nd C.).

647 393 *O God, You remember the faithfulness* ... An adaptation by CS of part of a prayer by R. Saadya Gaon (10th C.), from a manuscript reprinted in Halper, *Post-Biblical Hebrew Literature*, vol. 1, pp. 33f. The quotations are II Kings 13.23; Ps. 123.2; Ezek. 39.25; Lev. 26.9.

648 394 *Avinu Malkeinu* ... See No. 646.

THE SABBATH IN SUKKOT

649 395 *The Lord has brought you* ... Deut. 8.7, 9a, 10–14a, 17–18a; 10.12–13a, 18f.

650 395 *The glorious promise of spring* ... Freely adapted by CS from UPB, p. 184.

THE SABBATH IN CHANUKAH

651 397 *With grateful hearts* ... Adapted from UPB, p. 134.

652 397 *On the twenty-fifth day* ... From I Maccabees 1.54a, 59, 55, 52, 62f.; 2.15, 17–20, 22, 27f., 45, 48–52, 57, 61, 64; 3.1f., 4a, 6a, 7, 17f., 21, 23; 4.11, 14f., 24, 52ff., 56a, 58a, 59. Our trsl. is based on UPB, pp. 87ff., and RSV. We have made several adaptations for the sake of continuity, and have corrected the text to begin 'On the twenty-fifth day.' The text itself reads 'On the fifteenth day,' but that is probably an error.

SHABBAT ZACHOR

653 400 *How often our people* ... New, by CS. Based on a new prayer by JR and CS, in SOH, p. 284.

No. Page

654 400 *If the Eternal* . . . Ps. 124.2–3a, 4f., 7f.

655 401 *Those who trust* . . . Ps. 125.1f.

656 401 *Lord, how many* . . . Pss. 3.2f.; 140.6; 109.3a; 3.4; Jer. 30.10.

657 402 *O God, inspire us* . . . Based on SOH, p. 284.

PURIM

658 403 *We come before You* . . . Adapted by CS from UPB, pp. 136ff.

659 403 *Blessed is the Lord* . . . *to read the Megillah.* Cited in B. Megillah 21b.

660 404 *Blessed is the Lord* . . . *at this season.* B. Megillah 21b.

661 404 *Blessed is the Lord* . . . *this festive day.* This benediction, known as *Shehecheyanu,* is found in various places in the Talmud (e. g., B. Pesachim 7b). It is trad. recited at the commencement of festivals and on other happy occasions.

THE SABBATH IN PESACH

662 405 *Let every living soul* . . . The first three paragraphs are selected from *Nishmat Kol Chai* (See No. 500). The rest is by CS, adapted from a similar passage of his in SOH, p. 328.

663 405 *Great was our people's joy* . . . New, by CS, followed by Ps. 118.24.

IN REMEMBRANCE OF JEWISH SUFFERING

664 407 *All peoples have suffered* . . . Adapted from a passage by CS and JR in SOH, p. 287. The quotations are: C. N. Bialik, quoted in S. Halkin, *Modern Hebrew Literature,* p. 90; Job 13.15a (changed to 2nd person).

665 407 *A voice is heard in Ramah* . . . Jer. 31.15; Lam. 1.12a; 2.13; Ps. 13.2; 44.18, 23.

666 408 *And there was silence* . . . New, by CS. The quotation is Lev. 19.16.

667 409 *For the sin of silence* . . . New, by CS, followed by Obadiah, vv. 11–13a, 14, followed by 'Lord, You see it . . . ,' new, by CS.

668 410 *And I will make your seed* . . . Gen. Rabbah 41.9. The quotation is Gen. 13.16.

669 410 *We have been dust* . . . New, by CS.

670 411 *Take comfort* . . . Isa. 40.1, adapted; Lam. 3.21; Isa. 25.8; Jer. 31.15f.

671 411 *I believe* . . . See No. 285.

No. Page

THE SABBATH BEFORE YOM HA-ATSMA-UT

672 412 *As we stood at the edge* ... 'Against the Wind,' by Amir Gilboa (Russia-Israel, 1917–). The trsl. is by R. F. Mintz, in *Modern Hebrew Poetry*, p. 254, slightly revised by CS.

673 412 *Today we turn our thoughts* ... Slightly adapted from a prayer by JR in SOH, p. 285. It is followed by Ps. 137.5f.

674 412 *Blessed are the eyes* ... New, by CS, followed by Isa. 49.13; 51.3 (Cf. SOH, p. 285).

675 413 *Blessed is the match* ... By Hannah Senesh (See No. 456).

676 413 *Israel, born in pain* ... A revision by CS of his prayer in SOH, p. 286. It is followed by Ps. 122.6–9.

677 414 *Guardian of Israel* ... Slightly adapted from a prayer by CS in SOH, p. 286. It is followed by Isa. 2.3b.

For the Reading of the Torah

I

678 417 *There is none like You* ... *of all the worlds*. From the trad. introduction to the Reading of the Torah on Sabbaths, Festivals, and High Holy Days. Our first two paragraphs are cited in Soferim 14.8. They embody Pss. 86.8; 145.13; 29.11. Our third paragraph is a later addition. Unlike SOH (p. 135) we retain the trad. text, Ps. 51.20, which we trsl. somewhat freely, 'let Jerusalem be rebuilt.'

679 417 *Let us declare the greatness* ... The first half of the verse is based on Deut. 32.3. Its use in the Torah ritual is trad.; cf. Soferim 14.11, SRA, p. 58.

680 418 *For out of Zion* ... Isa. 2.3b. The use of this verse here is trad.

681 418 *Praised be the One* ... Trad. at this point. First alluded to in MV, p. 157.

682 418 *Hear O Israel* ... Deut. 6.4. *Our God is One* ... Not Scriptural. *O magnify the Lord with me* ... Ps. 34.4. The custom of reciting these three verses in this context is first mentioned in Soferim 14.9–11.

683 418 *Yours, Lord* ... I Chron. 29.11, the congregational response to the preceding.

684 419 *Reading of the Torah* ... The public reading of the Torah is very ancient and mentioned already in the Bible itself; cf. Deut. 31.10–13; Neh. 8.1–8. The custom arose of reading from the Torah on the

No. Page

following occasions: Sabbaths and Festivals, Fast Days, Mondays and Thursdays, New Moons, Chanukah, Purim, and the Intermediate Days of Pesach and Sukkot. This goes back to the early days of the synagogue. The Mishnah takes it for granted; cf., e. g., M. Meg. 3.6, 4.1f. But a fixed lectionary for the Sabbaths and Festivals emerged only in the Rabbinic period, and then gradually. In Palestine the Torah was divided into about 175 portions, so that it was read completely every 3 or 3½ years, a practice which continued until at least the twelfth C. Cf. J. Heinemann's discussion, *Tarbit* 33, p. 362. In Babylonia, a one-year cycle, consisting of 54 portions, was followed; this custom ultimately ousted the Palestinian one. Fixed lessons were also prescribed for the other occasions on which the Torah was read. In Reform Judaism the prevailing custom is to read each Sabbath (and, where daily services are conducted, on Monday and Thursday), a relatively short passage generally, but not always, selected from the trad. portion of the week. The custom, in many Reform synagogues, of trsl. the Torah-portion into the vernacular is a revival of an ancient practice, taken for granted in the Mishnah (Cf. M. Meg. 4.4).

685 419 *Praise the Lord ... Giver of the Torah.* The practice of reciting a benediction before (and after) the reading of the Torah is mentioned already in the Mishnah, Ber. 7.3; Meg. 4.1. The present version is cited in B. Ber. 11b in the name of R. Hamnuna (3rd C.).

686 419 *Blessed is the Lord ... Giver of the Torah.* The benediction trad. recited after the reading of the Torah. It is first cited in Soferim 13.8 but no doubt is much older.

687 419 *This is the Torah ...* Deut. 4.44; Num. 4.37. Trad. recited as the Torah is lifted up after the reading. The *Sefardim*, however, do this *before* the reading. On the practice, see Soferim 14.14 and Nachmanides on Deut. 27.26.

688 420 *The Reading of the Haftarah ...* The word *Haftarah* means 'conclusion' or 'dismissal,' and it is likely that at one time the *Haftarah* (also called שלמתא, 'completion') ended the service itself. The practice of 'concluding' the public reading of the Torah on Sabbaths and Festivals by reading, additionally, a portion from the prophets, is ancient, though not as ancient as the former. It is well attested in the Mishnah, e. g., Meg. 4.1f. However, a fixed lectionary established itself only in the course of centuries. The *Haftarot* were chosen because of their affinity of theme with the Torah reading, except for the three 'Haftarot of Rebuke' which precede Tish'a

be-Av, and the seven 'Haftarot of Consolation' which follow it. In Reform synagogues the trad. prophetic lectionary is not followed rigidly; often the *Haftarah* is chosen freely, in (closer) relation to the passage read from the Torah or to the theme of the sermon; and the Hagiographa are not excluded.

689 420 *Blessed is the Lord ... truth and righteousness.* The benediction trad. recited before the reading of the *Haftarah*, first cited in Soferim 13.9.

690 420 *Blessed is the Lord ... just and true.* The first sentence of the four trad. benedictions that follow the reading of the *Haftarah*, first cited in Soferim 13.10.

691 420 *For the Torah ...* The last of the four trad. benedictions recited after the reading of the *Haftarah*. The text, slightly shorter than here, is first cited in Soferim 13.14.

692 421 *Blessed is the Lord ... the Sabbath and its holiness.* The trad. text of the four benedictions that follow the *Haftarah*, here provided as an alternative to the shorter form above. *You are the faithful One ... the Shield of David.* Soferim 13.11–13. These two benedictions are excluded from UPB and SOH. Their antiquity is made clear by their close relationship to the prayers of the High Priest when reading the Scriptures on the Day of Atonement (See M. Yoma 7.1; M. Sota 7.2). We understand the references to Elijah and David to be metaphors of the coming of the Messianic age. The divine promise that David's light shall not forever be extinguished is alluded to in Pss. 89.36; 132.11. The trsl. of the third benediction is slightly abridged.

693 422 *Let us praise ...* Ps. 148.13f. First found in SRA, p. 59. We have trsl. the first word as first person plural (instead of 'Let *them* praise') so that the Reader and congregation may be associated in praise for the Torah.

694 423 *A Song of David ...* Ps. 29. The custom of reading this Ps. at this point (while carrying the Scroll in procession) has been traced back to the 11th C. So Elbogen, p. 201.

695 424 *The Torah of the Lord ...* Ps. 19.8–10; Prov. 4.2; 3.18; 3.17; Lam. 5.21. Trad. Ps. 19.8–9 is recited *before* the reading of the Torah. (There is an allusion to this in Soferim 14.14; cf. SRA, p. 59.) The Prov. verses are trad. recited in the present context, preceded by Num. 10.36; Ps. 132.8ff., and followed by Lam. 5.21. Our trsl. of Ps. 19.10 assumes that the word *yir-at*, 'fear,' should read *imrat*, 'word,' in the light of the context. Cf. Ps. 119.38; Isa. 5.24; Dahood, *The Anchor Bible, Psalms I*, pp. 123f.

No. Page

II

696 425 *Assemble the people* . . . Deut. 31.12–13a. The use of this passage to introduce the Torah Ritual was an innovation of SOH, p. 172. It was suggested by Herbert Richer.

697 425 *As for Me* . . . Isa. 59.21. Trad. found in a prayer attested in SRA, beginning 'A redeemer shall come to Zion' (See No. 897). It is utilized in the Torah Ritual by UPB (p. 97), SOH (pp. 172f.), LJPB (p. 360).

698 425 *O House of Jacob* . . . Isa. 2.5.

699 426 *Hear, O Israel . . . Our God is One* . . . See No. 682. Here we omit the 3rd verse mentioned in that Note.

700 426 *Yours, Lord* . . . See No. 683.

701 426 *The Reading of the Torah* . . . See No. 684.

702 426 *Praise the Lord . . . Giver of the Torah.* See No. 685.

703 427 *Blessed is the Lord . . . Giver of the Torah.* See No. 686.

704 427 *This is the Torah* . . . See No. 687.

705 427 *The Reading of the Haftarah* . . . See No. 688.

706 427 *Blessed is the Lord . . . truth and righteousness.* See No. 689.

707 428 *Blessed is the Lord . . . Sabbath and its holiness.* See Nos. 690 and 691.

708 429 *The Torah commanded us* . . . Deut. 33.4, with insertion (in H and E) of 'by God through Moses and the prophets,' following LJPB, p. 382 and SOH, p. 193. Adapted from the Torah Ritual according to the *Sefardi* liturgy.

709 429 *God's splendor* . . . Ps. 148.13c–14. Cf. No. 693.

710 429 *This is the covenant* . . . Jer. 31.33f. Cf. SOH, pp. 175f.; LJPB, p. 401.

711 430 *Behold, I have given you* . . . Prov. 4.2; 3.18, 17; Lam. 5.21. See No. 695.

III

712 431 *Our light is Torah* . . . New, by RL, quoting Prov. 6.23a; Isa. 54.13.

713 431 *They shall not hurt* . . . Isa. 11.9; Mic. 4.4. Utilized in the Torah Ritual of UPB, p. 94.

714 431 *This is the covenant* . . . Adapted by CS from UPB, p. 94, adding an allusion to Prov. 6.23a and quoting Mic. 6.8.

715 432 *O House of Jacob* . . . See No. 698.

716 432 *Hear, O Israel . . . Our God is One* . . . See No. 699.

717 432 *Yours, Lord* . . . See No. 683.

718 432 *The Reading of the Torah* . . . See No. 684.

719 432 *Praise the Lord . . . Giver of the Torah.* See No. 685.

720 433 *Blessed is the Lord . . . Giver of the Torah.* See No. 686.

No. Page
721 433 *This is the Torah* . . . See No. 687.
722 433 *The Reading of the Haftarah* . . . See No. 688.
723 433 *Blessed is the Lord* . . . *truth and righteousness.* See No. 689.
724 434 *Blessed is the Lord* . . . *Sabbath and its holiness.* See Nos. 690 and 691.
725 434 *Dwell, O Lord* . . . From *Forms of Prayer for Jewish Worship,* Reform Synagogues of Great Britain, vol. 1, p. 30. Based on a passage in the *Sefardi* Torah Ritual. *Lord our God, unite* . . . (p. 435) . . . *train for war.* New, by CS, q. Isa. 2.4.
726 435 *The Torah of the Lord* . . . See No. 695.

IV

727 437 *Happy is the one* . . . Prov. 3.13ff. Cf. SOH, p. 195, LJPB, p. 409. But in those PBs, the passage is used at the *conclusion* of the Torah Ritual.
728 437 *The world is sustained* . . . M. Avot 1.2. The use of this passage in the Torah Ritual is an innovation of the present PB.
729 437 *In this scroll* . . . New, by CS.
730 437 *Hear, O Israel* . . . *Our God is One* . . . See No. 699. *Yours, Lord* . . . See No. 683.
731 438 *The Reading of the Torah* . . . See No. 684.
732 438 *Praise the Lord* . . . *Giver of the Torah.* See No. 685.
733 438 *Blessed is the Lord* . . . *Giver of the Torah.* See No. 686.
734 439 *This is the Torah* . . . See No. 687.
735 439 *The Reading of the Haftarah* . . . See No. 688.
736 439 *Blessed is the Lord* . . . *truth and righteousness.* See No. 689.
737 439 *Blessed is the Lord* . . . *Sabbath and its holiness.* See Nos. 690 and 691.
738 440 *The world is sustained* . . . *by peace.* M. Avot 1.18. The use of this passage in the Torah Ritual is an innovation of the present PB.
739 440 *May it be God's will* . . . The concluding sentence of a passage from the Zohar, section *Vayakhel,* opening *Berich Shemei,* 'Blessed is the Master of the universe,' found in some recent Rituals before the Reading of the Torah. Our trsl. changes the Aramaic to the third person.
740 441 *When Torah entered the world* . . . Based on a reading by JR in SOH, pp. 257f., which was suggested by *Sabbath and Festival Prayer Book* (Rabbinical Assembly and United Synagogue of America, 1946), pp. 311f. It consists mainly of Rabbinic passages or allusions to them. The last two lines are new, by CS. Cf. No. 1122.
741 441 *It is a tree of life* . . . Prov. 3.18; Lam. 5.21. See No. 695.

V

No. Page

742 442 *The earth is the Lord's* ... Ps. 24.1–6. Trad. recited before the returning of the Scroll to the Ark on weekdays and Festivals occurring on weekdays. On the correct interpretation of this Ps. (which
has influenced our trsl.), see *The Problem of 'Curse' in the Hebrew
Bible*, by Herbert Chanan Brichto (*Journal of Biblical Literature
Monograph Series*, Vol. XIII, Society of Biblical Literature and
Exegesis, Philadelphia, 1963), pp. 64–7. On the trsl. of v. 6a, we
follow the new JPS. The basic meaning of דּוֹר (usually 'generation') in the present context is 'type.' For this suggestion we are
indebted to Prof. Brichto (in an oral communication); cf. Pss. 12.8;
14.5. Another line of reasoning leads to its trsl. as 'destiny' in SOH,
pp. 191ff., which was followed in *The New English Bible* where it is
trsl. as 'fortune'. Following most trsls. we add to the Hebrew of
v. 6b the English words 'O God of [Jacob]'.

743 442 *Lift up your heads* ... Ps. 24.7, 10, a continuation of the preceding.

744 443 *Let us exalt* ... Ps. 99.9. Trad. a continuation of 'Yours, Lord ...,'
No. 683. Already in SRA, p. 58. We have trsl. a second person
plural imperative as a first person plural cohortative.

745 443 *Hear, O Israel* ... *Our God is One* ... See No. 699.

746 443 *Yours, Lord* ... See No. 683.

747 443 *The Reading of the Torah* ... See No. 684.

748 444 *Praise the Lord* ... *Giver of the Torah.* See No. 685.

749 444 *Blessed is the Lord* ... *Giver of the Torah.* See No. 686.

750 444 *This is the Torah* ... See No. 687.

751 444 *The Reading of the Haftarah* ... See No. 688.

752 445 *Blessed is the Lord* ... *truth and righteousness.* See No. 689.

753 445 *Blessed is the Lord* ... *Sabbath and its holiness.* See Nos. 690 and 691.

754 446 *Let us declare the greatness* ... See No. 679.

755 446 *Praised be the One* ... Not Scriptural. Trad. recited, with several
Scriptural verses (Num. 10.35; Isa. 2.3b), after the Scroll has been
taken from the Ark; cf. No. 681. Here it is part of the ritual for *returning* the Scroll to the Ark.

756 446 *God's splendor* ... See No. 709.

757 446 *The Torah of the Lord* ... See No. 695.

Special Prayers

No. Page

758 451 *Into our hands* ... Freely adapted by CS from a prayer in UPB
p. 263. In the trad. liturgy, there is a benediction to be recited by
the father of a Bar Mitzvah after he has been called to the Reading
of the Torah. Called by its first words *Baruch Shepetarani*, 'Blessed
is the One who has rid me of the responsibility for this one (i. e.,
his son),' it comes from Gen. Rabbah 63.10, and in its curious way
expresses joy that the son now stands, religiously and morally, on
his own, with the privileges and responsibilities (and risks) of freedom of choice. For that benediction we offer the present replacement, to be recited, if desired, by either parent on behalf of a child
of either sex. Alternatively or additionally, the passage that follows
is offered as well.

759 451 *May the God of our people* ... Freely adapted from a blessing of
children by a parent in UPB, p. 377. Here it serves as an introduction to the *Shehecheyanu*, on which see No. 661. Offered here as
a blessing of a Bat or Bar Mitzvah in addition to, or in place of,
No. 758.

760 452 *Bless, O God, this congregation* ... The custom of reciting a prayer
for the congregation, and for the Community of Israel generally,
after the reading of the Torah, can be traced back to the earliest
PBs. The trad. *Ashkenazi* PB has two such prayers, one in Hebrew
and one in Aramaic. The custom of reciting a prayer for the Government has been traced back to the 14th, possibly the 11th or
12th C. (Abrahams, p. 160). Its underlying concept derives from
Jer. 29.7 and M. Avot 3.2. The present version combines these
prayers into a single prayer. It is new, by CS and ASD, and influenced by SOH, p. 156, which ultimately derives from the CCAR's
Blessing and Praise, 1923. We also pray, additionally, for the State
of Israel and its people, a custom that has become widespread in
recent times. Cf. UPB, pp. 148, 130.

761 452 *May He who saved Israel* ... Adapted by CS from a new prayer by
him in SOH, p. 341. Offered here as an additional prayer for the
Community of Israel on the Festivals.

762 453 *According to our calendar* ... Abridged from a prayer which has
been part of the *Ashkenazi* liturgy since the 18th C., having been
slightly adapted from an everyday private prayer composed by
Rav in the 3rd C. (B. Ber. 16b). The prayer begins actually with

No. Page

the following line ('O Lord our God, let ...'), but we have taken, in English, the liberty of placing the actual announcement of the beginning of the new month at the start of the prayer.

763 453 *O wondrous God* ... The substance of this prayer can be traced back to SRA, p. 90. In a longer form it was inserted into the Additional Service of the New Moon (*Rosh Chodesh*), and in a shorter form it came to be recited on the Sabbath preceding the New Moon, following the announcement of the day of the forthcoming week on which the new month would begin (which we have placed, in English, in the preceding passage, No. 762).

Services for The Festivals

FESTIVAL EVENING SERVICE

764 456 *It has been said* ... New, by CS. The quotation is Lev. 6.6.

765 456 *Blessed is the Lord* ... *Yom tov.* The custom of kindling lights of the eve of a Festival is taken for granted in the Talmud (Cf. B. Pesachim 102b); but the text of the benediction is not attested earlier than the Middle Ages (Cf. *Shulchan Aruch, Orach Chayim* 514.11).

766 456 *May we be blessed* ... See No. 191, of which this is a variation.

767 457 *It is written: Three times* ... Freely adapted by CS from LJPB, Vol. III, pp. 4f. It quotes Exod. 23.14ff., in a somewhat free trsl., and the *Shehecheyanu* (No. 661), also in a free rendering.

768 457 *A Song for the Sabbath Day* ... See No. 199.

769 459 *The Eternal is enthroned* ... See No. 200.

770 460 *With joyful hearts* ... New, by CS.

771 460 *Great was our people's joy* ... New, by CS, followed by Ps. 118.24.

772 461 *Blessed are those* ... A reading consisting of the following Scriptural verses: Ps. 106.3; Deut. 16.20; Lev. 25.35; Deut. 16.20; Lev. 25.42; Deut. 16.12; Exod. 23.9; Deut. 16.12; Lev. 22.32f.; Deut. 16.20, 12. Suggested by a similar passage in LJPB III, p. 15.

773 463 *Not without suffering* ... New, by CS.

774 463 *O give thanks to the Lord* ... Ps. 105.1–4, 7–10, 23, 42f.

775 465 *When Israel went forth* ... Ps. 114.

776 466 *Now summer's prospect* ... New, by CS, influenced by LJPB III, pp. 132ff.

777 466 *Endless are Your revelations* ... New, by CS.

No. Page

778 467 *It has been said: "Arise, shine* . . . Isa. 60.1ff. Cf. the use of this passage in LJPB III, p. 51.

779 467 *O God, Your light* . . . New, by CS. Suggested by LJPB III, p. 113. The quotations are Lev. 19.2b; Exod. 19.6; Deut. 30.11, 14; Jer. 31.31f.; Joel 3.1.

780 469 *On this day we give thanks* . . . New, by CS, with an allusion to Ps. 24.1.

781 469 *The glorious promise of spring* . . . Adapted by CS from UPB, p. 184.

782 470 *Help Your people* . . . *none else.* Ps. 28.9; I Kings 8.59; Joshua 4.24; Deut. 4.39. These vv. form part of the *Hoshanot,* a series of supplications based mainly on Ps. 118.25, for the *Ashkenazi* Ritual, by Elazar Kallir (7th–8th C. ?), on the theme of Divine Salvation. The prayers are recited while the worshippers go in procession around the sanctuary, each carrying a Lulav. According to M. Sukkah 4.5, such a processional during the days of Sukkot was a feature of worship during Temple days, the celebrants chanting Ps. 118.25 as they circled the Altar.

783 471 *Earth and sky* . . . Adapted from a prayer by HF.

784 472 *We have heard* . . . New, by CS; cf. UPB, p. 185.

785 472 *Our sages likened the Torah* . . . Based on Cant. Rabbah, ch. 1, and concluding with Prov. 3.18, 17. Suggested by Reconstructionist *Sabbath PB,* pp. 416–420.

786 474 *This day we complete* . . . New, by CS. Based on a prayer by CS in SOH, pp. 325f.

787 475 *Let the glory of God* . . . See No. 58.

788 475 *Praise the Lord* . . . See No. 52.

789 476 *Praised be the Lord* . . . *whose word makes evening fall.* See No. 53.

790 476 *Unending is Your love* . . . See No. 54.

791 477 *Hear, O Israel* . . . See No. 55.

792 478 *All this we hold* . . . See No. 56.

793 480 *Grant, O Eternal God* . . . See No. 57.

794 480 *The people of Israel* . . . See No. 208.

795 480 *And Moses declared* . . . Lev. 23.44.

796 481 *Eternal God, open my lips* . . . See No. 59.

797 481 *We praise You* . . . *Shield of Abraham.* See No. 60.

798 481 *Eternal is Your might* . . . See No. 61.

799 482 *You are holy* . . . See No. 62.

800 482 *In love and favor* . . . This is the Festival version of the *Kedushat Hayom* (See No. 215), somewhat abridged and somewhat freely trsl. It is alluded to already in the Talmud (B. Beitsah 17a, which

mentions the first paragraph and the concluding eulogy). The second paragraph (*Vatiten lanu*) is mentioned in B. Yoma 87b. On the third paragraph, which we abridge, see No. 76. The concluding paragraph is mentioned in J. Ber. 9.3. We combine Atzeret and Simchat Torah in our English rendering of the second and third paragraphs, since those days, distinct for other Jews outside Israel, are observed as one day by Reform Jews. Simchat Torah is mentioned for the first time by Hai Gaon (10–11th C.). Shemini Atzeret, 'The Eighth Day of Solemn Assembly,' is Biblical, and regarded as being in some sense an independent Festival from Sukkot, which it follows. See Lev. 23.36; Num. 29.35; B. Sukkah 48a.

801 484 *Be gracious* . . . See No. 75.

802 485 *We gratefully acknowledge* . . . See No. 77.

803 486 *Grant us peace* . . . See No. 80. On the English text, see No. 340.

804 486 *O God, guard my tongue* . . . Cf. No. 341.

805 486 *May the words* . . . See No. 82.

806 486 *May He who causes peace* . . . See No. 83.

807 487 *Praise the Lord* . . . Ps. 117. This and Ps. 118 are the last two Psalms of the *Hallel* (See No. 848). Although the *Hallel* is trad. recited only in the Festival morning service, we have, following SOH, pp. 326f., included this abridged version of its final portion also in the Festival evening service because of the increased importance which modern circumstances have given to the evening service.

808 487 *O give thanks to the Lord* . . . Ps., 118.1–4, 26, 28f. See preceding Note. For a fuller version of this Ps., see No. 854.

FESTIVAL MORNING SERVICE

809 491 *At the great festivals* . . . New, by CS; followed by Ps. 122.1–3, 6–9. We repeat v. 3, to bring out the possibilities in different trsl. The present ones were suggested by the *New English Bible* and the *Jerusalem Bible*.

810 492 *We rejoice now* . . . New, by CS, quoting Song of Songs 2.11–12b.

811 492 *Let My people go* . . . Adapted by CS from a prayer in SOH, p. 322, by CS and JR, which was based on LJPB, pp. 313f. The quotation is Exod. 7.26, etc.

812 493 *For now the winter is past* . . . From *Tal*, the prayer for 'Dew,' trad. inserted in the *Musaf* Service on the first day of Pesach. The present passage is a rearranged and abridged version of the one that appears in the *Sefardi* liturgy. In its original form, it contains

No. Page

        the nominal acrostic 'Solomon'; but its attribution to Solomon Ibn Gabirol is doubtful (Cf. Idelsohn, pp. 196, 343). The trsl. is by CS, who has also added Song of Songs 2.11f.

813 496 *This seventh day* ... Adapted by CS and ASD from a prayer by Samuel S. Cohon, in UPB, p. 182.

814 496 *Your way, O God* ... Ps. 77.14ff., 20f.

815 497 *My heart is ready* ... Ps. 57.8–12. This Ps. is not in the trad. liturgy. It was used for the first time, also in a Festival context, by SOH, p. 305.

816 498 *On this Chag Habikkurim* ... New, by CS.

817 498 *I, the Lord, am your God* ... Adapted by CS from his prayer in SOH, pp. 323f. The quotation is Exod. 20.2.

818 499 *I will give thanks* ... Ps. 111.1–3, 7–9b, 10. Verse 10c is utilized as a refrain here, though not in the original.

819 501 *Lord, who may abide* ... Pss. 15.1–5b (See No. 292); 101.7b, 6; 145.18; 43.3.

820 502 *In ancient times* ... Adapted by CS from SOH, pp. 324f., where it was adapted from LJPB, pp. 313f. The quotations are Amos 5.24 and Isa. 12.3.

821 503 *Let us listen* ... Ps. 85.9–14. See No. 172.

822 504 *Today we celebrate* ... New, by CS.

823 504 *God is in the faith* ... From a meditation by M. M. Kaplan, in Reconstructionist *Sabbath PB*, p. 391, slightly adapted. The quotation is Ps. 16.5, 11.

824 505 *God be gracious to us* ... Pss. 67.2–8; 68.25ff.

825 507 *Shout joyfully* ... Ps. 100. See No. 522.

826 507 *A Song for the Sabbath Day* ... Ps. 92. See No. 199.

827 509 *Lord our God, Source of life* ... New, by CS.

828 509 *Let the glory of God* ... See No. 58.

829 510 *Praise the Lord* ... See No. 52.

830 510 *Praised be the Lord* ... *the Maker of light.* See No. 100.

831 511 *Deep is Your love* ... See No. 101.

832 512 *Hear, O Israel* ... See No. 55.

833 513 *True and enduring* ... See No. 103.

834 515 *Eternal God, open my lips* ... See No. 59.

835 515 *We praise You* ... *Shield of Abraham.* See No. 60.

836 515 *Eternal is Your might* ... No. 61.

837 516 *O Source of life and blessing* ... Freely adapted by CS from UPB, p. 265, based on a *Tal* prayer by Elazar Kallir (7th–8th C. ?) which is trad. inserted in the *Gevurot* of the *Musaf* for the first day of Pesach

No. Page

(Cf. No. 812, for a *Tal* trad. in the *Sefardi* liturgy). The quotation is Isa. 44.3. In Israel, rain is almost unknown between Pesach and Shemini Atzeret. Only the dew provides moisture for growing things, and it is an ancient custom to pray for dew (*Tal*) on the first morning of Pesach, and for the fall rain (*Geshem*) on Shemini Atzeret.

838 517 *We sanctify Your name* ... See No. 510.

839 518 *In love and favor* ... See No. 800.

840 520 *Look with favor* ... See No. 337.

841 521 *Hear my prayer, O God* ... New, by CS.

842 521 *We gratefully acknowledge* ... See No. 77.

843 522 *Our God and God of all ages* ... The Priestly Benediction (Num. 6.24ff.) was recited daily in the Temple (M. Tamid 5.1). Later the last benediction of the *Tefillah*, known by the same name (called here *Birkat Shalom*; see No. 80), was substituted for the actual blessing by the priests; but the latter ceremony was retained on the Festivals, and the Reader also continued to recite the Priestly Blessing during the public repetition of the *Tefillah*, prefaced with the words which form our first paragraph. (These are already attested in MV, p. 67.) On the H and E beginning 'Grant peace,' see No. 542.

844 523 *O God, keep my tongue* ... See No. 81.

845 524 *May the words* ... See No. 82.

846 524 *May He who causes peace* ... See No. 83.

847 524 *Blessed is the Lord* ... *the Lulav.* The Lulav (palm branch, together with myrtle, and willow) and the Etrog (citron) are trad. taken in hand before the Hallel. The benediction is found in Tosefta Ber. 7.10. Trad., Lev. 23.40 is the source of the law concerning the 'Four Species' on Sukkot. Cf. B. Sukkah 46a.

HALLEL

848 525 *Blessed is the Lord our God* ... *to sing hymns of praise.* The word *Hallel* means 'praise' and is applied particularly to Psalms 113–118. This group of Psalms is also known as 'the Egyptian Hallel' (B. Ber. 56a) to distinguish it from 'the Great Hallel,' a name given to Ps. 136 (B. Ber. 4b). It was apparently recited already in the Temple (M. Pesachim 5.7). The trad. practice is to recite the whole *Hallel* on the eve of Pesach (as part of the Seder) and in the morning service on the first day of Pesach, on Shavuot, on the eight days

of Sukkot and on the eight days of Chanukah; and to recite a slightly shortened version (omitting Ps. 115.1–11 and Ps. 116.1–11) on *Rosh Chodesh* (New Moon) and on the last six days of Pesach. Our version of the Hallel is a slightly abridged one for all occasions, though the much shorter one we offer for the evening (See No. 807) might also be used on *Rosh Chodesh* and Chanukah mornings, on weekdays. The custom of reciting a benediction before the Hallel probably goes back to Mishnaic times and is assumed to be beyond debate in the Talmud. (B. Sukkah 39a). We have rendered the benediction somewhat freely.

849 525 *Halleluyah! Sing praises* . . . Ps. 113.1–8.

850 526 *When Israel went forth* . . . Ps. 114. Because the whole Hallel is rather long, one might recite this Psalm, with its emphasis on the Exodus, on Pesach, omitting Pss. 115 and 116, while reciting the latter on other occasions, omitting Ps. 114.

851 526 *Trust in the Lord* . . . Ps. 115.9, 12f., 15–18. See preceding Note. In v. 9, we have trsl. '*your* help and *your* shield' *ad sensum*, although the Masoretic text says '*their* help and *their* shield.'

852 527 *How can I repay* . . . Ps. 116.12f., 17. See No. 850.

853 527 *Praise the Lord* . . . Ps. 117. This and Ps. 118 are intended for all occasions on which Hallel is recited.

854 528 *O give thanks to the Lord* . . . Ps. 118.1–6, 8–12, 14–26, 28f. The three categories apostrophized in vv. 2–4 are ordinary Israelites, Israelites of priestly stock, and (probably) proselytes. In v. 12, our trsl. presupposes the acceptance of an emendation from LXX: בערו, 'blazed,' instead of דעכו, 'they were extinguished.' In v. 14 we have assumed that the word זמרת, trad. rendered 'song,' is to be understood in the light of a cognate Arabic word meaning 'to protect,' and we have therefore trsl. it 'shield.' (See D. Winton Thomas in *Record and Revelation*, ed. H. Wheeler Robinson, pp. 395f.)

FOR THE READING OF THE TORAH ON YOM TOV

855 531 *There is none like You* . . . *of all the worlds.* See No. 678.

856 531 *The Lord, the Lord God* . . . Exod. 34.6f. See No. 644.

857 532 *Let us declare the greatness* . . . See No. 679.

858 532 *For out of Zion* . . . See No. 680.

859 532 *Hear O Israel* . . . *let us exalt His name.* See No. 682.

860 532 *Yours, Lord* . . . See No. 683.

861 533 *The Reading of the Torah* . . . See No. 684.

READING OF THE TORAH ON ATZERET-SIMCHAT TORAH

No. Page

876 541 *Rejoice and be glad* ... Selected from a longer hymn which exists in various versions and is trad. chanted after the Scripture readings on Simchat Torah. It is found partially in MV.

877 542 *Reading of the Torah* ... See No. 684.

878 542 *Praise the Lord* ... *Giver of the Torah.* See No. 685. *Blessed is the Lord* ... *Giver of the Torah.* See No. 686.

879 543 *Let us be strong* ... Trad. chanted on completing any one of the five books of the Torah. Apparently based on II Sam. 10.12. Cf. B. Ber. 32b.

880 543 *Let us exalt* ... See No. 744. *This is the Torah* ... See No. 687.

881 543 *Reading of the Haftarah* ... See No. 688.

882 543 *Blessed is the Lord* ... *truth and righteousness.* See No. 689. *Blessed is the Lord* ... *just and true.* See No. 690. *For the Torah* ... (p. 544) See No. 868.

883 544 *The Torah commanded us* ... See No. 708.

884 545 *God's splendor* ... See No. 709.

885 545 *Behold, a good doctrine* ... See No. 711.

MEMORIAL SERVICE

The custom of commemorating the dead (*Hazkarat Neshamot*) on Yom Kippur is mentioned in Midrash Tanchuma (*Ha-azinu* 1, q. Deut. 21.8). Liturgical prayers in memory of the dead, especially martyrs, can be traced back to the 11th C., the period of the Crusades, and even before; see Abrahams, p. 232. The practice of reciting such prayers on the concluding days of the Pilgrimage Festivals later became popular, especially in Eastern Europe. (*Rabbi's Manual*, CCAR, 1961 ed., pp. 152f.). Such a service is known as *Hazkarat Neshamot*, 'Commemoration of souls,' or as *Yizkor*, from the opening word of the commemoration prayer (See No. 893). This Service is not found in the *Sefardi* liturgy, which has, instead, a single prayer called *Hashkavah*, recited in the Evening and Morning Services for Yom Kippur.

886 546 *The Lord is my shepherd* ... Ps. 23. We have retained 'the valley of the shadow of death' — even though the word should probably be vocalized צַלְמוּת and understood as 'deep darkness' — on account of its familiarity and because it has been so understood in Jewish trad. for many centuries.

887 547 *I lift up my eyes* ... Ps. 121.

888 547 *O God of life* ... New, by CS, influenced by UPB, p. 269, which is

No. Page

based on a prayer by Isaac M. Wise in his *Minhag America*. It contains allusions to Pss. 90 and 8, and to a prayer on which see No. 1070.

889 548 *Lord, what are we* . . . Pss. 144.3f.; 90.6, 3.

890 548 *Lord, You have been our refuge* . . . Ps. 90.1f., 4ff. (adapted), 10, 12, 16f.

891 549 *I have set the Eternal* . . . Ps. 16.8–11.

892 550 *O God, this hour revives* . . . New, by CS. Based on a prayer in UPB, pp. 271f., by Samuel S. Cohon, which goes back to a prayer by David Einhorn for the Yom Kippur Memorial Service. Cf. SOH, p. 352.

893 551 *May God remember* . . . The trad. commemoration prayer goes back partially to MV. The prayer for individuals is followed by a similar prayer for our martyrs, a widespread practice with roots in the period of the Crusades.

894 552 *In the rising of the sun* . . . Adapted from a Memorial Service compiled and ed. by RBG.

895 553 *O God full of compassion* . . . The *El Malei Rachamim*, as it is called from its opening words. Idelsohn, p. 232, says that it comes from 17th C. Eastern Europe. But somewhat similar dirges can be traced back to German lands in the Crusades (Abrahams, pp. 162f.). Our version is somewhat abridged.

Afternoon Service for Shabbat and Yom Tov

896 554 *Happy are those* . . . See No. 187.

897 557 *Your righteousness is everlasting* . . . A number of excerpts from a prayer known as *Uva Letsion* from its opening words. (Our version is rearranged, and the words appear later on, 'To Zion . . . will come'.) It is attested in SRA, pp. 38f. The complete version includes a form of *Kedushah*, 'Sanctification,' and a section in Aramaic repeating this. The prayer seems to have been used, in the Middle Ages, as a concluding prayer for the morning service in some congregations (See *Shulchan Aruch, Orach Chayim,* 132). Our version includes the following quotations: Pss. 119.142; 84.13; Jer. 17.7; Mic. 7.20; Isa. 59.20; Ps. 68.20; Isa. 59.21. In the passage beginning *Baruch Eloheinu,* 'Let us praise God,' we have, following SOH, p. 255, changed (in H and E) 'separated us from those who go astray' to 'called us to serve Him.'

Service for Tish'a be-Av and Yom Hasho-ah

The martyrdom of European Jewry under the Nazis has given a renewed impetus to the commemoration of Israel's suffering generally, and of this, the culminating tragedy, in particular. Gradually, by consensus, 27 Nisan, anniversary of the Warsaw Ghetto Rising, has come to be the main date for this commemoration, and it has been so proclaimed by the CCAR. Tish'a be-Av, as the trad. anniversary of the destruction of *both* Temples, has for many centuries been a day of fasting and lamentation.

No. Page

917 573 *In the presence of eyes* ... A poem, *Neder,* 'Oath,' by Avraham Shlonsky (Russia-Palestine/Israel, 1900–1974; leading Hebrew poet), in *Avraham Shlonsky: Yalkut Shirim,* ed. A. B. Yafeh, Yachdav, Tel Aviv, 1967. Trsl. by Herbert Bronstein.

918 574 *Ear of mankind* ... From a poem by Nelly Sachs (Germany-Sweden, b. 1891), entitled *Wenn die Propheten einbrachen,* 'If the prophets broke in,' in *O The Chimneys* (Farrar, Straus and Giroux, N. Y., 1967), p. 61.

919 574 *You must not say* ... From the 'Song of the Partisans,' Yiddish by Hirsh Glik, slightly adapted from a trsl. by Albert Friedlander, included in his anthology, *Out of the Whirlwind.*

920 575 *The universe whispers* ... See No. 375.

921 575 *I believe* ... See No. 285.

922 576 *Let the glory of God* ... See No. 58.

923 576 *Praise the Lord* ... See No. 52.

924 577 *Blessed is the Lord* ... *the night and its rest.* Slightly adapted from the UPB rendering of the *Ma-ariv Aravim,* p. 12. On the Hebrew (*Ma-ariv Aravim* and *Yotser*), see Nos. 53 and 100.

925 578 *We now proclaim* ... Adapted by CS from a prayer by Louis Witt, in UPB, p. 328, where, as here, it is a prelude to the *Shema.* On the Hebrew (*Ahavat Olam* and *Ahavah Rabbah*), see Nos. 54 and 101.

926 578 *Hear, O Israel* ... See No. 55.

927 579 *You shall love* ... See No. 429.

928 580 *You shall be holy* ... Lev. 19.2b (Cf. No. 430).

929 581 *And now this is the word* ... Isa. 43.1f., 5ff. On the Hebrew (*Geulah*), see Nos. 56 and 103.

930 582 *Be praised, O Lord* ... See No. 180.

931 582 *God of eternal might* ... See No. 306.

932 582 *You are holy* ... See No. 62.

933 583 *We sanctify Your name* ... See No. 107.

934 584 *Give us insight* ... See No. 184. Here it is slightly abridged.

935 584 *Answer us, O Lord* ... A prayer trad. inserted into the 7th benediction of the *Tefillah* on Fast Days, cited in B. Ta-anit 11b, 13b, and given in J. Ta-anit 2.2. We have altered the first sentence (in H and E) to make it yield the larger meaning required in the context of this service. The quotation is Isa. 65.24.

936 585 *Lord our God, You are the Comforter* ... A benediction found in J. Ber. 4.3, and intended for insertion on *Tish'a be-Av* in the 14th benediction of the *Tefillah* (See No. 72). SRA has it in slightly different form, p. 132. We have retained the trad. text, but we trsl.

No. Page

several verbs in the present or past tense, to reflect the altered circumstances of our times, in which our mourning, though intense, is tempered by the partial redemption we have experienced, especially through the creation of the State of Israel but also through the growth to maturity of American Jewry. The quotation is Zech. 2.9.

937 586 *Be gracious, O Lord* ... The SOH rendering of the *Avodah* (p. 53), slightly revised. On the Hebrew text, see No. 250.

938 586 *Eternal God* ... New, by CS. The conclusion is that of the *Avodah*, No. 75.

939 587 *O God of Israel's past* ... See No. 393.

940 587 *How can we give thanks* ... See No. 285.

941 588 *Let the day come* ... See No. 286. On the Hebrew (evening and morning *Birkat Shalom*), see Nos. 80 and 125.

942 588 *Our mission* ... By Elie Wiesel, in "Jewish Values in the Post-Holocaust Future: A Symposium," *Judaism*, Vol. 16, No. 3, Summer, 1967, p. 299.

943 589 *May the words* ... See No. 82. *May He who causes peace* ... See No. 83.

Service for Yom Ha-atsma-ut

The State of Israel came into being on 14 May 1948, 5 Iyar 5708. Because of the great importance of this event for world Jewry, its annual commemoration in the observance of Israel Independence Day (יוֹם הָעַצְמָאוּת) has become widely established among Jewish communities everywhere. The CCAR has proclaimed this day to be a Festival, and our service reflects this.

944 590 *Blessed is the match* ... See No. 675.

945 590 *Blessed is the Lord* ... *Shabbat*. See No. 190.

946 591 *For Zion's sake* ... Isa. 62.1; 35.1; 9.1.

947 591 *Blessed is the Lord* ... *this joyous day*. See No. 661.

948 591 *Give thanks to the Lord* ... Ps. 107.1–4a, 5f., 14, 35ff., 1. We use v. 1b as a refrain, a device found elsewhere (Cf. Pss. 118; 136). The present Psalm has its own refrain (v. 8, etc.) but it seemed less appropriate for the particular vv. in this selection.

949 593 *From the peak of Mt. Scopus* ... Words by A. Hameiri to a folktune. The second stanza is below; see No. 977.

No. Page
950 593 *Let the glory of God* ... See No. 58.
951 594 *Praise the Lord* ... See No. 52.
952 594 *Lord God of night and dawn* ... See No. 579. Here it serves as a *Ma-ariv Aravim* (See No. 53), and is very slightly abridged.
953 595 *You are manifest* ... See No. 580. Here it serves as an *Ahavat Olam* (See No. 54).
954 595 *With love for all* ... A form of *Ahavat Olam* found in *Siddur Rav Saadya Gaon* (Egypt-Palestine-Babylonia, 10th C.), p. 110, which is no longer found in the liturgy, and which we use here as a prelude to the *Shema*. We have added the concluding line (in H and E), and our trsl. is somewhat free. This passage might also be used when Yom Ha-atsma-ut occurs on the Sabbath, as an alternative to the preceding.
955 596 *Hear, O Israel* ... See No. 55.
956 597 *The hand of the Lord* ... Ezek. 37.1–6, 10ff., 13. The trsl. is slightly compressed. This serves as a *Ge-ulah*. On the Hebrew, see No. 56.
957 598 *Cause us, our Creator* ... See No. 163.
958 599 *Eternal God, open my lips* ... See No. 59.
959 599 *Blessed is the Lord ... Shield of Abraham.* This is one of the early forms of the old Palestinian *Avot* (See No. 180). See Solomon Schechter, 'Genizah Specimens,' in Petuchowski, ed., *Contributions to the Scientific Study of Jewish Liturgy*, p. 375.
960 599 *Life of the universe* ... The old Palestinian *Gevurot* (See No. 61). See Schechter, *ibid.*, p. 375.
961 600 *You are holy, inspiring awe* ... The old Palestinian *Kedushat Ha-shem* (See No. 62). See Schechter, *ibid.*, pp. 375f. This version has been preserved in the trad. liturgy for the High Holy Days.
962 600 *You are One* ... See No. 282. Here, however, we use only the beginning of this text.
963 600 *Our God and God of ages past* ... See No. 215.
964 601 *Lord our God, turn in compassion* ... From an alternative version of the trad. 11th Intermediate Benediction of the weekday *Tefillah*, printed in SOH, p. 474, Note 72. It is modelled after trad. forms and uses trad. phrases.
965 601 *Cause the plant of justice* ... See No. 73. Here we use it, without its concluding eulogy, as part of the introduction to the *Kedushat Hayom*, which follows.
966 601 *Our God ... be mindful* ... See No. 76. We have, for Yom Ha-atsma-ut, inserted (in H and E) 'day of Independence,' where appropriate. See, too, No. 800.

No. Page

967 602 *O Lord ... in reverence ...* This is the old Palestinian *Avodah*. See Schechter, in Petuchowski, *Contributions*, p. 376. On the English, see No. 309.

968 602 *For the glory of life ...* See No. 310.

969 602 *Let Israel Your people ...* See No. 252.

970 603 *Rabbi Joshua ben Levi ...* J. Chagigah 3.6. The Biblical reference is Ps. 122.3.

971 603 *The Holy One said ...* Num. Rabbah 23.7. We omit the proof-texts.

972 603 *No state is handed ...* Chaim Weitzmann (1874–1952, Russia-Britain-Palestine/Israel), first President of the State of Israel.

973 603 *If you will it ...* Theodor Herzl (1860–1904, Hungary-Austria), founder of 'Political Zionism.'

974 603 *O God, we are a people ...* New, by CS. The second paragraph is Isa. 52.7f., 10b.

975 604 *May the words ...* See No. 82.

976 604 *May He who causes peace ...* See No. 83.

977 605 *Wonderful are Your works ...* An abridged and slightly adapted version of a series of readings written and compiled by Jakob J. Petuchowski, for a service held in Jerusalem at the first Convention of the CCAR in Israel, 1970. The opening lines and the quotations which form the refrain are taken from the *Keter Malchut* of Solomon Ibn Gabirol (Spain, 1021?–1069?). It contains various Scriptural allusions, and the following major quotations: Lam. 2.1, 5; Pss. 137.1–6; 51.20 (Cf. No. 678); Isa. 40.1f.; 52.7ff.; Ps. 126; Isa. 11.9; Mic. 4.4 (Cf. No. 713). The conclusion is the second stanza of the song *Yerushalayim*, 'Jerusalem' (See No. 949). The trsl., by CS, is occasionally somewhat free. Several minor changes have been made in the Hebrew, at the suggestion of Prof. Petuchowski, to remove references that were specific to the first occasion of the use of this set of readings.

Concluding Prayers

ALEINU

978 615 *We must praise the Lord of all ...* This prayer is known from its opening word as *Aleinu*, lit., 'It is our duty.' The Scriptural quotations in it are Deut. 4.39; Exod. 15.18; Zech. 14.9. It is commonly attributed to Rav (3rd C.) as the reputed redactor of the section of the Rosh Hashanah liturgy relating to the blowing of the Sho-

No. Page

far, for it is in that context, introducing the *Malchuyot*, that it is first found (SRA, pp. 141f.). In Palestine it was early used as an introductory morning prayer (Cf. Elbogen, *Der Judische Gottesdienst*, p. 80). It is also found, in the first person *singular*, in a 3rd C. Palestinian Midrash, deriving from mystical circles. See G. G. Scholem, *Jewish Gnosticism, Merkabah Mysticism, and Talmudic Tradition* (N.Y., The Jewish Theological Seminary of America, 1960), p. 105. By the 13th C. it had also, in Western Europe, become a concluding prayer for all services throughout the year. J. Heinemann (*Hatefillah Bitkufat Hatannaim Veha-amoraim*, pp. 173ff.) has conjectured that the first half of the *Aleinu* (up to *Al Kein Nekaveh*, 'We therefore hope') may be a good deal older than Rav, going back to Temple times (See also Abrahams, p. 87). The first paragraph contains a passage which we trsl. *ad sensum*, '. . . who has set us apart . . . the nations.' Most Reform PBs have omitted or replaced this passage with a substitute (See Petuchowski, *Prayerbook Reform*, ch. 12). With this version of *Aleinu*, we attempt to restore its classical balance of particularism and universalism, and we offer as well a number of other versions, following.

979 617 *Let us adore* . . . This is the UPB version of *Aleinu* (pp. 71f.), somewhat adapted, and provided with the Hebrew extract from the *Aleinu* used in UPB II, p. 261.

980 618 *Let us revere* . . . A revision by CS of his free rendering of the *Aleinu*, with parts of the trad. text, which appears in *Gate of Repentance*, pp. 169f. The beginning Hebrew is as No. 979. The concluding passage ('Blessed be the name . . .') is Pss. 113.2; 72.19b.

981 620 *We praise Him who gave us life* . . . The beginning English is adapted from a passage by Herbert Bronstein; the last three paragraphs are by HF and CS. The Hebrew is from the *Aleinu* as it appears in SOH, pp. 364ff. The first paragraph substitutes, for the trad. Hebrew, 'he chose us to make known his unity, and called us to proclaim him King' (SOH, p. 364). This fourth *Aleinu* might be used on such special occasions as Yom Hasho-ah, or in a House of Mourning, etc.

BEFORE THE KADDISH

982 622 *Our thoughts turn* . . . By RIK, adapted.

983 622 *The origins of the Kaddish* . . . An abridgement of a passage by Leopold Kompert (1822–1866), in J. H. Hertz, *A Book of Jewish*

No. Page

Thoughts, Oxford University Press, Humphrey Milford, London, 1926, pp. 199f.

984 622 The contemplation of death ... By C. G. Montefiore, in Hertz, ibid., pp. 298f.

985 623 When cherished ties are broken ... Adapted by CS from a meditation by Israel Bettan, in UPB, pp. 74f.

986 624 O God, help me to live ... New, by RIK, slightly adapted.

987 624 What can we know of death ... Source unknown.

988 625 Judaism teaches us ... By J. L. Liebman.

989 625 It is hard to sing ... New, by RL.

990 625 This the profound praise ... New, by HF, quoting the first phrase of the Kaddish (See No. 997).

991 626 Eternal God, the generations ... Adapted by CS from a meditation by Solomon B. Freehof, in UPB, pp. 366f.

992 627 The light of life ... From A Common Service (See No. 344), slightly revised.

993 627 The Lord gives ... Adapted by CS from a meditation by Edward N. Calisch, in UPB, p. 75. The quotation is Job 1.21b.

994 627 In nature's ebb and flow ... Adapted by CS from a meditation by Samuel S. Cohon, in UPB, p. 73.

995 628 We have lived ... New, by CS and HC.

996 628 We recall the loved ones ... New, by RIK, slightly adapted.

997 629 Let the glory of God ... See No. 58. The present text is the Kaddish Yatom, 'Orphan's (Mourner's) Kaddish.' Our trsl. of the last sentence adds the words 'and all the world' (See No. 83). This form of the Kaddish is longer than the 'Reader's Kaddish,' the last two sentences being additional.

998 630 May the Source of peace ... Slightly adapted from UPB, p. 76. A variant on the sentiment trad. expressed to the mourners when they enter the synagogue during the Kabbalat Shabbat, before the recitation of Ps. 92: 'May the Presence comfort you among the other mourners for (or, of) Zion and Jerusalem' — a custom which may go back, in some form, to Temple times (so Idelsohn, p. 130). Cf. No. 198.

For Synagogue and Home

No. Page

HAVDALAH

The word *Havdalah* means 'separation' or 'differentiation' and refers especially to the ritual for 'ushering out' the Sabbath or a Festival. This custom seems to be as ancient as the *Kiddush*, going back to Pharisaic times. (Cf., e. g., M. Ber. 8.5 and Tosefta Ber. 6.7).

999 633 *Behold, God is my Deliverer* ... There is some variation among the rituals as to the introductory Scriptural passages for the *Havdalah*. We offer the following: Isa. 12.2f. (on the trsl. of זמרת see No. 854; we have also slightly adapted the trsl. of several vv., changing persons where it seemed necessary on grounds of English style); Pss. 3.9; 46.12; 84.13; 20.10; Esther 8.16; Ps. 116.13. The custom of prefacing the Havdalah ceremony with these Scriptural verses or a similar selection can be traced back to the 11th C. The accent is on *salvation* because the Messiah (or his forerunner, Elijah) was popularly expected to come following a Sabbath (on the Sabbath itself, which is a foretaste of the Messianic time, he would be redundant!), at the first opportunity, as the new week begins (Cf. Abrahams, p. 182).

1000 634 *Blessed is the Lord* ... *fruit of the vine.* See No. 1149. M. Ber. 8.5–8 refers to this and to the other Havdalah benedictions; Tosefta Ber. 6.7 (cited in B. Ber. 52a) mentions all three: wine, light, and spices.

1001 634 *Blessed is the Lord* ... *all the spices.* See preceding Note. The text of the benediction is cited in B. Ber. 43a. The use of spices in this context may go back to an ancient domestic custom, of bringing spices on burning coals into the room at the end of a meal (Cf. M. Ber. 6.6); this could, of course, only be done when the Sabbath was over (Cf. Levi, p. 204). Maimonides explains the custom as intended to 'cheer up' the 'additional soul' which, according to Rabbinic legend, dwells within the Jew during the Sabbath (B. Beitsah 16a; B. Ta-anit 27b); that 'over-soul' is saddened when the Sabbath departs, for it, in turn, must leave the Jew (*Mishneh Torah, Hilchot Shabbat* 29.29).

1002 634 *Blessed is the Lord* ... *the light of fire.* Lit., 'lights.' Because of the plural, it is customary to use a twisted candle, with two or more wicks (Cf. B. Pesachim 103b). The benediction is cited in M. Ber.

No. Page

8.5 as that recommended by the school of Hillel. The custom of lighting a candle at the conclusion of the Sabbath is probably due to the desire to kindle light as soon as the Sabbath, during which the kindling of fire was prohibited, was over. It has also been connected with the story of creation; in this view, the blessing of light at the start of the first day commemorates the first day of creation, whose feature was the creation of light (Cf. Gen. Rabbah 12.5; B. Pesachim 53b). It may be also connected with the legend that Adam was frightened when it grew dark at the end of the Sabbath, whereupon God taught him how to kindle a fire (B. Pesachim 54a; cf. Levi, p. 204).

1003 634 *We give thanks* ... Freely adapted by CS from a new prayer by JR in SOH, p. 410.

1004 634 *Eiliyahu hanavi* ... A trad. folk song that has become associated with Pesach and with the Havdalah, on account of their connection with the figure of Elijah and the theme of redemption.

1005 635 *Blessed is the Lord ... who separates the sacred from the profane.* This is the principal benediction of the Havdalah, from which its name is derived. It is cited in B. Pesachim 103b. We have omitted the phrase, 'between Israel and the other peoples,' as being too particularistic (especially in the context). Scriptural allusions include Gen. 1.4 and 2.1–3.

1006 636 *He who separates sacred from profane* ... An abridged version of a poem with an acrostic indicating that it was written by 'Isaac the Little,' whom it is, however, not possible to identify with certainty. It may have been R. Isaac ibn Giyyat (11th C. Spain; cf. F. L. Cohen in JE, Vol. VI, p. 187). It was probably intended originally for the concluding service of Yom Kippur; hence its penitential tenor.

1007 636 *Blessed is the Lord ... Creator of the fruit of the vine* ... See No. 1000.

1008 636 *We thank You* ... Very slightly abridged from a new prayer by JR and CS in SOH, p. 412.

1009 636 *Blessed is the Lord ... who separates* ... See No. 1005, of which this is an abridgement.

1010 637 *The Torah commands* ... This is an expanded version of the Havdalah, by ASD and CS. It might be used on special occasions and in 'camp' settings; in general, at communal as distinguished from family occasions. It begins with a slightly adapted quotation from Lev. 10.10. The 'day that is all Shabbat' is an allusion to the Sab-

No. Page

bath insertion in the fourth benediction of the *Birkat Hamazon*,
Grace after Meals. The concept goes back to the Mishnah (M.
Tamid 7.4). On the *Birkat Hamazon* in general, see Notes to SH,
Nos. 8–13.

1011 638 *The ancients took words* . . . New, by ASD and CS.

1012 638 *Behold, God is my Deliverer* . . . See No. 999.

1013 639 *Wine gladdens the heart* . . . New, by ASD and CS. Alludes to Ps.
104.15. On the benediction over wine, see No. 1000.

1014 639 *The added soul* . . . New, by ASD and CS. On the allusion to the
'added soul,' and on the benediction over spices, see No. 1001.

1015 640 *The Rabbis tell us* . . . New, by ASD and CS. On the allusion to
Adam, and on the benediction over light, see No. 1002.

1016 640 *Havdalah is not for the close of Shabbat alone* . . . New, by ASD and
CS. On the benediction, see No. 1005.

1017 641 *The light is gone* . . . New, by ASD and CS. Introduces the song,
Eiliyahu hanavi (See No. 1004).

1018 641 *A good week* . . . the refrain of *Hamavdil*, 'He who separates.' See
No. 1006.

CHANUKAH

1019 642 *These lights of Chanukah* . . . New, by CS, alluding to *Al Hanisim*,
'We give thanks for the . . . wonders' (See No. 78). It also quotes
briefly from SOH, p. 413, a new prayer by JR.

1020 642 *Blessed is the match* . . . See No. 675.

1021 642 *Zion hears and is glad* . . . Ps. 97.8.

1022 642 *Within living memory* . . . New, by CS.

1023 642 *Let the lights we kindle* . . . Suggested by SOH, p. 413, by JR.

1024 643 *Blessed is the Lord* . . . *the Chanukah lights.* Cited in B. Shabbat 23a.

1025 643 *Blessed is the Lord* . . . *who performed wondrous deeds* . . . Alluded
to in B. Shabbat 23a, partly cited in Soferim 20.6 and SRA, p. 99.

1026 643 *Blessed is the Lord* . . . *this season.* Alluded to in B. Shabbat 23a (Cf.
Rashi *ad loc.* and No. 661).

1027 643 *The people who walked in darkness* . . . Isa. 9.1a; Mic. 7.8; Ps. 18.29;
Ps. 112.4; Ps. 27.1; Prov. 6.23; Isa. 60.1; Isa. 60.19. The custom of reciting such verses while kindling the Chanukah lights is of recent
origin. Cf. SPJH, 1918 ed., p. 107 and SOH, pp. 416f. We follow
SOH, but in place of Ps. 37.5f. have Ps. 27.1 (Cf. SOH, p. 415, Note
588).

No. Page

1028 644 *We kindle these lights* ... First cited in Soferim 20.6. We have made one slight omission ('through the agency of Your holy priests').

AT A HOUSE OF MOURNING

1029 645 *We are assembled with our friends* ... Adapted by CS from UPB, p. 300.

1030 645 *I lift up my eyes* ... Ps. 121. Cf. No. 887.

1031 646 *As in the world around us* ... New, by CS. Cf. UPB, p. 301, which is based on a prayer by David Einhorn.

1032 646 *O Lord, God of the spirits* ... Adapted from SOH, p. 444.

1033 647 *O God full of compassion* ... See No. 895.

1034 647 *O Lord, Healer of the broken-hearted* ... Abrahams, p. 231, says that it is 'a recent composition, but it is similar to older forms.' The first sentence incorporates Ps. 147.3.

1035 648 *The Lord is my shepherd* ... Ps. 23. See No. 886.

1036 648 *Yitgadal Veyitkadash* ... The 'Orphan's *Kaddish.*' See No. 997.

Special Themes

NATURE

1037 651 *How wonderful, O Lord* ... Freely adapted by CS from SOH, p. 219, where it was freely adapted from LJPB, pp. 92f., which took it from *Prayer Book of the St. George's Settlement Synagogue,* ed. Basil Q. Henriques, 1929, p. 90. The quotations are Pss. 104.24a; 19.2.

1038 651 *Why should I wish to see* ... From Walt Whitman, 'Song of Myself,' section 48 (included in *Leaves of Grass,* 1855).

1039 652 *Praise the Lord, O my soul* ... Ps. 104.1f., 4, 10–11a, 12, 14–15a, 19–22, 24, 33.

1040 654 *To You the stars of morning* ... By Judah Halevi (See No. 287). The trsl. is slightly adapted from one by Olga Marx in *The Language of Faith,* ed. N. N. Glatzer, p. 54.

1041 654 *God is Lord of all creation* ... See No. 521.

1042 655 *And God saw* ... A composite passage by CS, freely adapting several Midrashim from Eccles. Rabbah 9 and Gen. Rabbah 9. The quotation is Gen. 1.31.

1043 655 *Light and splendor* ... By Leonard Cohen, from a poem, 'Three Good Nights,' in *Selected Poems,* p. 112.

No. Page

1044 656 *Of all created things* ... By Kathleen Raine, from a poem, 'Message from Home,' in *The Penguin Book of Religious Verse*, pp. 152ff.

OMNIPRESENCE

1045 658 *Why did the Holy One* ... From Exod. Rabbah 2.5, in the name of R. Joshua b. Korcha (2nd C.).

1046 658 *Earth's crammed with heaven* ... From Elizabeth Barrett Browning, 'Aurora Leigh,' Book vii.

1047 658 *Lord, You see through me* ... Ps. 139.1–4, 7–12.

1048 659 *Lord, where can I find You? Your glory fills the world* ... Trsl. by CS from David Frischmann's Hebrew version of Rabindranath Tagore's *Gitanjali*. Cf. CS's earlier trsl. in SOH, pp. 225ff. and Eugene Kohn's trsl. in Reconstructionist *Sabbath PB*, pp. 342–9.

1049 660 *Lord, where shall I find You? Your place is hidden* ... From a *piyyut* by Judah Halevi in *Selected Poems of Judah Halevi*, ed. Heinrich Brody (Jewish Publication Society of America, 1924), pp. 134f., trsl. CS and JR in *Gate of Repentance* (London, 1973), pp. 190f. Cf. SOH, pp. 227f. (The present trsl. is slightly revised).

1050 662 *Here in my curving arms* ... By John Hall Wheelock, 'This Quiet Dust,' in *The Bright Doom* (Charles Scribner's Sons, 1927).

1051 662 *Holy, Holy, Holy* ... Isa. 6.3.

QUEST

1052 663 *O incognito god* ... By A. M. Klein, 'Psalm XXIV,' in *Poems* (Jewish Publication Society of America, 1944), p. 30.

1053 663 *As a deer pants* ... Pss. 42.2f.; 43.3f.

1054 664 *Out of the deep springs* ... Adapted by CS from his trsl. in SOH, pp. 229f., of a poem by Jacob Cohen (1881–1959, Russia/Poland-Palestine/Israel).

1055 664 *O God, You are my God* ... Ps. 63.2–5a, 8.

1056 665 *O God, You are near* ... Adapted by CS from SOH, p. 231, where it is an adaptation of two prayers by IIM, in LJPB, pp. 184f. and 252.

1057 665 *How lovely are Your dwelling places* ... Ps. 84.1–8, 11–13. See No. 230.

HUMANITY

1058 667 *When God created us* ... Gen. 1.27–28a; 2.7a, c. The last verse is rendered freely.

1059 667 *Therefore was a single human being created* ... M. Sanhedrin 4.5. Some manuscripts of the Mishnah speak of the destruction or sal-

No. Page

vation of one human soul 'in Israel,' but following other ancient versions, we omit 'in Israel,' thus extending the scope of this passage to all humanity.

1060 667 *Then Isaac asked the Eternal* ... By Edmond Fleg, from a Midrashic source.

1061 668 *'You are My witnesses,' says the Lord* ... Midrash Tehillim, on Ps. 123.2. Attributed to R. Shimon b. Yochai (2nd C.). The quotation is Isa. 43.12.

1062 668 *The astonishing thing* ... By W. MacNeile Dixon, in *The Human Situation* (Edward Arnold & Co., London, agents).

1063 668 *Sovereign Lord* ... Ps. 8.2f., 4–10.

LONELINESS

1064 670 *I have been one acquainted with the night* ... A sonnet, 'Acquainted with the Night,' by Robert Frost.

1065 670 *Lord, many are tired* ... Revised by CS from his prayer in SOH, pp. 234f.

1066 671 *There are times* ... By CS, revised from SOH, p. 235.

1067 671 *... how strange we grow* ... Source unknown.

1068 671 *Could I meet one* ... By Hannah Senesh (See No. 456).

1069 672 *As the moon sinks* ... By an anonymous Japanese poet, trsl. Ishii and Obata, in *1001 Poems of Mankind*, compiled by H. W. Wells.

TRUST

1070 673 *O God, You have called us* ... Adapted by CS from his adaptation in SOH, pp. 87f., of a prayer which IIM (LJPB, pp. 153f.) took from Charles Voysey's *Theistic Prayer Book*.

1071 673 *The Most High dwells* ... Pss. 91.1f., 4f., 9f., 14ff. The trsl. is rather freely adapted, by several changes in person, for the purpose of this reading.

1072 674 *O Lord our God, in our great need* ... Adapted from SOH, p. 238, where it is adapted from LJPB, pp. 206f., which took it from JRU.

1073 674 *Lord, my heart is not proud* ... Ps. 131.

1074 675 *Those who trust in the Lord* ... Ps. 125.1f.

1075 675 *When evil darkens our world* ... New, by JR, in SOH, pp. 239f. (very slightly adapted).

1076 675 *I lift up my eyes* ... Ps. 121. Cf. No. 887.

No. Page

SINCERITY

1077 677 *It is told: Rabbi Chaim* ... Adapted from Newman, *The Hasidic Anthology*, p. 438. It is similar to a story told of the Baal Shem Tov in S. Ansky's *The Dybbuk* and cited in Newman, p. 450. Rabbi Chaim of Krosno (d. 1793), was a disciple of the Baal Shem Tov.

1078 677 *How may one approach* ... New, by CS. Influenced by SOH, p. 242, where it was adapted from LJPB, pp. 35f.

1079 677 *Happy are those* ... Ps. 119.2.

1080 677 *What is faithfulness* ... New, by CS. Cf. SOH, p. 242 (See No. 1078). It concludes by quoting Mic. 6.8, usually trsl. 'It has been told you, O man, what is good ...'

1081 678 *And now, O Israel* ... Deut. 10.12; Ps. 25.4–5a; Hos. 6.6; Deut. 4.29; Ps. 40.9; Mic. 6.6; Ps. 37.27–28a.

1082 678 *Send out Your light* ... Ps. 43.3.

1083 678 *Our Rabbis taught* ... B. Makkot 23b–24a (quoting Mic. 6.8; Isa. 56.1; Amos 5.4; Habakkuk 2.4); Sifra 89b (quoting Lev. 19.18 and Gen. 5.1); B. Shabbat 31a.

1084 679 *Lord our God* ... From J. Ber. 4.2, where it is reported by R. Pedat in the name of R. Jacob b. Idi as one of the three prayers by R. Eliezer (2nd C.).

1085 679 *Master of the universe* ... From *The Language of Faith*, ed. N. N. Glatzer, pp. 24–7, which took it from *Likkutei Tefillot*, a collection of personal prayers ascribed to R. Nachman of Bratzlav (See No. 6). The last verse is Ps. 51.12.

1086 680 *Purify our hearts* ... From the *Kedushat Hayom* (See No. 215).

RIGHTEOUSNESS

1087 681 *May He whose spirit is with us* ... Adapted from SOH, p. 246, where it is slightly adapted from LJPB, p. 87 (which took it from an early edition of UPB; now in UPB, p. 130) and from LJPB, p. 115.

1088 681 *We have learned* ... *And it has been written* ... Slightly adapted from Newman, *The Hasidic Anthology*, p. 62 and pp. 173f. The Biblical quotation is Lev. 6.6.

1089 681 *Speak to the whole community* ... Lev. 19.2; Mechilta to Exod. 15.2; Prov. 14.31; M. Avot 2.17, 15; Exod. 22.20; Lev. 19.14; Prov. 24.17, 29; Lev. 19.17a, 18b. Some of the latter vv. are freely adapted.

1090 682 *Seven things are an abomination* ... Prov. 6.16b–19.

1091 682 *These are the things that you shall do* ... Zech. 8.16f.

No. Page

1092 683 *These are the obligations* ... See No. 95.

1093 683 *Lord, who may abide* ... See No. 292.

JUSTICE

1094 685 *The world is sustained* ... M. Avot 1.18; Deut. 16.20; Hos. 10.12; Ps. 11.9; Lev. 25.10; Amos 5.15.

1095 685 *Thus says the Lord* ... Jer. 9.22f.

1096 686 *Our God and Creator* ... Freely adapted by CS from SOH, pp. 252f., where it is slightly adapted from LJPB, pp. 106f., which took it from CCAR, *Blessing and Praise*, 1923, pp. 36f.

1097 686 *Let justice roll down* ... Amos 5.24.

1098 686 *It is an easy thing* ... From William Blake, *Vala, or the Four Zoas*, Night the Second. (We have retained '&' for 'and' as Blake wrote it.)

1099 687 *You shall not steal* ... Lev. 19.11, 13ff.; Exod. 23.9; Lev. 19.34; Deut. 15.7b–8a; Isa. 1.16b–17.

1100 688 *When oppression is no more* ... Isa. 16.4b–5.

1101 688 *The Lord of Hosts is exalted* ... Isa. 5.16.

UNITY

1102 689 *The day will come* ... Hos. 2.18 (slightly adapted); Joel 2.21f.; Isa. 11.6–9.

1103 689 *God created us* ... Gen. 1.27.

1104 689 *Our tradition says* ... M. Sanhedrin 4.5 (Cf. No. 1059); Seder Eliyahu Rabbah, chapter 10, beginning.

1105 690 *Eternal God of all peoples* ... A revision by CS of his prayer in SOH, pp. 265f. The quotations are Isa. 45.22 and 19.24.

1106 690 *Laugh, laugh at all my dreams* ... By Saul Tchernichowsky (1875–1943, Russia-Palestine. One of the great Hebrew poets of the age.) The trsl. is a revision by CS of one by JR in SOH, p. 266.

1107 691 *Lord God of test tube and blueprint* ... From Norman Corwin, *On a Note of Triumph*.

1108 691 *Behold, how good it is* ... Ps. 133.1.

PEACE

1109 692 *The young soldiers do not speak* ... By Archibald Macleish, 'The Young Dead Soldiers,' in *The Human Season: Selected Poems, 1926–1972* (Houghton Mifflin Co., Boston, 1972), p. 18.

No. Page

1110 692 *The Holy One* ... M. Uktsin 3.12, q. Ps. 29.11. This, the last passage of the Mishnah, is a saying of R. Shimon b. Chalafta.

1111 692 *Our God, the Guide* ... See No. 185.

1112 693 *O God, You have called us* ... Adapted by CS from JR, in SOH, p. 281.

1113 694 *They shall beat their swords* ... Isa. 2.4b.

1114 694 *May it be Your will* ... From *The Language of Faith* (Schocken Books, New York, 1967), ed. N. N. Glatzer, p. 315, which took it from *Likkutei Tefillot*, a collection of personal prayers ascribed to R. Nachman of Bratzlav (See No. 6). The trsl. is revised from a new trsl. in SOH, p. 282.

1115 695 *Keep your tongue from evil* ... Ps. 34.14f.; M. Avot 1.12; B. Gittin 59b, quoting Prov. 3.17; Zech. 4.6b; Ps. 46.10; Isa. 32.16f.; 11.9; Mic. 4.4.

1116 695 *Grant us peace* ... See No. 340.

REVELATION

1117 696 *What is Torah?* ... New, by JR, in SOH, p. 255 (here slightly adapted).

1118 696 *Let us praise God* ... See No. 897.

1119 696 *One event stands out* ... New, by JR (slightly adapted here), in SOH, pp. 255f. The quotation is from Exod. Rabbah 29.9 and it alludes to Exod. 20.2. It also incorporates 'Praised be the One ... ,' on which see No. 681.

1120 697 *Blessed is the Lord* ... *who shares His wisdom* ... *who gives of His wisdom* ... These two benedictions are cited in B. Ber. 58a. The first is to be recited on seeing a Jewish sage, the second on seeing a Gentile sage.

1121 697 *Sinai was only the beginning* ... New, by JR (slightly adapted here), in SOH, p. 256.

1122 698 *The Torah is God's choicest gift* ... Slightly adapted from SOH, pp. 257f., where it is new, by JR, and suggested by *Sabbath and Festival PB* (Rabbinical Assembly and United Synagogue of America, 1946), pp. 311f. It contains the following allusions and quotations: B. Ber. 5a; Mechilta to Exod. 17.8 and adaptation of a modern Hebrew song (ארץ ישראל בלי תורה, היא כגוף בלי נשמה); Cant. Rabbah 1.2 and *Sifrei* to Deut. 11.22; *ibid.*; *Sifrei* to Num. 18.20 and M. Avot 6.1; *ibid.*; Gen. Rabbah 53.7; B. Gittin 59b; B. Sotah 14a; B. Shabbat 31a; Lam. Rabbah, Introduction, 2; J. Chagigah 1.7; M. Avot 3.3 and B. Ber. 6a; M. Pei-ah 1.1.

No. Page

1123 698 *If you study Torah* ... M. Avot 6.1 (omitting the proof-text, Prov. 8.14).

1124 699 *All your children* ... Isa. 54.13.

1125 699 *Let the glory of God* ... See No. 58. The present version of the *Kaddish* is an exapnded one, containing the invocation of blessing upon those who engage in the study and teaching of Torah. Abrahams (p. 100) considers it as dating from the 10th C. Since the *Kaddish* was originally recited at the end of a discourse, the interpolation would be needed only after the time when it had entered into general use as a prayer for mourners, etc. In the trad. liturgy, the 'Kaddish of our Teachers' is found at the conclusion of the morning service, and also, in some rituals, after the 'Morning Blessings' (See No. 94). Cf. No. 997.

THE TEN COMMANDMENTS

1126 701 The Ten Commandments appear twice in the Bible, with some variations: in Exod. 20 and Deut. 5. Ours (unlike SOH and LJPB) is the Exod. version. A more literal trsl. of their Hebrew name would be 'The Ten [Divine] Utterances.' In the Temple the Ten Commandments were recited every day before the *Shema* (M. Tamid 5.1). But in the synagogues this practice was officially discontinued 'on account of the insinuations of the heretics' (B. Ber. 12a), i. e., to avoid lending credence to the allegation that *only* the Ten Commandments were divinely revealed and authoritative (Rashi *ad loc.*). Nevertheless, many PBs have included the Ten Commandments as a supplementary reading (e. g., Baer, pp. 159f.). We take the 3rd Commandment to refer not to false swearing, but to misleading or malicious *truth*. This is already seen in the comment of R. Simon in Pesikta Rabbati, *Piska* 22.6 (See also 22.5). For a full discussion (which has influenced our trsl.) see *The Problem of Curse in the Hebrew Bible*, by Herbert Chanan Brichto, chapter 2, especially pp. 59–63. (For full citation, see Note No. 742.)

ISRAEL'S MISSION

1127 703 *Long ago* ... Slightly adapted from SOH, p. 259, where it was adapted from LJPB, p. 213.

1128 703 *If you truly listen to Me* ... Exod. 19.5f.; Isa. 42.1a; 43.10; 42.7; 49.6; Gen. 28.14b.

No. Page

1129 704 *The sense of being chosen* ... New, by CS, in SOH, p. 260, quoting Amos 3.2 and Isa. 11.9b. Here slightly revised.

1130 704 *For the mountains may depart* ... Isa. 54.10.

1131 705 *O God of Israel* ... Adapted from SOH, p. 261, where it was adapted from LJPB, p. 218, which took it from JRU.

1132 705 *I am a Jew because* ... Adapted from Edmond Fleg, *Why I am a Jew*, trsl. by Louise Waterman Wise, Bloch Publishing Co., New York, 1929, p. 77.

1133 706 *To be a Jew in the twentieth century* ... From Muriel Rukeyser, *Letter to the Front*.

1134 706 *How greatly we are blessed* ... From *Birchot Hashachar*. See No. 601.

REDEMPTION

1135 707 *I believe* ... See No. 285.

1136 707 *And I tell you* ... A. Nissenson, *Not Stone*, slightly adapted from a trsl. from the Yiddish by Joseph Leftwich, *The Golden Peacock*, p. 364.

1137 708 *Pour down, O heavens* ... Isa. 45.8.

1138 708 *And it will be said* ... Isa. 25.9; 40.4f.; Joel 3.1; Isa. 60.18f.; 11.9.

1139 710 *All the world* ... An anonymous poem, found in MV, pp. 386f., and included in the Additional Service (*Musaf*) for the High Holy Days. We have slightly adapted Israel Zangwill's trsl. of stanzas 1, 2, and 4.

DOUBT

1140 711 *Cherish your doubts* ... By Robert T. Weston. From *Hymns for the Celebration of Life* (The Beacon Press, Boston, 1964), No. 421.

1141 711 *You are just, O Eternal One* ... Jer. 12.1f., 4. The Hebrew of v. 4 is somewhat obscure. Our trsl. is based on the one in the *New English Bible*, which follows LXX.

1142 712 *Then the Eternal answered Job* ... Job 38.1f., 4–5a, 6b–11, 17f., 31, 33.

1143 713 *Again, I considered all the acts* ... Eccles. 4.1ff.

1144 713 *I do not know how to ask You* ... A saying of R. Levi Yitzchak of Berditchev (c. 1740–1809; a leading Chasidic R., noted for his compassionate love of Israel, which led him to call God to account for Jewish suffering). Adapted from Buber, *Tales of the Hasidim*, Vol. 1, pp. 212f.

1145 714 *I call heaven and earth to witness* ... Deut. 30.19–20a.

1146 714 *Surely, if you do right* ... Gen. 4.7.

No. Page

1147 714 *There are many who say* ... Ps. 4.7–9. In v. 7, following many authorities, we take נסה to be equivalent to נשא.

1148 715 *Let the glory of God* ... See No. 58. The *Kaddish* here affirms our faith in the ultimate triumph of good over evil.

Kiddush

1149 719 *For the eve of Shabbat: The seventh day* ... New, by CS. Based on UPB, p. 93 (Cf. SOH, p. 401). The quotation is Exod. 20.9f. A variation of this prayer will be found in SH; see SH Notes No. 28. *Blessed is the Lord* ... *Creator of the fruit of the vine.* The benediction to be said before drinking wine — M. Ber. 6.1. Wine is a symbol of joy (Cf. Ps. 104.15); and since the Sabbath is a day of joy (Cf. Isa. 58.13), wine became associated especially with the Sabbath. Thus the commandment: 'Remember the Sabbath day and sanctify it' (Exod. 20.8), was taken by the Rabbis to mean 'Remember it over wine' (B. Pesachim 106a). So originated the ritual of the *Kiddush*, which is short for *Kiddush Hayom*, 'The Sanctification of the Day.' It consists of the blessing over the wine, followed by a prayer giving thanks for the Sabbath and proclaiming its sanctity. The Mishnah (e. g., M. Ber. 8.1) testifies to its antiquity. It was and it essentially a *home* rite, preceding the evening meal; but the practice of reciting *Kiddush* also in the synagogue (originally for the benefit of travellers who might eat and sleep there) began already in Talmudic times (B. Pesachim 101a). Rav Amram quotes his predecessor, Natronai Gaon, to the effect that 'they make *Kiddush* in the synagogues even when no travellers are present who eat there' (SRA, p. 65). Today this is the general practice. *Blessed is the Lord* ... *for the Sabbath and its holiness.* The essential themes of this prayer are stipulated in B. Pesachim 117b. The full text, practically as now, appears in SRA, p. 66.

1150 720 *For the morning of Shabbat:* Originally, the Shabbat Morning *Kiddush* consisted only of the benediction for wine — so B. Pesachim 106a, which calls it 'The Great Kiddush,' either in irony or from a desire to increase its importance. Later, a number of Biblical passages were added to it. *The people of Israel* ... Exod. 31.16f. *Therefore the Lord blessed* ... Exod. 20.11 (trad. Exod. 20.8–11 is used). *Blessed is the Lord* ... *fruit of the vine.* See No. 1149.

No. Page

1151 721 *For the eve of Yom Tov: Blessed is the Lord . . . and the Festivals.* The custom of reciting *Kiddush* over a cup of wine on the eve of Festivals, as on Sabbath eve (See No. 1149), as well established in the days of the Talmud (Cf. B. Pesachim 105a). The prescribed text is partly cited in Soferim 19.3 and is found fully (almost as now) in SRA, p. 173. *Blessed is the Lord . . . this season.* See No. 661. *Blessed is the Lord . . . in the Sukkah.* Cited in B. Sukkah 46a. Alludes to Lev. 23.42: 'You shall dwell in booths seven days.' *Blessed is the Lord . . . from the earth.* The blessing for bread (and, in general, therefore, before meals) is based on Ps. 104.14, and is cited in M. Ber. 6.1.

1152 723 *For the morning of Yom Tov: The people of Israel . . .* Exod. 31.16f. *Therefore the Lord blessed . . .* Exod. 20.11. *These are the appointed seasons . . .* Lev. 23.4 (also utilized in the *Sefardi* Ritual as an insertion before the *Tefillah* of the evening service on Festivals; cf. No. 795); *And Moses declared . . .* Lev. 23.44 (this is the insertion before the *Tefillah* of the Festival evening service in the *Ashkenazi* Ritual; see No. 795); *Blessed is the Lord . . . fruit of the vine.* See No. 1149. *Blessed is the Lord . . . in the Sukkah.* See No. 1151. *Blessed is the Lord . . . from the earth.* See No. 1151.

NOTES TO SONGS

No. Page

1 729 *Adon Olam* ... This doctrinal hymn, emphasizing the transcendence, unity, and immanence of God, is known from its opening words as *Adon Olam*, 'The Eternal Lord.' Its author is unknown, but it is generally believed to date from the 11th or 12th C.

2 730 *The Lord of All* ... Very slightly adapted from a metrical version of *Adon Olam* (See No. 1) by F. De Sola Mendes. *Union Hymnal*, pp. 77, 80.

3 730 *Ein Keiloheinu* ... This simple hymn occurs already in SRA, p. 39, where, however, the order of the first two stanzas is reversed. Likewise in MV. The change was probably made in order to let the first three stanzas express acrostically the word 'Amen,' followed by *Baruch Ata* (the first words of the next two stanzas).

4 731 *Yigdal* ... This hymn has been attributed to Daniel b. Judah of Rome (14th C.). It is a brief summary in verse of the 'Thirteen Principles of the Jewish Faith' as expounded by Moses Maimonides in his Commentary on the Mishnah (to Sanhedrin 10.1). In verse 12 we have (following UPB, vol. II, p. 165) changed the first half ('He will send our Messiah at the end of days') to (H & E) 'At the end of days He will send an everlasting redemption.' In the last verse we have followed UPB, SOH, etc., in changing (H & E) 'In His great love God will resurrect the dead' to 'He has implanted eternal life within us' (Cf. the benediction after the reading of the Torah, ST Note No. 686).

5 732 *We Praise the Living God* ... This is a metrical version of *Yigdal* (See No. 4) by Newton Mann. *Union Hymnal*, p. 56, here revised by Malcolm H. Stern.

6 733 *Queen Sabbath* ... See ST Note No. 319.

7 734 *Yom Zeh Leyisra·eil* ... See ST Note No. 419. 'Gift of new soul' is an allusion to the Rabbinic idea that on the Sabbath the Jew acquires 'an additional soul' (B. Beitsah 16a; B. Ta-anit 27b).

8 735 *Shalom Aleichem* ... See ST Note No. 294.

9 736 *Lecha Dodi* ... See ST Note No. 198.

10 737 *Come, O Sabbath Day* ... By Gustav Gottheil (1827–1903), Rabbi in Berlin, Manchester and New York. *Union Hymnal*, p. 123, here revised by Malcolm H. Stern.

NOTES TO SHAAREI TEFILLAH

No. Page

11 738 *Come, O Holy Sabbath Evening* ... By Harry H. Mayer. *Union Hymnal*, p. 108, here revised by Malcolm H. Stern.

12 738 *O Holy Sabbath Day* ... Slightly adapted from a hymn by Isaac S. Moses, in *Union Hymnal*, p. 126.

13 739 *How Good It Is* ... Slightly adapted from a hymn by Florence Weisberg, in *Union Hymnal*, p. 114, *Union Songster*, p. 112. This is a metrical version of Ps. 92 with the refrain from *Lecha Dodi* (See ST Note No. 198).

14 740 *Yah Ribon* ... See ST Note No. 373.

15 740 *Yom Zeh Mechubad* ... A *Zemirah* ('Table Song') by Israel Najara. See ST Note No. 373.

16 741 *Menucha Vesimcha* ... A *Zemirah* ('Table Song') with nominal acrostic. It is the work of one Moses, not otherwise identified. However, another of his *Zemirot* (*Kol Mekadeish Shevi·i*) is found in MV, p. 147. Birnbaum, in his edition of the *Siddur*, thinks it likely that he is R. Moses b. Kalonymus (Mayence, 10th C.).

17 742 *Yedid Nefesh* ... See ST Note No. 260. This is from the first stanza of the text.

18 742 *Eileh Chameda Libi* ... From *Yedid Nefesh*; see ST Note No. 260. The full text is suggested by Abrahams, whose version is grammatically correct. Here we follow the better-known text, to accommodate musical arrangements.

19 742 *Vatik* ... From *Yedid Nefesh*; see ST Note No. 260 and No. 18, above.

20 742 *Ki Eshmera Shabbat* ... By Abraham Ibn Ezra (Spain, 13th C.; poet and Biblical exegete). We use only the refrain from this *Zemirah* ('Table Song').

21 743 *Deror Yikra* ... By Dunash Halevi ben Labrat (Morocco-Spain, 10th C.). Slightly adapted from a trsl. by David Goldstein, in *The Jewish Poets of Spain* (Penguin Books, 1971), p. 31, stanzas 1, 2, and 4.

22 743 *Vetaheir Libeinu* ... From the *Kedushat Hayom*; see ST Note No. 215.

23 744 *Magein Avot* ... See ST Note No. 224.

24 744 *Tov Lehodot* ... Ps. 92.2f.

25 745 *Anim Zemirot* ... See ST Note No. 598.

26 745 *Shachar Avakeshecha* ... See ST Note No. 546.

27 746 *Ashreinu* ... See ST Note No. 601.

28 746 *Veha·eir Eineinu* ... From the *Ahavah Rabbah* (See ST Note No. 101).

29 747 *Baruch Eloheinu* ... See ST Note No. 897. Here we retain the trad. text for singing.

30 747 *Ata Echad* ... See ST Note No. 282.

111

No. Page
31 747 *Shomeir Yisra·eil* ... A *Piyyut* (liturgical poem) of unknown date and authorship. It is part of the *Tachanun*, a series of penitential prayers ('petitions for grace') in the trad. weekday morning and afternoon services.
32 748 *Lo Yisa Goi* ... Isa. 2.4c.
33 748 *Esa Einai* ... Ps. 121.1f. The trsl. is meant to be sung.
34 749 *Mi Ha·ish* ... Ps. 34.13ff.
35 749 *Veheishiv Leiv Avot* ... Mal. 3.23–24a.
36 749 *I·ve·du* ... Ps. 100.2.
37 750 *Pitechu Li* ... Ps. 118.19.
38 750 *Ma Navu* ... Isa. 52.7f.
39 750 *David Melech* ... B. R.H. 25a.
40 751 *Amar Rabbi Akiva* ... Sifra 89b (quoting Lev. 19.18).
41 751 *Amar Rabbi Elazar* ... B. Ber., end (64a).
42 751 *Im Ein Ani Li Mi Li* ... M. Avot 1.14.
43 751 *Al Shelosha Devarim* ... M. Avot 1.2.
44 752 *Rad Halaila* ... By Y. Orland.
45 752 *Hoshia Et Amecha* ... See ST Note No. 782.
46 753 *Ani Ma·amin* ... See ST Note No. 285.
47 753 *If Our God Had Not Befriended* ... A metrical version of Ps. 124 by Edward Churton. *Union Hymnal*, p. 130.
48 754 *Spring-Tide of the Year* ... By Alice Lucas (1851–1935, eldest sister of Claude G. Montefiore). *Union Hymnal*, p. 136.
49 754 *God of Might* ... By Gustav Gottheil (See No. 10). *Union Hymnal*, p. 125.
50 755 *In the Wilderness* ... Based on Exod. Rabbah 29.9 (Cf. ST Note No. 1119), adapted by Judith K. Eisenstein. See *Union Songster*, pp. 226f.
51 755 *Could We with Ink* ... Slightly adapted from Israel Zangwill's rendering of a portion of *Akdamut*, an acrostic *piyyut* (liturgical poem) in praise of the God of Revelation and Creation, in Aramaic, written by R. Meir b. Isaac (France, 11th C.), and recited on the first day of Shavuot in the *Ashkenazi* Ritual. See *Union Songster*, pp. 228f.
52 755 *From Heaven's Heights the Thunder Peals* ... By Isaac M. Wise, slightly adapted by CS. *Union Hymnal*, p. 150.
53 756 *Ein Adir* ... *Sefardi* folk song.
54 757 *Take Unto You* ... By Alice Lucas (See No. 48). We have changed 'thou' to 'You,' etc. The quotation is from Lev. 23.40. *Union Hymnal*, pp. 208f.

No. Page

55 757 *Mi Yemaleil* ... The Hebrew is of unknown origin; the English is slightly adapted from Ben M. Edidin. On the first Hebrew phrase, cf. Ps. 106.2. See *Union Songster*, pp. 260f.

56 758 *Ma·oz Tsur* ... This is the first stanza of the trad. Chanukah hymn, which has an acrostic showing it to be the work of a poet named Mordechai, possibly of the 13th C.

57 758 *Rock of Ages* ... An English adaptation by Marcus Jastrow (1829–1903) and Gustav Gottheil (See No. 10) of a German Chanukah hymn by Leopold Stein (1810–1882). We have changed 'thou' to 'You,' and made one other change: 'Maccabees' for 'martyr-race,' in the third stanza.

58 759 *Al Hanisim* ... See ST Note No. 78.

59 760 *Utsu Eitsa* ... Isa. 8.10.

60 760 *Shoshanat Ya·akov* ... Abridged from an alphabetical acrostic dating from the Gaonic Age, the concluding lines of which are older, being cited in J. Meg. 3.7.

61 761 *Father, Hear the Prayer* ... By L. M. Willis, slightly adapted. We use the first and third stanzas. *Union Hymnal*, p. 46.

62 761 *When this Song of Praise* ... By William Cullen Bryant. We have changed 'Thy' to 'Your.' *Union Hymnal*, p. 106.

63 761 *O Lord, Where Shall I Find You?* ... Slightly adapted by CS from the trsl. by Solomon Solis-Cohen of a poem by Judah Halevi (Cf. ST Note No. 1049). *Union Hymnal*, pp. 22f.

64 762 *O God Our Help* ... A metrical version of Ps. 90 by Isaac Watts. *Union Hymnal*, p. 50.

65 762 *O Worship the King* ... Slightly adapted from a metrical version of Ps. 104 by Robert Grant. *Union Hymnal*, p. 61.

66 763 *There Lives A God!* ... A trsl., by James K. Gutheim, of a hymn from the *Hamburg Temple Hymnal*. *Union Hymnal*, p. 62.

67 763 *America the Beautiful* ... By Katherine Lee Bates.

68 764 *The National Anthem* ... By Francis Scott Key.

69 764 *God of our People* ... By Daniel C. Roberts. *Union Hymnal*, p. 306. We have changed 'fathers' to 'people.'

70 765 *Hatikvah* ... By Naftali Herz Imber (Poland–U.S., 1856–1909).

A Table of Scriptural Readings[1]

THE READINGS given in this Table for the fifty-four sidrot into which the Torah is divided, and for the corresponding haftarot, are those prescribed by tradition. Occasionally the Sefardi rite differs from the Ashkenazi in the choice of haftarah. In those instances the Sefardi reading is given in parentheses. Alternative readings are suggested for the haftarot and for several sidrot.

On Shabbat afternoon, and Monday and Thursday mornings, the first parasha of the sidra for the coming Shabbat is read. This parasha is indicated in the Table by an asterisk.

In some years several or all of the following sidrot are combined: Vayakheil-Pikudei, Tazria-Metsora, Acharei-Kedoshim, Behar-Bechukotai, Chukat-Balak, Matot-Masei, Nitsavim-Vayeilech. When this occurs, read the haftarah assigned to the second sidra, except that when Nitsavim-Vayeilech are joined, Isaiah 61.10–63.9 (the haftarah for Nitsavim) is the traditional reading.

The readings given for holidays are in accordance with the practice of the Reform synagogue.

For those congregations which conduct daily services, readings have been suggested for the intermediate days of Sukkot and Pesach, as well as for Chanukah, Purim, and Tish'a be-Av.

In the traditional synagogue, appropriate selections from two Sifrei Torah are read on holidays and special Sabbaths, and, on rare occasions, selections from three are read. Some of these selections have been indicated in the Table. Choice may be made from the regular weekly portion, from the special reading or readings for the day, or excerpts from all may be read.

Reform Jews throughout the world observe Pesach and Sukkot for seven days, and Shavuot and Shemini Atzeret-Simchat Torah for one day. This is also the practice in traditional congregations in Israel. Traditional Jews in the Diaspora add an extra day to these festivals. When, in the Diaspora, the eighth day of Pesach or the second day of Shavuot falls on Shabbat, Reform congregations read the sidra assigned to the following week in the standard religious calendars. However, in order to preserve uniformity in the reading of the Torah throughout the entire community, it is suggested that on these occasions, the sidra be spread over two weeks, one portion to be read while traditional congregations are observing the festival, and another portion to be read the following Shabbat.

	Torah	Haftarah
בראשית	Genesis 1.1–6.8	*Isaiah 42.5–43 11* *(42.5–21)* *Psalm 19.1–15* *Psalm 104.1–30* *Psalm 139.1–18* *Job 38.1–11*
	*Genesis 1.1–13	
נח	Genesis 6.9–11.32	*Isaiah 54.1–55.5* *(54.1–10)* *Isaiah 14.12–20* *Isaiah 44.1–8* *Jeremiah 31.31–36* *Zephaniah 3.9–20* *Psalm 104.24–35*
	*Genesis 6.9–22	
לך לך	Genesis 12.1–17.27	*Isaiah 40.27–41.16* *Joshua 24.1–14* *Isaiah 51.1–16* *Joel 2.21–3.2* *Psalm 105.1–15*
	*Genesis 12.1–13	
וירא	Genesis 18.1–22.24	*II Kings 4.1–37* *(4.1–23)* *Ezekiel 18.1–32* *Micah 6.1–8* *Psalm 111.1–10* *Job 5.17–27*
	*Genesis 18.1–14	
חיי שרה	Genesis 23.1–25.18	*I Kings 1.1–31* *Jeremiah 32.1–27* *Psalm 15.1–5* *Psalm 45.1–18* *Proverbs 31.10–31*
	*Genesis 23.1–16	

	Torah	Haftarah
תולדות	Genesis 25.19–28.9	Malachi 1.1–2.7
		I Kings 5.15–26
		Psalm 5.1–13
		Proverbs 4.1–23
	*Genesis 25.19–26.5	
ויצא	Genesis 28.10–32.3	Hosea 12.13–14.10
		(11.7–12.12)
		I Samuel 1.1–28
		I Kings 19.1–12
		Jeremiah 31.1–17
		Psalm 27.1–14
		Psalm 62.1–9
		Psalm 139.1–18
		Proverbs 2.1–9
		Ruth 4.9–17
	*Genesis 28.10–22	
וישלח	Genesis 32.4–36.43	Hosea 11.7–12.12
		(Obadiah 1.1–21)
		Isaiah 44.6–21
		Isaiah 45.1–7
		Jeremiah 10.1–16
		Jeremiah 31.10–26
		Psalm 27.1–14
		Psalm 37.1–40
	*Genesis 32.4–13	
וישב	Genesis 37.1–40.23	Amos 2.6–3.8
		I Kings 3.5–15
		Psalm 34.1–23
		Psalm 63.1–12
	*Genesis 37.1–11	
מקץ	Genesis 41.1–44.17	I Kings 3.15–4.1
		Judges 7.2–23
		Isaiah 19.19–25
		Psalm 67.1–8
		Proverbs 10.1–7
		Daniel 2.1–23
	*Genesis 41.1–14	

	Torah	*Haftarah*
ויגש	Genesis 44.18–47.27	*Ezekiel 37.15–28*
		Amos 8.4–11
		Psalm 71.1–24
		Psalm 72.1–20
	*Genesis 44.18–30	
ויחי	Genesis 47.28–50.26	*I Kings 2.1–12*
		Psalm 22.24–32
		Job 5.17–27
		Ecclesiastes 12.1–14
		I Chronicles 28.1–10
	*Genesis 47.28–48.9	
שמות	Exodus 1.1–6.1	*Isaiah 27.6–28.13; 29.22–23*
		(Jeremiah 1.1–2.3)
		I Samuel 3.1–21
		Isaiah 6.1–13
		Joel 2.21–3.2
	*Exodus 1.1–17	
וארא	Exodus 6.2–9.35	*Ezekiel 28.25–29.21*
		Isaiah 42.5–17
		Isaiah 52.1–10
		Jeremiah 1.1–10
		Ezekiel 31.1–12
		Psalm 78.38–55
	*Exodus 6.2–13	
בא	Exodus 10.1–13.16	*Jeremiah 46.13–28*
		Isaiah 19.19–25
		Psalm 105.7–45
		Ezra 6.16–22
	*Exodus 10.1–11	
בשלח	Exodus 13.17–17.16	*Judges 4.4–5.31*
		(5.1–31)
		Joshua 4.4–18
		Isaiah 63.7–16
		Psalm 78.1–29
		Psalm 106.1–12
		Psalm 124.1–8
	*Exodus 13.17–14.8	

274

	Torah	Haftarah
יתרו	Exodus 18.1–20.23	Isaiah 6.1–7.6; 9.5–6 (6.1–13) I Kings 3.3–15 Isaiah 43.1–12 Jeremiah 7.1–23 Jeremiah 31.23–36 Psalm 19.1–15
	*Exodus 18.1–12	
משפטים	Exodus 21.1–24.18	Jeremiah 34.8–22; 33.25–26 Jeremiah 17.5–14 Amos 5.6–24
	*Exodus 21.1–19	
תרומה	Exodus 25.1–27.19	I Kings 5.26–6.13 I Kings 7.51–8.21 I Kings 8.22–43 I Chronicles 22.1–13
	*Exodus 25.1–16	
תצוה	Exodus 27.20–30.10	Ezekiel 43.10–27 Joshua 24.1–28 Isaiah 61.1–11 Isaiah 65.17–66.2 Psalm 42.1–12 Psalm 43.1–5
	*Exodus 27.20–28.12	
כי תשא	Exodus 30.11–34.35	I Kings 18.1–39 (18.20–39) Jeremiah 31.31–36 Ezekiel 20.1–20 Psalm 27.1–14 Psalm 81.1–17 Psalm 106.1–23
	*Exodus 30.11–22	

	Torah	*Haftarah*
ויקהל	Exodus 35.1–38.20	*I Kings 7.40–50*
		(7.13–26)
		I Chronicles 29.9–20
	*Exodus 35.1–20	
פקודי	Exodus 38.21–40.38	*I Kings 7.51–8.21*
		(7.40–50)
		I Kings 8.10–30
		II Chronicles 5.1–14
	*Exodus 38.21–39.1	
ויקרא	Leviticus 1.1–5.26	*Isaiah 43.21–44.23*
		Isaiah 1.10–20, 27
		Isaiah 33.13–22
		Psalm 50.1–23
	*Leviticus 1.1–13	
צו	Leviticus 6.1–8.36	*Jeremiah 7.21–8.3; 9.22–23*
		Hosea 6.1–6
		Malachi 1.6–14; 2.1–7
		Malachi 3.1–6
	*Leviticus 6.1–11	
שמיני	Leviticus 9.1–11.47	*II Samuel 6.1–7.17*
		(6.1–19)
		Isaiah 61.1–11
		Psalm 39.1–14
		Psalm 51.1–21
		Psalm 73.1–28
		Daniel 1.1–21
	*Leviticus 9.1–16	
תזריע	Leviticus 12.1–13.59	*II Kings 4.42–5.19*
		Job 2.1–10
	*Leviticus 12.1–13.5	
	Deuteronomy 12.28–13.5	

	Torah	*Haftarah*
מצרע	Leviticus 14.1–15.33	*II Kings 7.3–20* *Psalm 103.1–22* *Proverbs 10.11–23*
	*Leviticus 14.1–12 Deuteronomy 26.12–19	
אחרי מות	Leviticus 16.1–18.30	*Ezekiel 22.1–19* *(22.1–16)* *Isaiah 58.1–14* *Isaiah 59.1–21* *Ezekiel 22.17–31*
	*Leviticus 16.1–17	
קדשים	Leviticus 19.1–20.27	*Amos 9.7–15* *(Ezekiel 20.2–20)* *Jeremiah 22.1–9, 13–16* *Psalm 15.1–5* *Job 29.1–17*
	*Leviticus 19.1–14	
אמר	Leviticus 21.1–24.23	*Ezekiel 44.15–31* *Isaiah 56.1–8* *Ezekiel 36.16–28* *Malachi 1.1–14* *Nehemiah 8.1–18*
	*Leviticus 21.1–15	
בהר	Leviticus 25.1–26.2	*Jeremiah 32.6–27* *Jeremiah 31.1–13* *Jeremiah 34.8–16* *Nehemiah 5.1–13*
	*Leviticus 25.1–13	
בחקתי	Leviticus 26.3–27.34	*Jeremiah 16.19–17.14* *Zephaniah 3.1–20* *Psalm 116.1–19* *Job 36.1–15*
	*Leviticus 26.3–13	

	Torah	Haftarah
במדבר	Numbers 1.1–4.20	Hosea 2.1–22
		II Samuel 24.1–14
		Malachi 2.4–10
		Psalm 107.1–16
		I Chronicles 15.1–15
	*Numbers 1.1–19	
נשא	Numbers 4.21–7.89	Judges 13.2–25
		Judges 16.4–21
		Jeremiah 35.1–19
		Psalm 67.1–8
		Ezra 3.8–13
	*Numbers 4.21–33	
בהעלתך	Numbers 8.1–12.16	Zechariah 2.14–4.7
		Joel 2.21–3.5
		Psalm 68.1–11, 33–36
		Psalm 77.1–21
		Psalm 81.1–11
		II Chronicles 5.1–14
	*Numbers 8.1–14	
שלח לך	Numbers 13.1–15.41	Joshua 2.1–24
		Joshua 14.6–14
		Jeremiah 17.19–18.8
		Ezekiel 20.1–22
		Psalm 106.1–27, 44–48
	*Numbers 13.1–20	
קרח	Numbers 16.1–18.32	I Samuel 11.14–12.22
		Judges 9.1–21
		Isaiah 56.1–8
		Psalm 106.13–46
	*Numbers 16.1–13	
חקת	Numbers 19.1–22.1	Judges 11.1–33
		Ezekiel 36.21–38
		Psalm 42.1–12
		Psalm 78.1–24
	*Numbers 19.1–17	

	Torah	*Haftarah*
בלק	Numbers 22.2–25.9	*Micah 5.6–6.8*
		Joshua 24.1–14
		Isaiah 54.11–17
		Habakkuk 3.1–19
	*Numbers 22.2–12	
פינחס	Numbers 25.10–30.1	*I Kings 18.46–19.21*
		Joshua 17.1–5
		Joshua 22.11–34
		Joshua 23.1–14
		Judges 1.1–15
		Ezekiel 45.18–25
	*Numbers 25.10–26.4	
מטות	Numbers 30.2–32.42	*Jeremiah 1.1–2.3*
		Joshua 22.1–10
		Joshua 22.11–34
	*Numbers 30.2–17	
מסעי	Numbers 33.1–36.13	*Jeremiah 2.4–28; 3.4; 4.1–2*
		(2.4–28; 4.1–2)
		Joshua 20.1–9
		Jeremiah 33.1–27
	*Numbers 33.1–10	
דברים	Deuteronomy 1.1–3.22	*Isaiah 1.1–27*
		Amos 2.1–11
		Lamentations 3.19–41
	*Deuteronomy 1.1–11	
ואתחנן	Deuteronomy 3.23–7.11	*Isaiah 40.1–26*
		Jeremiah 7.1–23
	*Deuteronomy 3.23–4.8	
עקב	Deuteronomy 7.12–11.25	*Isaiah 49.14–51.3*
		Isaiah 50.1–10
		Jeremiah 2.1–9
		Jeremiah 26.1–16
		Zechariah 8.7–23
	*Deuteronomy 7.12–21	

SCRIPTURAL READINGS

	Torah	Haftarah
ראה	Deuteronomy 11.26–16.17	*Isaiah 54.11–55.5*
		Joshua 8.30–35
		I Kings 22.1–14
		Isaiah 26.1–12
		Jeremiah 23.13–32
		Jeremiah 34.8–17
		Psalm 15.1–5
		Psalm 24.1–10
	*Deuteronomy 11.26–12.10	
שפטים	Deuteronomy 16.18–21.9	*Isaiah 51.12–52.12*
		I Samuel 8.1–22
		Jeremiah 23.13–32
		Ezekiel 34.1–31
	*Deuteronomy 16.18–17.13	
כי תצא	Deuteronomy 21.10–25.19	*Isaiah 54.1–10*
		Isaiah 5.1–16
		Isaiah 59.1–21
		Proverbs 28.1–14
		Proverbs 30.1–9
	*Deuteronomy 21.10–21	
כי תבוא	Deuteronomy 26.1–29.8	*Isaiah 60.1–22*
		Joshua 4.1–24
		Isaiah 35.1–10
		Isaiah 49.14–26
	*Deuteronomy 26.1–15	
נצבים	Deuteronomy 29.9–30.20	*Isaiah 61.10–63.9*
		Joshua 24.1–28
		Isaiah 51.1–16
		Jeremiah 31.27–36
	*Deuteronomy 29.9–28	
וילך	Deuteronomy 31.1–30	*Isaiah 55.6–56.8*
		On Shabbat Shuvah: Hosea 14.2–10, Micah 7.18–20, Joel 2.15–27
	*Deuteronomy 31.1–3	

280

	Torah	*Haftarah*
האזינו	Deuteronomy 32.1–52	*II Samuel 22.1–51* *Psalm 78.1–38* *On Shabbat Shuvah: Hosea* *14.2–10, Micah 7.18–20,* *Joel 2.15–27*
	*Deuteronomy 32.1–12	
וזאת הברכה	Deuteronomy 33.1–34.12	*Joshua 1.1–18* *(1.1–9)*
	*Deuteronomy 33.1–7	
Shabbat Shuvah	Weekly portion	*Hosea 14.2–10, Micah* *7.18–20, Joel 2.15–27* *(Hosea 14.2–10, Micah* *7.18–20)*
Sukkot		
1st day	Leviticus 23.33–44	*Zechariah 14.7–9, 16–21* *Isaiah 35.1–10* *Isaiah 32.1–8, 14–20*
2nd day	Leviticus 23.39–44	
3rd day (if Shabbat) (if weekday)	Exodus 33.12–34.26 Exodus 23.14–17	*Ezekiel 38.18–39.7*
4th day	Exodus 34.21–24	
5th day (if Shabbat) (if weekday)	See readings for 3rd day Deuteronomy 16.13–17	
6th day (if Shabbat) (if weekday)	See readings for 3rd day Deuteronomy 31.9–13	

SCRIPTURAL READINGS

	Torah	Haftarah
7th day	Deuteronomy 11.10–15	

NOTE: *The Book of Ecclesiastes is read on the Shabbat during Sukkot.*

Atzeret-Simchat Torah	Deuteronomy 34.1–12	Joshua 1.1–18
	Genesis 1.1–2.3	(1.1–9)

Chanukah		
1st day	Numbers 6.22–7.17	
2nd day	Numbers 7.18–29	
3rd day	Numbers 7.24–35	
4th day	Numbers 7.30–41	
5th day	Numbers 7.36–47	
6th day	Numbers 7.42–53	
7th day	Numbers 7.48–59	
8th day	Numbers 7.54–8.4	
1st Shabbat during Chanukah	Weekly portion	Zechariah 4.1–7
2nd Shabbat during Chanukah	Weekly portion	I Kings 7.40–50
		I Kings 8.54–66

NOTE: *The first day of Tevet falls on the sixth or seventh day of Chanukah. The special reading for Rosh Chodesh may be added to that for Chanukah or substituted for it. If Rosh Chodesh and Shabbat coincide, three Sifrei Torah may be taken from the Ark. A selection from the regular weekly portion is read first.*

Shabbat Shekalim	Weekly portion	II Kings 12.5–16
	Exodus 30.11–16	(11.17–12.17)

Shabbat Zachor	Weekly portion	Esther 7.1–10; 8.15–17,
	Deuteronomy 25.17–19	or 9.20–28

SCRIPTURAL READINGS

	Torah	*Haftarah*
Purim	Exodus 17.8–16	

NOTE: *The Book of Esther is read on Purim.*

Shabbat Parah	Weekly portion Numbers 19.1–9	*Ezekiel 36.22–36*
Shabbat Hachodesh	Weekly portion Exodus 12.1–20	*Ezekiel 45.16–25*
Shabbat Hagadol	Weekly portion	*Malachi 3.4–24*
Pesach		
1st day	Exodus 12.37–42; 13.3–10	*Isaiah 43.1–15*
2nd day	Exodus 13.14–16	
3rd day		
(*if Shabbat*)	Exodus 33.12–34.26	*Ezekiel 37.1–14* *Song of Songs 2.7–17*
(*if weekday*)	Exodus 23.14–17	
4th day	Exodus 34.18–23	
5th day		
(*if Shabbat*)	See readings for 3rd day	
(*if weekday*)	Numbers 9.1–5	
6th day	Leviticus 23.1–8	
7th day	Exodus 14.30–15.21	*II Samuel 22.1–51* *Isaiah 11.1–6, 9; 12.1–6*

NOTE: *The Song of Songs is read on the Shabbat during Pesach.*

Yom Hasho-ah	Deuteronomy 4.30–40	*II Samuel 1.17–27* *Psalm 9.1–21* *Psalm 116.1–19* *Psalm 118.5–24*
Yom Ha-atsma-ut	Deuteronomy 8.1–18 Deuteronomy 11.8–21 Deuteronomy 26.1–11 Deuteronomy 30.1–16	*Isaiah 60.1–22* *Isaiah 10.32–12.6* *Isaiah 65.17–25*
Shavuot	Exodus 19.1–8; 20.1–14	*Isaiah 42.1–12*

NOTE: *The Book of Ruth is read on Shavuot.*

283

SCRIPTURAL READINGS

	Torah	*Haftarah*
Tish'a be-Av		
Morning	Deuteronomy 4.25–41	*Jeremiah 8.13–9.23*
Afternoon	Exodus 32.11–14; 34.1–10	*Isaiah 55.6–56.8*
		(Hosea 14.2–10, Micah 7.18–20)

NOTE: *The Book of Lamentations is read on Tish'a be-Av.*

Rosh Chodesh		
Weekday	Numbers 28.11–15	
Shabbat and Rosh Chodesh	Weekly portion	*Isaiah 66.1–13, 23*
Shabbat when Rosh Chodesh is next day	Weekly portion	*I Samuel 20.18–42*

NOTE: *In the traditional calendar, when a month has thirty days, the thirtieth day and the first day of the new month are observed as Rosh Chodesh. It is suggested that in the Reform synagogue Rosh Chodesh should be observed on the first day of the new month.*

[1]*A Table of Scriptural Readings* ... We follow UPB and others in providing a suggested Scriptural lectionary of Torah and Haftarah Readings, for the entire year. Our lectionary is new, compiled by ASD, based on the trad. one, UPB, and other sources. The lectionary in the second edition of UPB was prepared by Kaufmann Kohler, that in the third edition by Solomon B. Freehof.

LITURGY COMMITTEE

OF THE

CENTRAL CONFERENCE OF AMERICAN RABBIS

A. Stanley Dreyfus,
Chairman

JAY R. BRICKMAN   NORMAN D. HIRSH
HERBERT BRONSTEIN   GUNTER HIRSCHBERG
HARVEY J. FIELDS   LAWRENCE A. HOFFMAN
FREDRIC S. POMERANTZ

JOSEPH B. GLASER, *ex-officio*
W. GUNTHER PLAUT, *ex-officio*
MALCOLM H. STERN, *ex-officio*
GEORGE WEINFLASH, *for the American Conference of Cantors*

★   ★

Lawrence A. Hoffman

Editor of Gates of Understanding

★   ★

Chaim Stern

Editor of Gates of Prayer